THE ARTIFICIAL INTELLIGENCE HANDBOOK FOR BUSINESS ANALYSTS

Future-Proof Your Skills; Save a Wealth of Time; and Secure Your Job.

Includes: 1000+ optimized ChatGPT Prompts & Strategies for Business Analysts to Elevate Your Business Tasks and Innovate Successfully.

Author: Jeroen Erné

COPYRIGHT © 2023 BY JEROEN ERNÉ

Disclaimer:
This book is designed to provide advice only on the subjects covered. While we try to specify the advice, information, and subjects specifically for your job function and job industry, there is no one-size-fits-all solution. No claims can be made based on the contents of this book. In the case you're looking

for one-on-one personal training tailored for yourself or your colleagues, general AI consultancy, or AI implementations, please contact the author via their email or website.

Dedication:
To those in the workforce who are committed to excellence, and who understand the pivotal role of artificial intelligence in shaping the future of employment. May this book serve as your guide to not just surviving, but thriving in a landscape forever transformed by technology.

INTRODUCTION

In the dynamic world of business analysis, staying ahead of the curve is not just an option, it's a necessity. "The Artificial Intelligence Handbook for Business Analysts" is your gateway to mastering this landscape. This book is a treasure trove of knowledge, exploring the revolutionary role of ChatGPT and AI in the realm of business analytics.

At the heart of this book is ChatGPT, an AI marvel that is redefining the tools and techniques at the disposal of business analysts. You will learn not just what ChatGPT is, but also how it can automate and refine aspects of your role. With over 1000 tailored prompts, this book equips you to leverage AI for tasks ranging from analyzing market trends to predicting financial performances.

The content is meticulously crafted to address the multifaceted challenges you face daily. Whether it's segmenting customer groups for targeted marketing, optimizing supply chains, or developing pricing strategies, ChatGPT emerges as a powerful ally. It provides clarity in complex data analysis, aids in risk assessment, and offers insights into stakeholder needs.

But this book is more than just an AI manual. It's a journey into the future of business analysis, where AI and human expertise blend to create unprecedented efficiency and effectiveness. We present this knowledge with an authoritative yet relatable tone, understanding that the transition to AI-augmented analytics is as much about practical application as it is about technological sophistication.

Dive into the pages of this handbook to transform the way you approach business analysis. Embrace the power of AI and ChatGPT, and redefine what's possible in your profession. Welcome to a world where data meets intuition, and where your analytical capabilities are supercharged by the power of artificial intelligence.

COMPLIMENTARY RESOURCES

Elevate your game with this book purchase from Amazon or your preferred platform. Here's what you'll unlock:

☐ 1 month free at CompleteAITraining.com, where you'll:

☐ Tap into custom ChatGPTs designed for your field, boosting efficiency and insight;

☐ Dive into a curated collection of prompts, sharpening your AI skills tailored to your profession;

☐ Access comprehensive courses to become an AI whiz, setting you apart in your industry;

☐ Ask unlimited questions to our AI strategy GPT, guiding your AI journey with expert advice;

☐ Explore video tutorials, audiobooks, and eBooks, enriching your learning experience on the go or at home.

You can request access to the complimentary resources at https://completeaitraining.com/free-resources-amazon .

WHAT IS CHATGPT?

ChatGPT, developed by OpenAI, is a chatbot designed to replicate natural conversation. It allows users to engage with it by asking questions or making requests using prompts. This user-friendly and intuitive tool has quickly become popular, serving as an alternative to conventional search engines and a valuable resource for AI writing, among other applications.

What does"GPT" stand for?

The abbreviation "GPT" in ChatGPT stands for generative pre-trained transformer. In the realm of AI, training involves teaching a computer system to identify patterns and make decisions based on input data, much like a teacher imparting information to students and assessing their comprehension.

A transformer is a neural network that is specifically trained to analyze the context of input data and assign importance to each component accordingly. Due to its contextual learning capabilities, this model is commonly employed in natural language processing (NLP) to generate text that closely resembles human writing. (In AI, a model refers to a collection of mathematical equations and algorithms that enable a computer to analyze data and make decisions.)

Unlike older AI chatbots that could provide detailed responses to questions, ChatGPT adopts a dialog format, enabling it to address follow-up and clarifying queries. Additionally, it can identify and reject inappropriate or hazardous requests, such as those pertaining to illegal activities.

HOW DOES CHATGPT WORK?

ChatGPT employs natural language processing (NLP), an AI technology that comprehends, examines, and produces language akin to human speech. The extensive language model (LLM) underwent training by amalgamating two significant sources:

1. A vast corpus of text excerpts sourced from web pages and program code preceding 2022.

2. Dialogues contributed by actual individuals, showcasing exemplary responses to given prompts, subsequently evaluating model outputs based on response excellence.

FEATURES AND LIMITATIONS OF CHATGPT AND OTHER GENERATIVE AI

ChatGPT is a remarkable leap forward in generative AI, offering numerous capabilities to expedite specific tasks when utilized strategically. However, it is crucial to acknowledge its limitations in order to effectively harness this technology and maximize its potential impact.

FEATURES OF CHATGPT

ChatGPT offers a range of powerful features for Business Analysts:

• It can generate text that closely resembles the style and structure of the input data.

• It can provide responses to prompts or input text, whether it's crafting a story or answering a question.

• It supports text generation in multiple languages.

• It allows for the modification of text style, whether formal or informal.

• It can ask clarifying questions to better grasp the intent behind the input data.

• It responds in a way that aligns with the conversation's context, offering follow-up instructions and understanding references to previous questions.

Similar to ChatGPT, other generative AI models excel in tasks involving images, sounds, and video.

LIMITATIONS AND RISKS OF CHATGPT

While ChatGPT is a powerful tool, it does have its limitations. Firstly, transformer models like ChatGPT lack common sense reasoning ability. This means they may struggle with complexity, nuance, and questions related to emotions, values, beliefs, and abstract concepts. These limitations can manifest in various ways:

• The model doesn't fully understand the meaning of the text it generates. Although some output may sound humanlike, it's important to remember that ChatGPT is not human. Consequently, it may struggle with nuances, ambiguity, sarcasm, or irony. Moreover, it can produce text that seems plausible but is actually incorrect or nonsensical. Additionally, it cannot verify the accuracy of its own output.

• There is a risk of generating biased, discriminatory, or offensive text. ChatGPT's performance depends on the input data it was trained on. Since it was trained on a large amount of text data from the internet, including biased content, this bias can be reflected in the generated text.

• The model may provide outdated information. Its knowledge is limited to events before 2021, and it is not connected to the wider internet. For tasks like code generation, it might rely on outdated examples that no longer adhere to modern cybersecurity standards.

• The output can be formulaic. ChatGPT has a tendency to generate text that resembles existing phrases and may overuse certain expressions. This can result in flat and unimaginative text or, in extreme cases, even plagiarism or copyright infringement.

• Availability of the tool can be an issue. Due to its immense popularity, ChatGPT's servers may experience capacity problems. In such cases, you may receive a message stating that "ChatGPT is at capacity."

CAN I USE CHAT GPT FOR FREE?

Indeed, the answer is affirmative. OpenAI has generously made ChatGPT accessible to all, free of charge. Nevertheless, it is important to note that the free tier does come with certain restrictions, particularly during periods of high demand when its capacity may be limited.

While the current state of affairs allows for free usage, it is crucial to acknowledge that this may not be a permanent arrangement. OpenAI benefits greatly from the invaluable feedback received from users like yourself, which aids in refining and enhancing the AI language model. Additionally, this initiative serves to encourage widespread adoption of this remarkable technology across various industries.

By offering ChatGPT for free, OpenAI not only fosters innovation but also empowers businesses and professionals, including Business Analysts, to leverage the potential of AI in their respective domains.

WHAT IS CHATGPT PLUS?

Alongside the free tier, OpenAI has unveiled ChatGPT Plus, a subscription plan priced at $20 per month. This plan brings forth added advantages, including quicker response times, priority access to new features and enhancements, and expanded API usage limits. Its purpose is to elevate your Chat GPT experience, guaranteeing optimal outcomes from your interactions with the chatbot.

GPT-3 VS GPT-3.5 VS GPT-4: WHAT DOES IT ALL MEAN?

GPT is short for "Generative Pre-trained Transformer." It's an AI language model developed by OpenAI. The term "Generative" means that the model can generate text based on input. "Pre-trained" indicates that the model has been trained on a large dataset and fine-tuned using human feedback and reinforcement learning. "Transformer" refers to the neural network design used in GPT, which has become the foundation for many advanced natural language processing models.

In essence, GPT is the language model used by the ChatGPT AI bot to understand context and generate coherent, human-like text. The numbers following GPT, such as "GPT-3.5" or "GPT-4," represent different versions of the model. GPT-4 is the latest version used by ChatGPT.

While GPT-3 showed impressive results in AI language processing, GPT-3.5 pushed the boundaries further by improving both processing and output quality. However, GPT-4 takes it even further and is much more concise than 3.5. In fact, it was able to pass the law bar exam effortlessly!

Now that we've covered the basics, let's move on to the next section where we'll explain the exact steps to start using ChatGPT.

SIGNING UP FOR CHATGPT

So you're ready to dive into ChatGPT? Great! This guide will walk you through every step. Don't worry, it's simple. Just make sure you have a browser like Google Chrome or Firefox, or really, any browser you like to use on your computer or phone.

Step 1: Head over to chat.openai.com. You'll see a "Sign up" button right there. Click it.

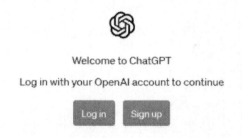

Step 2: You'll see a form asking for your email and password. Fill it out. If you want to make it even easier, you can use your Google or Microsoft account to sign up.

Create your account

Please note that phone verification is required for
signup. Your number will only be used to verify
your identity for security purposes.

Email address

Continue

Already have an account? Log in

OR

G   Continue with Google

▦   Continue with Microsoft Account

Step 3: Before you move ahead, you've got to check your
email to make sure it's really you. So, go ahead and open that
verification email.

Verify your email

We sent an email to
████████@yahoo.com.
Click the link inside to get started.

Resend email

Step 4: Once you've verified your email, you'll be asked to give a
few more details. Just basic stuff

Tell us about you

First name | Last name

Birthday (MM/DD/YYYY) 📅

Continue

By clicking "Continue", you agree to our Terms and
acknowledge our Privacy policy

Step 5: Almost there! Now they'll ask for your mobile number.
You'll get a text with a code. Put that code in.

Verify your phone number

🇺🇸 ⌄ | +1 (415) 123-4567

Send code

Step 6: Boom! You're in. Welcome to ChatGPT!

Quick heads-up: The free version of ChatGPT can sometimes be a bit slow or log you out if lots of people are using it. If you want to skip the line and make things smoother, you might want to look into getting the premium version. We'll talk about how to do that in the next section.

HOW TO SIGN UP
FOR CHATGPT PLUS

If you're finding the free version of ChatGPT pretty neat but want to kick things up a notch—think faster replies, extra features, and first dibs on the cool new stuff—then ChatGPT Plus is what you're after. Upgrading is a cinch, and here's how to do it:

Step 1: Once you're logged in, look at the bottom-left corner of your dashboard. There's a button saying "Upgrade to Plus." Give it a click.

 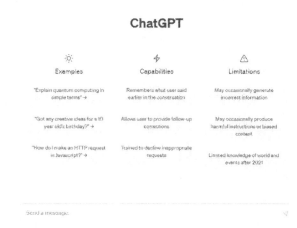

Step 2: You'll then see another button that says "Upgrade Plan." Go ahead, click it too.

Your plan ✕

Free plan

Your current plan

⊘ Available when demand is low

⊘ Standard response speed

⊘ Regular model updates

ChatGPT Plus USD $20/mo

Upgrade plan

⊘ Available even when demand is high

⊘ Faster response speed

⊘ Priority access to new features

I need help with a billing issue

Now you'll go through the steps to put in your payment info and finish subscribing.

It's $20 a month, but what you get is more than worth it. Faster replies, no waiting—even during busy times—and you even get the latest from OpenAI, like the super-advanced GPT-4 model.

So, if you want the best experience ChatGPT has to offer, ChatGPT Plus is the way to go.

USING CHATGPT

Alright, you've mastered the art of ChatGPT. In this section, we'll delve into the essential knowledge that will empower you to maximize its potential and wield ChatGPT with finesse. We'll explore the art of crafting impeccable prompts and navigating seamless back-and-forth exchanges. Get ready to unlock the full potential of ChatGPT and become a true virtuoso in its utilization.

WHAT IS A CHATGPT PROMPT?

OpenAI recently launched their new ChatGPT system, a machine learning tool designed for natural language communication. It has the ability to imitate human conversations and engage with individuals accordingly. ChatGPT can adapt to ongoing conversations and learn to provide appropriate responses. With increased usage, the system improves over time.

A ChatGPT prompt serves as an opening statement or question to initiate a conversation with the AI assistant, ChatGPT. This AI language model has been extensively trained on a vast amount of data and can generate responses that resemble human language. These prompts typically revolve around specific topics like technology, health, education, entertainment, and more.

Using natural language processing techniques, ChatGPT comprehends the prompt and generates a coherent and relevant response. ChatGPT prompts can be utilized for various purposes, such as gathering information, problem-solving, or simply engaging in a friendly chat. The quality of the response may vary depending on the topic, complexity of the prompt, and the training data of the AI model. The ultimate aim of a ChatGPT prompt is to initiate a friendly and captivating conversation with the AI assistant while obtaining the desired information in a natural language format.

CHATGPT PERFECT PROMPT BASICS

To write the perfect ChatGPT prompts, it's important to know some general rules. Here are tips for crafting ideal prompts:

1. Choose a clear and specific topic: Select a topic that aligns with your interests, questions, or goals. Avoid broad or ambiguous topics to keep the conversation focused and engaging.

2. Ask open-ended questions: Encourage discussion and reflection by posing questions that require thoughtful and elaborate answers, rather than simple yes or no responses.

3. Provide context: Help the AI assistant or human responder understand the purpose, scope, and goals of your prompt by offering some background information. This can lead to a more personalized and helpful response.

4. Be courteous and respectful: Foster a friendly and supportive conversation environment by using polite and respectful language. This enhances the quality of the response and builds a positive relationship with the assistant.

5. Use clear and concise language: Opt for straightforward and concise language that is easy to understand. This minimizes misunderstandings and enables the chatbot or human responder to provide relevant and helpful responses.

By following these tips, you can create relevant, engaging, and focused prompts for ChatGPT.

WRITE PERFECT PROMPTS FOR CHATGPT IN 5 SIMPLE STEPS

Ready to take your ChatGPT experience to the next level? The secret lies in becoming a master of prompt writing. In this chapter, we'll guide you through five straightforward steps that will lay the foundation for your success. But that's not all. As you progress through this book, we'll equip you with an extensive collection of prompts tailored to your unique role and industry. So, stay with us on this journey, because our goal isn't just to enhance your ChatGPT interactions—it's to bring about a transformative experience.

1. Narrow down your topic

To narrow your ChatGPT prompt, follow these steps:
• Brainstorm ideas: Start with broad themes or topics you're interested in, like sports, music, travel, technology, health, or finance.
• Identify specific topics: Find sub-topics within your chosen theme, such as artificial intelligence, cybersecurity, or social media for technology.
• Consider the audience: Think about what your target audience finds interesting or relevant to engage them and get

insightful responses.
• Research the topic: Make sure you have enough knowledge on the subject to ask informed and relevant questions.
• Define the scope: Ensure your prompt is specific and focused, avoiding broad or vague prompts that may confuse the AI assistant.

2. Use action words

Using action words is crucial for crafting an impeccable ChatGPT prompt. These words ensure that the prompt is precise, explicit, and captivating. They effectively convey the prompt's purpose and motivate the AI assistant to deliver informative and insightful responses. Below, you'll find a comprehensive list of action words to employ when composing the ideal ChatGPT prompts:

• Identify
• Describe
• Explain
• Compare
• Contrast
• Discuss
• Analyze
• Evaluate
• Recommend
• Suggest
• Propose
• Predict
• Assess
• Interpret
• Apply
• Demonstrate
• Illustrate
• Elaborate
• Justify
• Validate

3. Provide context for the AI

When crafting the perfect ChatGPT prompt, it's crucial to provide context for your topic. This helps the AI assistant grasp the background, purpose, and scope of the prompt. Here are some tips to ensure you provide ample context:

• Define your topic: Start by offering a clear and concise definition. This familiarizes the AI assistant with the topic, enabling it to focus on the specific issue or question at hand.

• Provide additional information: Share details about the topic's history, current status, and future trends. This gives the AI assistant more context and background.

• Explain the purpose: Highlight why the topic is relevant or important to you and why you're interested in discussing it with the AI assistant. This helps focus the conversation and make the prompt more engaging.

• Outline goals or objectives: Clearly outline what you hope to achieve or the specific information you're seeking. This ensures the AI assistant understands your intentions.

• Use supporting examples: Illustrate your topic with relevant examples or anecdotes. This adds depth and detail to the issues you wish to discuss.

4. Define what output you want

To optimize your time, it's crucial to clearly define the desired output for ChatGPT in your prompt. Consider these key aspects to ensure the output meets your needs:

• Tone: Specify whether you prefer a formal, informal, friendly, or professional response from ChatGPT.

• Language: Indicate the language you expect ChatGPT to use in its response. If you have a specific language requirement, mention it in your prompt.

• Length: Define the desired response length, whether it's a concise answer, a paragraph, or a more extensive reply.

• Format: Specify the expected response format, such as text, audio, or video.

• Depth of Detail: Clearly define the level of detail you need in the response. If you require a thorough analysis of a specific topic, include it in the prompt.

• Personalization: Determine the desired level of personalization in the response. Would you like ChatGPT to address you by name, offer recommendations based on your interests, or engage in a conversation resembling human interaction?

5. Interact with the AI

To craft an impeccable ChatGPT prompt, it's crucial to master the art of interacting with ChatGPT to obtain optimal responses. Here are some valuable tips for engaging with ChatGPT effectively:

• Pose Follow-Up Questions: Don't hesitate to ask more targeted follow-up questions if you require additional details on specific parts of the response. This will refine and clarify the response.

• Fine-Tune Answers: If ChatGPT provides an answer that doesn't quite meet your expectations, offer feedback and refine the question or prompt. This will result in a more accurate and focused response.

• Seek Clarification: If the response is unclear or ambiguous, request clarification. This ensures a more precise and tailored response that aligns with your needs.

• Provide Feedback: Share feedback on the quality and relevance of the response received from ChatGPT. This feedback personalizes future interactions and leads to better-informed responses.

• Specify: Clearly communicate your intent or purpose in the conversation, instructing the AI to be more specific. Define what you expect from the AI Assistant to receive the desired response.

• Stay Engaged: Maintain an active presence in the conversation with ChatGPT by asking relevant questions, fostering an informative dialogue, and consistently providing feedback.

By adhering to these tips for crafting perfect prompts and refining your interactions with the AI chatbot, you'll achieve superior results with greater efficiency than ever before!

EXAMPLES OF BAD CHATGPT PROMPTS

Here are some examples of poor ChatGPT prompts:
• "Tell me anything you know." – This prompt lacks specificity and context for the AI assistant to work with.
• "I don't know what to ask. What do you want to talk about?" – This prompt places the entire burden of the conversation on the AI assistant without providing direction or context.
• "Can you write me a story?" – This vague prompt lacks specific details or context for the AI assistant to work with.
• "Do my homework." – This prompt is unethical, inappropriate, and does not encourage insightful or meaningful responses from the AI assistant.
• "What color am I thinking of?" – This meaningless and irrelevant prompt does not provide any feedback or learning from the interaction.
• "Talk to me about nothing." – This unconstructive and vague prompt prevents the AI assistant from initiating an engaging conversation without any context.
• "Why are you so dumb?" – This disrespectful and inappropriate prompt hinders engagement with the AI assistant.

In general, poor ChatGPT prompts are overly general or vague, lack context or clarity, use inappropriate language, or are simply irrelevant to engage the AI assistant. The prompts should be focused, clear, and appropriate to generate valuable insights and learning.

EXAMPLES OF GOOD CHATGPT PROMPTS

Here are some examples of effective ChatGPT prompts:

• "Define zero waste practices and suggest ways individuals can incorporate them into their daily lives."

• "Recommend innovative technologies, tools, and best practices to enhance supply chain processes and reduce waste."

• "Explore how businesses can utilize data analytics to gain a better understanding of customer needs and enhance sales and marketing outcomes."

• "Share instances of how Machine Learning models are being utilized in the healthcare industry to enhance diagnosis, treatment, and patient outcomes."

• "Discuss strategies to enhance environmental sustainability in food production and distribution, including effective initiatives and policies."

• "Analyze the pros and cons of remote work and propose practices that companies should implement to ensure its success."

• Effective ChatGPT prompts are focused, specific, and encourage in-depth engagement from the AI assistant. They provide sufficient background, context, and guidance for the assistant to develop informative and insightful responses. Additionally, they aim to address real-world problems rather than posing meaningless questions.

WHAT ARE CHATGPT CUSTOM INSTRUCTIONS?

Custom Instructions enable you to personalize your ChatGPT interactions, ensuring the model captures your unique tone, style, and expertise. Instead of relying solely on its extensive yet general database, ChatGPT takes direct guidance from you to shape its responses.

This feature also eliminates the inconvenience of repeatedly inputting or copying important details and preferences every time you use ChatGPT. Custom Instructions enforce your guidelines, writing style, and instructions, optimizing your interactions and saving you valuable time.

At a fundamental level, Custom Instructions can be used to maintain a consistent voice and style across blog posts, emails, and marketing materials. For those in development and programming roles, Custom Instructions empower you to guide ChatGPT in generating code with a unified and efficient style.

For instance, imagine a teacher creating a lesson plan without having to constantly mention that they are teaching 3rd-grade science. Similarly, a developer aiming for streamlined Python code can state their preference just once, and ChatGPT will consistently take it into account.

HOW DO I
USE CUSTOM
INSTRUCTIONS?

Utilizing ChatGPT's Custom Instructions for content creation is a simple yet powerful method that can bring about significant advantages. Whether you're composing blog articles, social media posts, or promotional materials, establishing personalized guidelines can enhance your productivity and enhance the excellence of your work.

STEPS TO ACTIVATE CHATGPT CUSTOM INSTRUCTIONS

Below the 2 quick steps on how to set up ChatGPT custom Instructions.

Step 1. Click the three dots next to your name and select "Custom instructions."

Step 2. Set up custom instructions

Custom instructions ⓘ

What would you like ChatGPT to know about you to provide better responses?

0/1500

How would you like ChatGPT to respond?

0/1500

Enabled for new chats ⬤   Cancel   Save

If you're looking for ChatGPT to function in a specific role, you can indicate that in your custom instructions. Here's how you could add that element:

"ChatGPT, act as a job function assistant, focusing on administrative tasks. Please respond in a formal tone, summarizing your thoughts in bullet points. Keep your responses concise and within 100 words. Confirm your understanding of our mission and vision before proceeding with the conversation."

In this example, specifying "act as a job function assistant focusing on administrative tasks" gives ChatGPT a role to play, guiding the nature of its responses to fit within the scope of typical administrative assistance. This can be particularly useful if you want the conversation to focus on a specific set of tasks or functions.

Besides that you can set custom instructions for how you would like ChatGPT to respond, you could specify things like tone, format, or any special requirements. Here are some examples:

• Tone: "Please respond in a formal/business tone."
• Format: "Summarize your responses in bullet points."
• Depth: "Provide detailed explanations for any technical terms used."
• Length: "Keep responses concise, not exceeding 100 words."
• Interactivity: "Ask follow-up questions to clarify any unclear points."
• Focus: "Please focus on the practical applications of our offerings."
• Verification: "Confirm your understanding of our mission and vision before proceeding."

So a custom instruction could look something like:
"ChatGPT, please respond in a formal tone, summarizing your thoughts in bullet points. Keep your responses concise and within 100 words. Confirm your understanding of our mission and vision before proceeding with the conversation."

Example custom instructions for: "What would you like ChatGPT to know about you to provide better responses?"

In order to receive more personalized and accurate responses from ChatGPT, you might consider providing some background information or specifying your preferences and needs. Here's how you could phrase those custom instructions:

Prompt:
Hello, ChatGPT. Meet [Company Name]—our mission is to [Business Mission] and our vision is [Business Vision]. We are in the [industry], and we specialize in [brief description].

Key USPs:
[USP 1]
[USP 2]
[USP 3]

KPIs we track:
[KPI 1]
[KPI 2]
[KPI 3]

Our offerings:
[Product/Service 1]: [Brief Benefit]
[Product/Service 2]: [Brief Benefit]
[Product/Service 3]: [Brief Benefit]

Please confirm your understanding and keep these details in mind for our conversation. Feel free to ask questions.
Note that custom instructions fields can contain a maximum of 1500 characters.

Example custom instructions for: "How would you like ChatGPT to respond?"

To specify ChatGPT's role, include it in your custom instructions. For example:

"ChatGPT, act as a job function assistant, focusing on administrative tasks. Respond formally, summarizing in bullet points. Keep responses concise within 100 words. Confirm understanding of our mission and vision before proceeding."

By specifying "act as a job function assistant focusing on administrative tasks," you guide ChatGPT's responses to align with typical administrative assistance. This is helpful when focusing on specific tasks or functions.

Custom instructions can also include tone, format, or special

requirements. Examples:
· Tone: "Respond in a formal/business tone."
· Format: "Summarize responses in bullet points."
· Depth: "Provide detailed explanations for technical terms."
· Length: "Keep responses concise, under 100 words."
· Interactivity: "Ask follow-up questions for clarity."
· Focus: "Emphasize practical applications of our offerings."
· Verification: "Confirm understanding of our mission and vision."

A custom instruction may look like this:
"ChatGPT, respond formally, summarizing in bullet points. Keep responses concise within 100 words. Confirm understanding of our mission and vision before proceeding."

CHATGPT'S ADVANCED DATA ANALYSIS FEATURE - ANALYSE DATA WITHIN MINUTES.

CHATGPT ADVANCED DATA ANALYSIS UNVEILED

Welcome to the expansive and ever-evolving realm of AI. Today, we shall acquaint ourselves with the groundbreaking Advanced Data Analysis tool of ChatGPT. Prepare to embark on a journey that transcends mere text generation, delving into a domain where executing code, unraveling complex problems, and effortlessly managing file uploads and downloads become second nature. The future, my esteemed colleagues, is not a distant tomorrow – it is upon us today. Let us wholeheartedly embrace it with ChatGPT's Advanced Data Analysis, as I take you on a guided tour of its awe-inspiring capabilities.

TRANSCENDING THE STANDARD CHATGPT LIMITATIONS

In the realm of AI's ever-evolving impact on technology, ChatGPT emerges as a true testament to innovation. However, it has encountered its fair share of limitations - grappling with mathematical conundrums, lacking the ability to generate or comprehend images, and occasionally producing hallucinatory responses. But fret not, for those days are now behind us. Enter the realm of Advanced Data Analysis, where you can effortlessly conquer all of the aforementioned challenges and so much more, with utmost finesse and accuracy.

A DATA ANALYST SITTING NEXT TO YOU

Do not fear the intricacy, as even the most cutting-edge tools have their origins in simplicity. Advanced Data Analysis, previously referred to as the Code Interpreter, serves as a guiding light, enriching ChatGPT's capabilities to execute mathematical computations, scrutinize data, decipher Python code, and beyond. Therefore, fret not about the complexities, as Advanced Data Analysis ensures your security and proficiency.

ACTIVATING ADVANCED DATA ANALYSIS IN CHATGPT

Turning on the Advanced Data Analysis is simple.

Please note, this feature is only available in the paid version of ChatGPT Plus.

If you have an account, just follow these steps:
1. Logging In: Easily sign in to your ChatGPT Plus account.
2. Navigating to Settings: Head to the settings page. This is your control center in ChatGPT.

3. Selecting the Beta Option: Choose "Beta." You'll see various options here, including the Advanced Data Analysis.

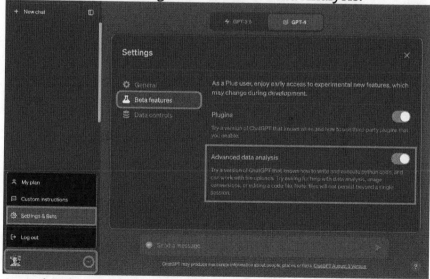

4. Activation: Just click to activate the Advanced Data Analysis plugin, like flipping on a light switch.

5. Now you can upload a file.

6. Select any file you want to use from your computer.

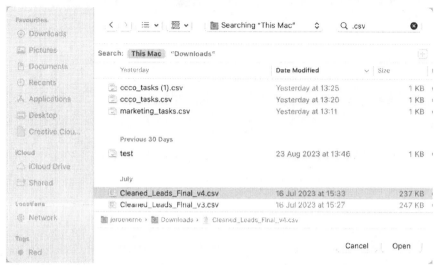

7. And now you can interact with that file. You can make new versions, data visualisations, analaysis. etc.

🗂 Advanced Data Analysis

Cleaned_Leads_Final_v4.csv
Spreadsheet

Make a new CSV with new leads from the Restaurant Industry and only add CEOs, General Directors and Founders to the new sheet.

To begin processing the CSV file and extracting leads from the Restaurant Industry with titles of CEOs, General Directors, and Founders, let's first load the CSV file and examine its contents. This will help us understand the structure of the data and identify the relevant columns for filtering the leads. Shall we proceed?

↻ Regenerate

⊕ Yes   ▶

ChatGPT may produce inaccurate information about people, places, or facts. ChatGPT September 25 Version

PRACTICAL EXAMPLES

Unleash the boundless opportunities of ChatGPT's Advanced Data Analysis. Picture yourself effortlessly uploading data, crafting impactful visualizations, and effortlessly downloading the results. With a reservoir of formidable power at your fingertips, you can analyze extensive datasets, detect anomalies, and make enlightened decisions based on accurate, trustworthy data in mere moments. The authority to unlock these potentials is firmly within your grasp, waiting to be unleashed.

Uploadable File Types:
- Text Files (.txt, .csv, .json, .xml, etc.)
- Image Files (.jpg, .png, .gif, etc.)
- Document Files (.pdf, .docx, .xlsx, .pptx, etc.)
- Code Files (.py, .js, .html, .css, etc.)
- Data Files (.csv, .xlsx, .tsv, .json, etc.)
- Audio Files (.mp3, .wav, etc.)
- Video Files (.mp4, .avi, .mov, etc.)

The Analysis possibilities.
Embark on a multitude of tasks and analysis when you upload your chosen file type:

- File Transformation: Seamlessly transition between file types, merging and converting as needed.

- Inquisitive Analysis: Question your data, uncovering hidden layers and invaluable insights.
- Advanced Analytics: Navigate through vast amounts of data, exploring trends, patterns, and data-driven pathways for decision-making.
- Data Visualization: Bring your data to life with vibrant, clear, and informative visuals, enhancing understanding and interpretation.
- Anomaly Detection: Identify and analyze anomalies within your data, providing clarity and ensuring data reliability.
- Predictive Analytics: Harness your data to anticipate and prepare for future trends and events.
- Text Analysis: Delve into textual data for sentiment analysis, keyword extraction, and more, revealing the sentiments and themes within.
- Image and Video Analysis: Extract valuable information from images and videos, analyzing content, patterns, and features.
. Maintain a similar writing style.

JOURNEY AHEAD

In the upcoming chapters, we will delve into the multitude of tasks that can be achieved using Advanced Data Analysis prompts. These comprehensive guides will expertly steer you through the vast realm of advanced data analytics, ensuring confidence and clarity every step of the way.

The future never stands still, but with Advanced Data Analysis, you're not merely progressing towards it; you're beckoning the future towards yourself. Stay tuned for more insights in a similar writing style.

USING AI TO CREATE YOUR VISUALS (PHOTO'S, IMAGES, ART ETC)

Creating visually appealing and relevant imagery has always been a crucial part of storytelling, marketing, and conveying complex ideas. The emergence of artificial intelligence (AI) has greatly expanded the possibilities of image creation. AI now allows us to effortlessly generate photo-realistic images, 3D renders, cartoons, explainer visuals, and descriptive imagery, which used to be a laborious task. Two remarkable AI tools in this field are Midjourney and DALL-E.

Midjourney
Midjourney is an artificial intelligence program and service developed by San Francisco-based independent research lab Midjourney, Inc. It transforms natural language descriptions, known as "prompts," into a wide range of image styles. Whether you need a serene landscape, a complex architectural design in 3D, or a simple cartoon for a children's book, Midjourney makes these creative endeavors easily accessible. Explore Midjourney: https://www.midjourney.com.

DALL-E
DALL-E, DALL-E 2, and DALL-E 3 are text-to-image models

created by OpenAI using deep learning techniques. They generate digital images from natural language descriptions, or "prompts." With a simple text prompt, these models can produce a variety of images, from photo-realistic visuals to stylized cartoons and intricate 3D renders. For example, a prompt like "a futuristic city skyline" could result in a highly detailed 3D render or a stylized cartoon, depending on the specified parameters. Explore DALL-E: https://openai.com/dall-e-2.

Although the journey of creating images using AI tools like DALL-E and the envisioned Midjourney is filled with endless creative possibilities, it may require some learning. For video instructions on how to leverage these AI tools for image creation, visit jeroenerne.com/AI-images. This link provides a visual guide that can help you better understand and navigate the process of AI-assisted image generation, making the transition from textual description to visual representation a breeze.

CHATGPT FOR BUSINESS ANALYSTSS

Welcome to this transformative guide for Business Analystss. If you want to boost efficiency and innovation, you're in the right place. This book introduces ChatGPT, an AI-powered tool that will be your essential ally.

What's Ahead
In the upcoming chapters, we'll explore the specific tasks that define your role. Each chapter provides focused instructions and tailored prompts to help you tackle the unique challenges of your industry and job.

Tailored Prompts for Your Role
We've carefully curated over 1000 prompts to assist you with everything from routine tasks to complex projects. This isn't a one-size-fits-all solution; it's a targeted toolkit to enhance your day-to-day operations. As a book owner, you can request a document with all these prompts at https://jeroenerne.com/prompt/ for easy copying and pasting.

MARKET TREND
ANALYSIS

DECIPHERING MARKET TRENDS

In the dynamic landscape of business analysis, artificial intelligence (AI) and tools like ChatGPT are revolutionizing how we approach market trend analysis. The key lies in harnessing AI's power to dissect vast amounts of market data, transforming them into actionable insights for strategic planning. This process not only accelerates the analysis but also enhances its accuracy, leading to more informed decision-making.

Imagine Sarah, a business analyst at a mid-sized tech firm. Tasked with identifying upcoming market trends in the tech industry, she turns to AI-driven tools like ChatGPT. With these tools, Sarah can swiftly sift through global market reports, social media chatter, and financial news, gaining a comprehensive view of emerging trends. For instance, she notices a rising interest in sustainable tech solutions across various social platforms. By cross-referencing this with financial reports and market data, she validates this trend as a potential growth area.

Sarah's experience underscores the value of AI in trend analysis. It's not just about faster data processing; it's about the depth and breadth of analysis. AI tools can identify subtle patterns and correlations that might escape human analysts, offering a richer, more nuanced understanding of market dynamics.

For business analysts, integrating AI into their toolkit is no longer optional; it's imperative for staying ahead in a rapidly evolving market. By embracing AI-driven tools, analysts like Sarah can provide their organizations with the foresight to navigate market changes proactively rather than reactively.

In conclusion, AI's role in market trend analysis is transformative. It enables analysts to delve deeper into market data, uncover hidden trends, and offer strategic insights that drive business growth. As AI continues to evolve, its impact on business analysis will only deepen, making it an indispensable part of the analyst's arsenal.

Note: Note that within this chapter, when exploring the strategies, tasks, and ideas, you have the opportunity to employ ChatGPT's Advanced Data Analysis feature. If you seek a more in-depth understanding of this feature, please consult the earlier chapter that elucidates its capabilities.

Task: Data collection

Gathering relevant data on market trends from various sources such as industry reports, market research studies, and online publications.

Example Prompt 1:
ChatGPT, please gather and summarize the key findings from the latest industry report on market trends in our target

industry. Include information on emerging technologies, consumer preferences, and competitive landscape.

Example Prompt 2:

ChatGPT, analyze and extract relevant data from market research studies conducted in the past year. Focus on trends related to customer behavior, purchasing patterns, and market segmentation. Provide a concise summary of the findings.

Example Prompt 3:

ChatGPT, search online publications and extract data on the latest market trends in our industry. Pay particular attention to articles discussing disruptive innovations, changing consumer demands, and shifts in market dynamics. Compile the information in a comprehensive report.

Example Prompt 4:

ChatGPT, utilize advanced data processing capabilities to analyze and compare market trends across multiple sources. Identify common themes, patterns, and discrepancies in the data collected from industry reports, market research studies, and online publications. Present the findings in a visually appealing format for easy interpretation.

Task: Data cleaning and preprocessing

Removing any inconsistencies or errors in the collected data to ensure accuracy and reliability.

Example Prompt 1:

Develop a ChatGPT model that can identify and correct common data inconsistencies and errors in the collected dataset. Train the model using a combination of clean and noisy data samples to ensure accurate and reliable data cleaning and preprocessing.

Example Prompt 2:

Design a ChatGPT system that can automatically detect and handle missing values in the collected dataset. Implement advanced data processing techniques to impute missing values and ensure the accuracy and reliability of the preprocessed data.

Example Prompt 3:
Create a ChatGPT-based solution that can identify and rectify inconsistent data formats within the collected dataset. Utilize advanced data processing functionality to standardize data formats and eliminate any inconsistencies, ensuring the accuracy and reliability of the preprocessed data.

Example Prompt 4:
Build a ChatGPT model capable of identifying and resolving duplicate records in the collected dataset. Leverage advanced data processing techniques such as fuzzy matching and record linkage to detect and remove duplicate entries, ensuring the accuracy and reliability of the preprocessed data.

Task: Data analysis

Analyzing the collected data to identify patterns, trends, and insights related to market trends.

Example Prompt 1:
Using ChatGPT's Advanced Data processing functionality, analyze the collected market data to identify patterns and trends in consumer behavior. Provide insights on how these trends can impact the market and suggest potential strategies for businesses to capitalize on them.

Example Prompt 2:
Leveraging ChatGPT's Advanced Data processing functionality, conduct a comprehensive analysis of the collected data to identify emerging market trends. Highlight any significant shifts in consumer preferences, purchasing behavior, or market dynamics, and provide actionable insights for businesses to adapt their strategies accordingly.

Example Prompt 3:

Utilize ChatGPT's Advanced Data processing functionality to analyze the collected market data and identify key patterns and insights related to competitor analysis. Identify market gaps, competitive advantages, and potential threats, and provide recommendations on how businesses can position themselves effectively in the market.

Example Prompt 4:

With the help of ChatGPT's Advanced Data processing functionality, perform a deep dive analysis of the collected data to uncover hidden insights and correlations related to market trends. Identify any untapped market opportunities, potential customer segments, or emerging niche markets, and provide strategic recommendations for businesses to capitalize on these findings.

Task: Competitor analysis

Examining the strategies, products, and performance of competitors in the market to understand their impact on current market trends.

Example Prompt 1:

Using ChatGPT's Advanced Data processing functionality, analyze and compare the marketing strategies employed by our top three competitors in the market. Highlight the key tactics they use to attract customers and gain market share, and provide insights on how these strategies impact current market trends.

Example Prompt 2:

Leveraging ChatGPT's Advanced Data processing functionality, conduct a comprehensive analysis of our competitors' product portfolios. Identify the strengths and weaknesses of their offerings, compare them to our own products, and provide recommendations on how we can improve our product lineup to stay competitive in the market.

Example Prompt 3:

With the help of ChatGPT's Advanced Data processing

functionality, evaluate the financial performance of our main competitors over the past three years. Analyze their revenue growth, profitability, and market share trends, and assess the impact of these factors on the current market landscape. Provide actionable insights on how we can adapt our business strategies to counter their influence.

Example Prompt 4:

Utilizing ChatGPT's Advanced Data processing functionality, examine the online presence and customer engagement strategies of our competitors. Analyze their social media activities, customer reviews, and online reputation to understand how they are influencing current market trends. Provide recommendations on how we can enhance our own online presence and engage with customers more effectively to stay ahead of the competition.

Task: Consumer behavior analysis

Studying consumer preferences, buying patterns, and demographics to identify shifts in market trends and understand customer needs.

Example Prompt 1:

Using ChatGPT's Advanced Data processing functionality, analyze consumer behavior data to identify emerging market trends and understand changing customer preferences. Provide insights on how these trends can impact your business strategy and suggest potential product or service enhancements to meet evolving customer needs.

Example Prompt 2:

Leverage ChatGPT's Advanced Data processing functionality to conduct a comprehensive analysis of consumer buying patterns across different demographics. Identify key factors influencing purchasing decisions and recommend strategies to optimize your marketing efforts and improve customer engagement.

Example Prompt 3:

With the help of ChatGPT's Advanced Data processing functionality, analyze consumer preferences and demographics to uncover hidden patterns and correlations. Provide actionable insights on how to tailor your product offerings and marketing campaigns to better align with customer needs and increase market share.

Example Prompt 4:
Utilize ChatGPT's Advanced Data processing functionality to perform a deep dive into consumer behavior data, including online interactions and purchase history. Identify customer segments with specific preferences and buying patterns, and propose personalized marketing strategies to enhance customer satisfaction and drive sales growth.

Task: Industry analysis

Assessing the overall industry landscape, including market size, growth rate, and key players, to determine the broader market trends.

Example Prompt 1:
Using ChatGPT's Advanced Data processing functionality, analyze the market size and growth rate of the industry over the past five years. Identify any significant trends or patterns that can help assess the overall industry landscape.

Example Prompt 2:
Leveraging ChatGPT's Advanced Data processing functionality, provide an in-depth analysis of the key players in the industry. Identify their market share, competitive advantages, and growth strategies to understand their impact on the broader market trends.

Example Prompt 3:
With the help of ChatGPT's Advanced Data processing functionality, analyze the historical data and industry reports to identify the emerging trends and disruptive technologies that are

shaping the industry landscape. Assess their potential impact on market size and growth rate.

Example Prompt 4:
Utilizing ChatGPT's Advanced Data processing functionality, conduct a comparative analysis of the industry's sub-sectors. Evaluate their respective market sizes, growth rates, and key players to determine the overall industry landscape and identify potential growth opportunities.

Task: Technology analysis

Evaluating emerging technologies and their potential impact on market trends, such as artificial intelligence, blockchain, or Internet of Things (IoT).

Example Prompt 1:
ChatGPT, analyze the potential impact of artificial intelligence on market trends in the next five years. Consider factors such as adoption rates, industry disruptions, and potential challenges faced by businesses.

Example Prompt 2:
ChatGPT, evaluate the role of blockchain technology in shaping market trends. Discuss its potential applications, benefits, and challenges faced by businesses in adopting blockchain solutions.

Example Prompt 3:
ChatGPT, analyze the impact of the Internet of Things (IoT) on market trends. Explore the potential benefits, risks, and challenges associated with the widespread adoption of IoT devices across industries.

Example Prompt 4:
ChatGPT, assess the emerging technologies that are likely to have a significant impact on market trends in the next decade. Provide an overview of these technologies, their potential applications, and the potential disruptions they may cause in various industries.

Task: Economic analysis

Examining economic indicators, such as GDP, inflation rates, and interest rates, to understand their influence on market trends.

Example Prompt 1:

ChatGPT, analyze the relationship between GDP growth and market trends over the past decade. Provide insights on how changes in GDP have influenced market performance and identify any patterns or correlations between the two.

Example Prompt 2:

Using ChatGPT's advanced data processing functionality, examine the impact of inflation rates on market trends in the last five years. Identify any sectors or industries that have been particularly affected by inflation and provide recommendations for investors based on these findings.

Example Prompt 3:

ChatGPT, analyze the historical relationship between interest rates and market trends. Identify any instances where changes in interest rates have led to significant shifts in market performance and provide an explanation for these patterns.

Example Prompt 4:

Using ChatGPT's advanced data processing capabilities, conduct a comparative analysis of GDP growth, inflation rates, and interest rates in different countries. Identify any global trends or patterns that can help investors understand the potential impact of these economic indicators on market trends across various regions.

Task: Social media analysis

Monitoring social media platforms to track discussions, sentiments, and influencers related to market trends.

Example Prompt 1:

Develop a ChatGPT model that can analyze social media conversations and identify key market trends by tracking discussions, sentiments, and influencers. The model should be able to process large volumes of social media data and provide real-time insights to support decision-making in marketing strategies.

Example Prompt 2:
Create a ChatGPT system that can monitor social media platforms and extract relevant data to analyze discussions, sentiments, and influencers related to market trends. The system should be capable of filtering and categorizing social media content, identifying emerging trends, and providing comprehensive reports on the impact of these trends on the market.

Example Prompt 3:
Design a ChatGPT-based solution that can automatically track and analyze social media conversations to identify sentiment patterns and influential users in relation to market trends. The solution should leverage advanced data processing techniques to extract meaningful insights, such as sentiment analysis, topic modeling, and network analysis, to support effective social media monitoring and decision-making.

Example Prompt 4:
Build a ChatGPT-powered tool that can perform real-time social media analysis, tracking discussions, sentiments, and influencers relevant to market trends. The tool should utilize advanced data processing functionality to identify sentiment shifts, detect emerging trends, and provide actionable insights for businesses to adapt their marketing strategies accordingly.

Task: Reporting and visualization

Presenting the findings of the market trend analysis in a clear and visually appealing manner, using charts, graphs, and reports.

Example Prompt 1:

Generate a visually appealing report summarizing the market trend analysis for the past quarter, including charts and graphs that highlight key findings and insights.

Example Prompt 2:
Create a detailed presentation showcasing the market trend analysis results, utilizing ChatGPT's advanced data processing functionality to generate interactive charts and graphs.

Example Prompt 3:
Produce a comprehensive report that presents the findings of the market trend analysis, using ChatGPT's advanced data processing capabilities to generate visually appealing charts and graphs that effectively communicate the trends.

Example Prompt 4:
Utilize ChatGPT's advanced data processing functionality to generate visually appealing reports and visualizations that effectively communicate the market trend analysis findings, ensuring clarity and ease of understanding for stakeholders.

Idea: Competitor Analysis

ChatGPT can assist in gathering and analyzing data on competitors' market trends, including their product offerings, pricing strategies, and customer feedback.

Example Prompt 1:
Prompt: "As a business analyst, I need ChatGPT to assist me in gathering and analyzing data on our competitors' market trends. Please provide a detailed analysis of our top three competitors, including their product offerings, pricing strategies, and customer feedback. Additionally, identify any emerging trends or opportunities that we can leverage in our own business strategy."

Example Prompt 2:
Prompt: "ChatGPT, I require your support as a business analyst to

conduct a comprehensive competitor analysis. Please gather data on our main competitors' product offerings, pricing strategies, and customer feedback. Analyze this information and provide a comparison report highlighting our strengths and weaknesses in relation to our competitors. Additionally, identify any gaps in the market that we can capitalize on to gain a competitive advantage."

Example Prompt 3:

Prompt: "As a business analyst, I need ChatGPT's advanced data processing functionality to assist me in analyzing our competitors' market trends. Please gather data on our top five competitors' product offerings, pricing strategies, and customer feedback. Based on this analysis, provide recommendations on potential areas of improvement for our own product offerings and pricing strategies. Additionally, identify any emerging trends that we should be aware of to stay ahead in the market."

Example Prompt 4:

Prompt: "ChatGPT, I require your assistance as a business analyst to gather and analyze data on our competitors' market trends. Please collect information on our main competitors' product offerings, pricing strategies, and customer feedback. Based on this data, provide insights on how we can differentiate ourselves from our competitors and attract more customers. Additionally, identify any potential threats or challenges posed by our competitors' strategies and suggest countermeasures to mitigate them."

Idea: Consumer Behavior Analysis

ChatGPT can help in understanding consumer preferences, buying patterns, and emerging trends by analyzing social media conversations, online reviews, and customer surveys.

Example Prompt 1:

Prompt: As a business analyst, I need ChatGPT's advanced data processing functionality to analyze social media conversations *and identify emerging consumer trends. Please provide insights on the latest preferences and buying patterns in the fashion industry based on social media discussions and online reviews.*

Example Prompt 2:
Prompt: ChatGPT, as a business analyst, I require your assistance in understanding consumer preferences and buying patterns in the technology sector. Analyze customer surveys and online reviews to identify the most sought-after features in smartphones and laptops, and provide insights on emerging trends in this market.

Example Prompt 3:
Prompt: As a business analyst, I need ChatGPT's advanced data processing capabilities to analyze social media conversations and customer surveys in the food and beverage industry. Please provide insights on the changing consumer preferences and emerging food trends, such as plant-based diets or gluten-free options, based on the gathered data.

Example Prompt 4:
Prompt: ChatGPT, as a business analyst, I require your support in analyzing social media conversations and online reviews to understand consumer preferences and buying patterns in the travel and tourism industry. Please provide insights on emerging travel trends, popular destinations, and factors influencing consumer decision-making when choosing accommodations or travel experiences.

Idea: Industry Research

ChatGPT can aid in conducting comprehensive research on industry trends, including market size, growth rate, key players, and technological advancements.

Example Prompt 1:
As a business analyst, I need ChatGPT to conduct industry research on the automotive sector. Please provide a detailed analysis of the current market size, growth rate, key players, and

any technological advancements in the industry.

Example Prompt 2:
ChatGPT, I require your assistance as a business analyst to research the e-commerce industry. Please gather information on the market size, growth rate, major players, and any recent technological advancements that have impacted the sector.

Example Prompt 3:
As part of my industry research, I need ChatGPT to analyze the healthcare sector. Please provide insights into the market size, growth rate, key players, and any significant technological advancements that have shaped the industry.

Example Prompt 4:
ChatGPT, I'm conducting industry research on the renewable energy sector. Can you assist me by gathering data on the market size, growth rate, major players, and any notable technological advancements that have influenced the industry?

Idea: Market Segmentation

ChatGPT can support the identification and analysis of different market segments based on demographic, psychographic, and behavioral factors, helping businesses target specific customer groups effectively.

Example Prompt 1:
Prompt: As a business analyst, I need ChatGPT to assist me in identifying and analyzing different market segments based on demographic factors. Please provide a detailed analysis of the various customer groups within our target market, considering factors such as age, gender, income level, and location. Additionally, suggest effective strategies for targeting each segment.

Example Prompt 2:
Prompt: ChatGPT, using its advanced data processing

functionality, I require your support in conducting market segmentation analysis based on psychographic factors. Please analyze our target market and identify distinct customer groups based on their interests, values, attitudes, and lifestyle choices. Furthermore, provide recommendations on how businesses can effectively tailor their marketing messages to resonate with each segment.

Example Prompt 3:
Prompt: I need ChatGPT to assist me in analyzing market segments based on behavioral factors. Utilizing its advanced data processing capabilities, please identify and analyze different customer groups within our target market based on their purchasing behavior, brand loyalty, usage patterns, and decision-making processes. Additionally, suggest strategies for businesses to effectively engage and retain each segment.

Example Prompt 4:
Prompt: ChatGPT, as a business analyst, I require your support in conducting a comprehensive market segmentation analysis that considers demographic, psychographic, and behavioral factors. Please analyze our target market and identify distinct customer groups based on a combination of these factors. Provide insights into the characteristics, preferences, and needs of each segment, along with recommendations on how businesses can effectively target and serve these specific customer groups.

Idea: Demand Forecasting
ChatGPT can assist in predicting future market demand by analyzing historical sales data, economic indicators, and consumer behavior patterns.

Example Prompt 1:
Prompt: "As a business analyst, I need ChatGPT to assist in predicting future market demand for our product. Please analyze the historical sales data, economic indicators, and consumer

behavior patterns to forecast the demand for the next quarter. Provide insights on potential factors influencing the demand and any recommendations to optimize our production and inventory management."

Example Prompt 2:
Prompt: "ChatGPT, we are planning to launch a new product in the market. Can you help us forecast the demand for this product by analyzing historical sales data, economic indicators, and consumer behavior patterns? Please provide insights on the expected demand trends, potential market saturation, and any recommendations to effectively position our product in the market."

Example Prompt 3:
Prompt: "Our company is expanding into a new region, and we need to estimate the market demand for our existing product in that region. ChatGPT, please analyze historical sales data, economic indicators specific to the region, and consumer behavior patterns to forecast the demand for the next year. Additionally, provide insights on any regional factors that may impact the demand and suggestions to tailor our marketing strategies accordingly."

Example Prompt 4:
Prompt: "As a business analyst, I'm tasked with predicting the demand for our product during the upcoming holiday season. ChatGPT, please analyze historical sales data, economic indicators during previous holiday seasons, and consumer behavior patterns to forecast the demand for this year's holiday season. Additionally, provide insights on any emerging trends or shifts in consumer preferences that may impact the demand, and recommendations to optimize our marketing and production strategies for the holiday season."

Idea: Pricing Analysis

ChatGPT can help in analyzing pricing trends, competitor pricing strategies, and customer willingness to pay, enabling businesses to optimize their pricing models.

Example Prompt 1:

Prompt: As a business analyst, I need ChatGPT's advanced data processing functionality to analyze pricing trends in the market. Please provide insights on the current pricing trends for our industry, including any notable changes or patterns observed over the past year. Additionally, identify any factors that may have influenced these trends and suggest potential adjustments to our pricing model to optimize profitability.

Example Prompt 2:

Prompt: ChatGPT, using its advanced data processing capabilities, I need your assistance in analyzing competitor pricing strategies. Please gather and analyze data on our key competitors' pricing models, including their pricing structures, discounts, and promotional offers. Based on this analysis, provide recommendations on how we can position our pricing strategy to gain a competitive advantage and attract more customers.

Example Prompt 3:

Prompt: ChatGPT, I require your support as a business analyst to assess customer willingness to pay for our products/services. Utilize your advanced data processing functionality to analyze customer feedback, reviews, and purchase patterns to determine the price sensitivity of our target market. Based on this analysis, suggest pricing adjustments or bundling strategies that can maximize customer satisfaction and revenue generation.

Example Prompt 4:

Prompt: As a business analyst, I need ChatGPT's advanced data processing capabilities to optimize our pricing models. Please analyze historical sales data, customer demographics, and market trends to identify potential pricing segments or customer groups with varying willingness to pay. Based on this analysis, propose personalized pricing strategies or dynamic pricing models that can cater to different customer segments and enhance overall profitability.

Idea: Product Trend Analysis

ChatGPT can support businesses in identifying emerging product trends, analyzing customer preferences, and predicting future demand for specific products or features.

Example Prompt 1:

Prompt: "As a business analyst, I need ChatGPT to perform product trend analysis for our company. Please analyze customer preferences and identify emerging product trends in the electronics industry. Additionally, predict the future demand for wireless earbuds with noise-canceling features."

Example Prompt 2:

Prompt: "ChatGPT, as a business analyst, I require your assistance in conducting product trend analysis for our fashion retail company. Analyze customer preferences and identify emerging product trends in the apparel industry. Furthermore, predict the future demand for sustainable and eco-friendly clothing options."

Example Prompt 3:

Prompt: "As a business analyst, I need ChatGPT to support our market research efforts by analyzing customer preferences and identifying emerging product trends in the food and beverage industry. Please predict the future demand for plant-based protein alternatives and provide insights on consumer preferences for different flavors and packaging options."

Example Prompt 4:

Prompt: "ChatGPT, as a business analyst, I require your expertise in product trend analysis for our automotive company. Analyze customer preferences and identify emerging product trends in the electric vehicle market. Additionally, predict the future demand for electric SUVs with autonomous driving capabilities."

Idea: Market Entry Strategy

ChatGPT can aid in developing market entry strategies by analyzing market trends, competitive landscape, and customer needs, helping businesses make informed decisions.

Example Prompt 1:

As a business analyst, I need ChatGPT to analyze the current market trends, competitive landscape, and customer needs in the automotive industry to help develop a market entry strategy for a new electric vehicle manufacturer. Provide insights on the demand for electric vehicles, key competitors, and customer preferences to guide our decision-making process.

Example Prompt 2:

ChatGPT, please analyze the market trends, competitive landscape, and customer needs in the e-commerce sector to assist in developing a market entry strategy for a new online fashion retailer. Identify emerging trends, major players in the industry, and customer preferences to help us make informed decisions on product offerings and marketing strategies.

Example Prompt 3:

As a business analyst, I require ChatGPT's advanced data processing capabilities to analyze market trends, competitive landscape, and customer needs in the healthcare industry. Provide insights on the latest healthcare innovations, key competitors, and customer demands to support the development of a market entry strategy for a telemedicine platform.

Example Prompt 4:

ChatGPT, please assist in developing a market entry strategy for a new sustainable energy company by analyzing market trends, competitive landscape, and customer needs in the renewable energy sector. Identify emerging technologies, major competitors, and customer preferences to help us make informed decisions on product development and market positioning.

Idea: SWOT Analysis

ChatGPT can assist in conducting a SWOT (Strengths, Weaknesses, Opportunities, Threats) analysis to evaluate the internal and external factors impacting a business and identify market trends that can be leveraged.

Example Prompt 1:

Prompt: Conduct a SWOT analysis for a new startup in the e-commerce industry. Evaluate the strengths and weaknesses of the company's internal operations, identify potential opportunities in the market, and assess the threats posed by competitors. Additionally, ask ChatGPT to provide insights on emerging market trends that the startup can leverage to gain a competitive advantage.

Example Prompt 2:

Prompt: Perform a SWOT analysis for a well-established retail chain. Assess the strengths and weaknesses of the company's brand reputation, supply chain management, and customer loyalty programs. Request ChatGPT to identify potential opportunities in the market, such as expanding into new geographical regions or diversifying product offerings. Also, ask for insights on the threats posed by emerging e-commerce platforms and changing consumer preferences.

Example Prompt 3:

Prompt: Help a small manufacturing company conduct a SWOT analysis to evaluate its internal capabilities and external market conditions. Request ChatGPT to identify the strengths and weaknesses of the company's production processes, supply chain efficiency, and workforce skills. Additionally, ask for insights on potential opportunities in the market, such as partnerships with complementary businesses or adopting sustainable manufacturing practices. Lastly, seek ChatGPT's input on the threats posed by global economic fluctuations and evolving industry regulations.

Example Prompt 4:
Prompt: Assist a technology startup in conducting a SWOT analysis to assess its internal resources and external market dynamics. Ask ChatGPT to evaluate the strengths and weaknesses of the company's technological expertise, intellectual property portfolio, and team composition. Request insights on potential opportunities in the market, such as strategic alliances with established industry players or leveraging emerging technologies. Also, seek ChatGPT's perspective on the threats posed by rapid technological advancements and potential cybersecurity risks.

Idea: Brand Perception Analysis

ChatGPT can help in analyzing brand sentiment, customer perceptions, and online reputation to understand how market trends affect brand image and customer loyalty.

Example Prompt 1:
Prompt: As a business analyst, use ChatGPT's advanced data processing functionality to analyze brand sentiment and customer perceptions for a specific brand. Provide insights on how market trends are affecting the brand's image and customer loyalty.

Example Prompt 2:
Prompt: Utilize ChatGPT's advanced data processing capabilities to conduct a comprehensive brand perception analysis for a selected company. Analyze customer reviews, social media mentions, and online reputation to identify key factors influencing brand sentiment and customer loyalty. Provide recommendations on how the company can improve its brand image in light of market trends.

Example Prompt 3:
Prompt: Leverage ChatGPT's advanced data processing functionality to analyze the brand perception of a particular product or service. Analyze customer feedback, online reviews,

and social media conversations to understand how market trends are impacting the brand's image and customer loyalty. Provide actionable insights on how the brand can adapt its strategies to enhance customer perceptions and strengthen brand loyalty.

Example Prompt 4:
Prompt: As a business analyst, use ChatGPT's advanced data processing capabilities to conduct a real-time brand perception analysis for a specific industry. Analyze customer sentiment, online reputation, and market trends to assess how different brands within the industry are perceived by customers and how these perceptions impact customer loyalty. Provide a comparative analysis and recommendations for brands to improve their market position and customer loyalty based on the insights gained.

Idea: Technology Adoption Analysis

ChatGPT can support businesses in analyzing the adoption rate of new technologies within the market, identifying potential opportunities or threats for their products or services.

Example Prompt 1:
Prompt: As a business analyst, I need ChatGPT to analyze the adoption rate of new technologies within the market and identify potential opportunities or threats for our products or services. Please provide a detailed analysis of the current adoption rate of artificial intelligence (AI) technologies in the healthcare industry, highlighting any emerging trends or challenges that may impact our business.

Example Prompt 2:
Prompt: ChatGPT, using its advanced data processing functionality, please analyze the adoption rate of blockchain technology across various industries. Identify the sectors where blockchain adoption is rapidly increasing and provide insights into potential opportunities for our company to leverage this

technology in our products or services.

Example Prompt 3:

Prompt: Our company is considering investing in Internet of Things (IoT) technologies. ChatGPT, as a business analyst, I need your support to analyze the current adoption rate of IoT in the manufacturing sector. Please provide an in-depth analysis of the key players, market trends, and potential risks associated with IoT adoption in this industry.

Example Prompt 4:

Prompt: As a business analyst, I want ChatGPT to analyze the adoption rate of cloud computing technologies in the financial services sector. Please provide a comprehensive analysis of the current market landscape, including the major players, key trends, and potential opportunities or threats that our company should be aware of when considering the adoption of cloud computing solutions in our services.

Idea: Market Trend Monitoring

ChatGPT can continuously monitor market trends by analyzing real-time data from various sources, providing businesses with up-to-date insights to adapt their strategies accordingly.

Example Prompt 1:

As a business analyst, I need ChatGPT to continuously monitor market trends by analyzing real-time data from various sources. Please provide a summary of the current market trends in the technology industry and highlight any emerging technologies that businesses should be aware of.

Example Prompt 2:

ChatGPT, using its advanced data processing functionality, please analyze real-time data from social media platforms, news articles, and industry reports to provide an overview of the current market trends in the fashion industry. Identify any shifts in consumer preferences, emerging fashion trends, and popular brands that businesses should consider when adapting their strategies.

Example Prompt 3:

In order to adapt our marketing strategies, we need ChatGPT to monitor market trends in the food and beverage industry. Utilizing its advanced data processing capabilities, please analyze real-time data from online reviews, restaurant ratings, and social media discussions to identify any emerging food trends, popular cuisines, or changes in consumer preferences that businesses should take into account.

Example Prompt 4:

As a business analyst, I require ChatGPT to continuously monitor market trends in the automotive industry. By analyzing real-time data from industry reports, customer reviews, and social media discussions, please provide insights on the current market trends, such as the demand for electric vehicles, emerging technologies in autonomous driving, and any shifts in consumer preferences that businesses should consider when adapting their strategies.

COMPETITOR ANALYSIS

UNDERSTANDING YOUR COMPETITION

In today's cutthroat business world, understanding your competitors is not just an option, it's a necessity. Artificial Intelligence, particularly tools like ChatGPT, has become a game-changer in competitor analysis. It equips business analysts with unparalleled insights into competitors' strengths, weaknesses, and market strategies.

Take, for example, Alex, a business analyst at a burgeoning e-commerce company. His challenge is to understand how his company stacks up against its rivals. Using AI-driven analysis, Alex delves into a wealth of data: social media sentiment, customer reviews, and market reports. ChatGPT, with its ability to process and analyze large volumes of text, becomes his ally in this quest.

Alex uncovers patterns in competitors' customer engagement strategies and identifies gaps in their services. He notices, for instance, a recurring complaint about slow customer service in a rival company. This insight opens up an opportunity for his company to capitalize on, by focusing on speedy and efficient customer service.

This example illustrates the potency of AI in competitor

analysis. It's not merely about collecting data; it's about extracting meaningful patterns and actionable insights from that data. AI tools like ChatGPT allow analysts to move beyond surface-level observations to deeper, strategic insights about competitors' operations.

In sum, AI empowers business analysts to conduct more comprehensive and insightful competitor analyses. This level of understanding is crucial for businesses to carve out a competitive edge in their respective markets. As AI technologies evolve, their role in shaping business strategies through competitor analysis will only grow more significant.

Note: It's important to remember that the strategies, tasks, and ideas presented in this chapter can be enhanced with the use of ChatGPT's Advanced Data Analysis feature. For a comprehensive understanding of this tool, kindly review the chapter that expounds on its functionalities.

Task: Competitor Identification

ChatGPT can help in identifying potential competitors by analyzing industry trends, market research, and customer feedback.

Example Prompt 1:
ChatGPT, analyze the latest industry trends and provide a list of potential competitors in the market based on these trends.

Example Prompt 2:
Using ChatGPT's advanced data processing functionality, identify potential competitors by analyzing market research reports and extracting key insights.

Example Prompt 3:
Leverage ChatGPT's ability to analyze customer feedback and identify competitors that are frequently mentioned or compared to our business.

Example Prompt 4:
Utilize ChatGPT's advanced data processing capabilities to analyze industry data and provide a comprehensive list of potential competitors based on market dynamics and customer preferences.

Task: Competitor Profiling

ChatGPT can assist in creating detailed profiles of competitors, including their products/services, pricing strategies, target markets, and strengths/weaknesses.

Example Prompt 1:
ChatGPT, analyze the pricing strategies of our top three competitors in the market and provide a detailed comparison of their pricing models, including any discounts, promotions, or bundling options they offer.

Example Prompt 2:
ChatGPT, gather information on our competitors' target markets and demographics. Provide insights into their customer profiles, including age groups, geographical locations, and any specific segments they focus on.

Example Prompt 3:
ChatGPT, analyze the strengths and weaknesses of our main competitors' products/services. Provide a comprehensive overview of their key features, unique selling points, and any areas where they may be lacking compared to our offerings.

Example Prompt 4:
ChatGPT, conduct a thorough analysis of our competitors' marketing strategies. Identify their key marketing channels,

messaging tactics, and any partnerships or collaborations they have engaged in. Additionally, provide insights into any recent marketing campaigns they have launched and their impact on the market.

Task: Market Share Analysis

ChatGPT can provide insights on competitors' market share by analyzing available data, industry reports, and customer surveys.

Example Prompt 1:
Using ChatGPT's Advanced Data processing functionality, analyze the available data on competitors' market share in the industry and provide insights on their performance trends over the past year.

Example Prompt 2:
Leveraging ChatGPT's Advanced Data processing capabilities, conduct a comprehensive analysis of industry reports and customer surveys to determine the market share of key competitors and identify any emerging trends.

Example Prompt 3:
With the help of ChatGPT's Advanced Data processing functionality, analyze the available data on competitors' market share and provide a comparative analysis of their performance against industry benchmarks.

Example Prompt 4:
Utilizing ChatGPT's Advanced Data processing capabilities, analyze customer surveys and industry reports to gain insights into competitors' market share, identify potential growth opportunities, and recommend strategies to improve market position.

Task: Product Comparison

ChatGPT can help in comparing your products/services with those of competitors, highlighting key features, advantages, and areas for improvement.

Example Prompt 1:
Compare our product/service with our top competitor and provide a detailed analysis of the key features and advantages of each. Additionally, identify areas for improvement in our product/ service based on the comparison.

Example Prompt 2:
Using ChatGPT's advanced data processing functionality, analyze our product/service and three of our main competitors' offerings. Highlight the unique features and advantages of each, and provide recommendations on how we can enhance our product/service to stay competitive in the market.

Example Prompt 3:
Leveraging ChatGPT's advanced data processing capabilities, conduct a comprehensive comparison between our product/ service and three key competitors. Focus on identifying the key differentiators, advantages, and areas for improvement for each offering, and provide actionable insights on how we can position ourselves better in the market.

Example Prompt 4:
With the help of ChatGPT's advanced data processing functionality, perform a detailed analysis of our product/ service and two of our closest competitors. Highlight the strengths and weaknesses of each offering, emphasizing the key features and advantages that set us apart. Additionally, provide recommendations on how we can further improve our product/ service to gain a competitive edge.

Task: Pricing Analysis

ChatGPT can assist in analyzing competitors' pricing strategies, including pricing models, discounts, promotions, and pricing elasticity.

Example Prompt 1:

ChatGPT, analyze our competitors' pricing models and identify any unique strategies they employ to set their prices. Also, provide insights on how their pricing models differ from ours and suggest potential improvements for our pricing strategy.

Example Prompt 2:

ChatGPT, examine our competitors' discount and promotion strategies and determine their effectiveness in attracting customers. Additionally, suggest innovative discount and promotion ideas that we can implement to gain a competitive edge in the market.

Example Prompt 3:

ChatGPT, analyze the pricing elasticity of our products compared to our competitors'. Provide insights on how sensitive customers are to price changes and recommend optimal pricing points to maximize revenue while maintaining a competitive position in the market.

Example Prompt 4:

ChatGPT, conduct a comprehensive pricing analysis of our competitors' products and services. Identify any pricing gaps or opportunities where we can adjust our prices to gain a competitive advantage. Additionally, suggest potential pricing strategies that align with market trends and customer preferences.

Task: SWOT Analysis

ChatGPT can help in conducting a SWOT (Strengths, Weaknesses, Opportunities, Threats) analysis of competitors, identifying their competitive advantages and vulnerabilities.

Example Prompt 1:

ChatGPT, analyze the strengths of our top three competitors in the market and identify their competitive advantages.

Example Prompt 2:
ChatGPT, evaluate the weaknesses of our main competitors and highlight any vulnerabilities that we can exploit.

Example Prompt 3:
ChatGPT, identify potential opportunities in the market that our competitors might be overlooking and suggest strategies to capitalize on them.

Example Prompt 4:
ChatGPT, analyze the threats posed by our competitors and provide insights on how we can mitigate those threats to maintain our competitive edge.

Task: Marketing Strategies

ChatGPT can provide insights on competitors' marketing tactics, such as advertising campaigns, social media presence, content marketing, and partnerships.

Example Prompt 1:
Analyze the advertising campaigns of our top three competitors and provide insights on their messaging, target audience, and channels used. Additionally, identify any unique strategies or creative approaches they have employed.

Example Prompt 2:
Examine the social media presence of our main competitors, including their follower growth, engagement rates, and content strategy. Highlight any successful tactics they have implemented and suggest potential improvements for our own social media strategy.

Example Prompt 3:
Evaluate the content marketing efforts of our competitors by analyzing their blog posts, articles, and other content assets. Identify the topics they focus on, the formats they use, and any patterns or trends that emerge. Provide recommendations on how

we can differentiate our content strategy.

Example Prompt 4:
Research the partnerships formed by our competitors and assess their impact on their marketing efforts. Identify key collaborations, sponsorships, or influencer partnerships that have contributed to their success. Propose potential partnership opportunities for our own brand to enhance our marketing strategies.

Task: Customer Analysis

ChatGPT can assist in analyzing competitors' customer base, demographics, preferences, and satisfaction levels through online reviews, surveys, and social media monitoring.

Example Prompt 1:
Using ChatGPT's Advanced Data processing functionality, analyze competitors' customer base by extracting and categorizing demographic information from online reviews, surveys, and social media posts. Provide insights on age groups, gender distribution, and geographical locations of their customers.

Example Prompt 2:
Leverage ChatGPT's Advanced Data processing functionality to identify and analyze competitors' customer preferences by extracting and analyzing sentiment from online reviews, surveys, and social media conversations. Provide insights on popular product features, customer expectations, and areas for improvement.

Example Prompt 3:
Utilize ChatGPT's Advanced Data processing functionality to assess competitors' customer satisfaction levels by analyzing sentiment and sentiment trends in online reviews, surveys, and social media posts. Provide insights on overall customer satisfaction, common pain points, and areas where competitors excel.

Example Prompt 4:

With the help of ChatGPT's Advanced Data processing functionality, conduct a comprehensive customer analysis of competitors by combining demographic information, preferences, and satisfaction levels extracted from online reviews, surveys, and social media monitoring. Provide a holistic view of their customer base, identify potential target segments, and suggest strategies to improve customer satisfaction and loyalty.

Task: Innovation Assessment

ChatGPT can help in assessing competitors' innovation capabilities, R&D investments, patents, and new product launches.

Example Prompt 1:

ChatGPT, analyze the R&D investments of our top three competitors in the past five years and provide a summary of their innovation capabilities.

Example Prompt 2:

Using ChatGPT's advanced data processing functionality, assess the patent portfolio of our main competitors and identify any emerging trends or areas of focus.

Example Prompt 3:

Evaluate the new product launches of our competitors in the last year and compare them to our own product offerings. Provide insights on potential gaps or areas where we can improve.

Example Prompt 4:

Leveraging ChatGPT's capabilities, analyze the innovation strategies of our competitors and identify any potential threats or opportunities for our business. Provide recommendations on how we can enhance our own innovation capabilities.

Task: Competitive Benchmarking

ChatGPT can provide benchmarks for key performance indicators (KPIs) to compare your business's performance against competitors, such as sales growth, customer retention, and market share.

Example Prompt 1:
ChatGPT, analyze and compare our sales growth against our top three competitors in the past year. Provide insights on the areas where we are performing better and areas where we need improvement.

Example Prompt 2:
ChatGPT, gather data on customer retention rates for our industry and compare our customer retention rate with our closest competitor. Identify the factors contributing to their higher retention rate and suggest strategies to improve our own.

Example Prompt 3:
ChatGPT, analyze market share data for our industry and provide a detailed comparison of our market share against our top five competitors. Identify the reasons behind any significant differences and recommend actions to increase our market share.

Example Prompt 4:
ChatGPT, analyze our customer satisfaction scores and compare them with our main competitor. Identify the key drivers of customer satisfaction for both companies and suggest areas where we can outperform our competitor to enhance customer loyalty.

Idea: Competitor Landscape Analysis

ChatGPT can provide a comprehensive overview of the competitive landscape by gathering information on key competitors, their market share, product offerings, and customer feedback.

Example Prompt 1:
Prompt: "Perform a competitor landscape analysis for our

company's industry. Gather information on the top 5 competitors, their market share, product offerings, and customer feedback. Provide a comprehensive overview of each competitor, highlighting their strengths and weaknesses."

Example Prompt 2:
Prompt: "Assess the competitive landscape in the market segment we are targeting. Identify the top 3 competitors and their market share. Additionally, gather information on their product offerings and customer feedback. Provide insights on how our company can differentiate itself from these competitors."

Example Prompt 3:
Prompt: "Conduct a competitor analysis for our new product launch. Identify the main competitors in the market, their market share, and product offerings. Furthermore, gather customer feedback on these competitors' products. Provide recommendations on how our product can position itself effectively against these competitors."

Example Prompt 4:
Prompt: "Analyze the competitive landscape in the e-commerce industry. Identify the top 5 competitors, their market share, and product offerings. Additionally, gather customer feedback on their products and services. Provide an in-depth comparison of each competitor, highlighting their unique selling points and areas for improvement."

Idea: Competitor Pricing Analysis

ChatGPT can assist in analyzing competitor pricing strategies, identifying pricing gaps, and recommending optimal pricing strategies to stay competitive in the market.

Example Prompt 1:
Prompt: "As a business analyst, I need assistance in analyzing competitor pricing strategies and identifying pricing gaps. Please use ChatGPT's advanced data processing functionality to provide

insights and recommendations on optimal pricing strategies to help our company stay competitive in the market."

Example Prompt 2:
Prompt: "ChatGPT, I require your support as a business analyst to conduct a competitor pricing analysis. Utilize your advanced data processing capabilities to analyze our competitors' pricing strategies, identify any gaps in our pricing, and recommend optimal pricing strategies that will enable us to maintain a competitive edge in the market."

Example Prompt 3:
Prompt: "In order to stay competitive in the market, our company needs to analyze competitor pricing strategies and identify any gaps in our own pricing. As a business analyst, I request your assistance, ChatGPT, to leverage your advanced data processing functionality and provide us with a comprehensive analysis of competitor pricing, along with recommendations for optimal pricing strategies."

Example Prompt 4:
Prompt: "As a business analyst, I am tasked with conducting a competitor pricing analysis to ensure our company remains competitive in the market. ChatGPT, I need your support in analyzing our competitors' pricing strategies, identifying any pricing gaps, and recommending optimal pricing strategies that will help us maintain a strong position in the market. Please utilize your advanced data processing capabilities to provide us with valuable insights and recommendations."

Idea: Competitor SWOT Analysis

ChatGPT can generate a SWOT (Strengths, Weaknesses, Opportunities, Threats) analysis for each competitor, helping businesses understand their relative advantages and disadvantages.

Example Prompt 1:

Prompt: As a business analyst, I need ChatGPT to generate a SWOT analysis for our main competitor, XYZ Company. Please provide a detailed analysis of their strengths, weaknesses, opportunities, and threats in comparison to our business.

Example Prompt 2:
Prompt: Help me analyze the relative advantages and disadvantages of our top three competitors in the market. Generate a comprehensive SWOT analysis for each competitor, highlighting their strengths, weaknesses, opportunities, and threats. This analysis will assist us in understanding our position in the market and identifying areas for improvement.

Example Prompt 3:
Prompt: Our company is planning to enter a new market, and we need to assess the competition. Can you provide a SWOT analysis for the top five competitors in this market? Focus on their strengths, weaknesses, opportunities, and threats, and highlight any key insights that can help us develop a competitive advantage.

Example Prompt 4:
Prompt: We are considering a strategic partnership with a potential competitor. Before proceeding, we need to evaluate their strengths, weaknesses, opportunities, and threats. Please generate a SWOT analysis for this competitor, emphasizing their relative advantages and disadvantages compared to our business. This analysis will help us make an informed decision regarding the partnership.

Idea: Competitor Product Analysis

ChatGPT can analyze competitor products, features, and functionalities, providing insights on how to improve existing products or develop new ones to outperform competitors.

Example Prompt 1:
Prompt: As a business analyst, I need ChatGPT to analyze the features and functionalities of our main competitor's product,

XYZ, and provide insights on how we can improve our existing product to outperform them. Please analyze XYZ's key features, strengths, weaknesses, and suggest areas where we can enhance our product to gain a competitive edge.

Example Prompt 2:

Prompt: ChatGPT, please conduct a detailed analysis of our competitor's product, ABC, and compare it with our own product. Identify the unique features and functionalities of ABC that make it stand out in the market. Based on this analysis, provide recommendations on how we can modify our existing product or develop new features to surpass ABC and attract more customers.

Example Prompt 3:

Prompt: We are planning to launch a new product to compete with our rival company's offering, DEF. As a business analyst, I need ChatGPT to analyze the key features and functionalities of DEF and provide insights on how we can develop our new product to outperform it. Please analyze DEF's strengths, weaknesses, and suggest innovative features or improvements that can give us a competitive advantage in the market.

Example Prompt 4:

Prompt: Our competitor recently released a new version of their product, LMN, which has gained significant attention in the market. As a business analyst, I need ChatGPT to analyze the new features and functionalities of LMN and provide insights on how we can enhance our existing product to stay ahead of the competition. Please identify the unique selling points of LMN and suggest improvements or additions to our product to ensure we remain competitive in the industry.

Idea: Competitor Marketing Analysis

ChatGPT can analyze competitor marketing campaigns, messaging, and channels to identify effective strategies and tactics that can be adopted or improved upon.

Example Prompt 1:
As a business analyst, I need ChatGPT to analyze competitor marketing campaigns and identify effective strategies and tactics that can be adopted or improved upon. Please provide a detailed analysis of our top three competitors' marketing messaging and channels, highlighting any unique approaches or successful campaigns that we can learn from.

Example Prompt 2:
ChatGPT, I require your assistance as a business analyst to conduct a comprehensive competitor marketing analysis. Please analyze the marketing campaigns, messaging, and channels of our main competitors and provide a comparative analysis of their strategies. Identify any gaps or opportunities for improvement in our own marketing efforts based on their successful tactics.

Example Prompt 3:
In order to enhance our marketing strategies, I need ChatGPT to analyze our competitors' marketing campaigns, messaging, and channels. Please provide a detailed report on the most effective strategies and tactics employed by our competitors, along with recommendations on how we can adopt or improve upon them to gain a competitive advantage.

Example Prompt 4:
As a business analyst, I'm seeking ChatGPT's expertise in competitor marketing analysis. Please analyze the marketing campaigns, messaging, and channels of our key competitors and provide insights on their successful strategies. Additionally, suggest innovative approaches or tactics that we can implement to differentiate ourselves and outperform our competitors in the market.

Idea: Competitor Customer Analysis

ChatGPT can gather and analyze customer feedback and reviews about competitors, helping businesses understand customer preferences, pain points, and areas for improvement.

Example Prompt 1:

As a business analyst, I need ChatGPT to gather and analyze customer feedback and reviews about our competitors in the electronics industry. Please provide a summary of the top three pain points customers have mentioned in their reviews, along with any common areas for improvement that our competitors should focus on.

Example Prompt 2:

ChatGPT, as a business analyst tool, I require your assistance in analyzing customer feedback and reviews about our competitors in the fashion industry. Please compile a comprehensive report highlighting the most frequently mentioned customer preferences and the key areas where our competitors are excelling. Additionally, identify any pain points that customers have expressed, which we can leverage to improve our own offerings.

Example Prompt 3:

In my role as a business analyst, I need ChatGPT to help me understand customer preferences and pain points by analyzing feedback and reviews about our competitors in the food delivery market. Please provide an overview of the top three customer preferences that our competitors are successfully catering to, as well as any common pain points that customers have expressed. This analysis will help us identify potential areas for improvement and gain a competitive edge.

Example Prompt 4:

As a business analyst, I require ChatGPT's advanced data processing functionality to analyze customer feedback and reviews about our competitors in the travel industry. Please generate a detailed report summarizing the most frequently mentioned customer preferences and pain points. Additionally, identify any emerging trends or areas for improvement that our competitors have overlooked, which we can capitalize on to enhance our own offerings and attract more customers.

Idea: Competitor Partnership Analysis

ChatGPT can identify potential partnerships or collaborations with competitors that can mutually benefit both businesses, such as joint marketing campaigns or shared distribution channels.

Example Prompt 1:
As a business analyst, I need ChatGPT to analyze potential partnerships or collaborations with competitors that can mutually benefit both businesses. Please provide a list of competitor companies in the same industry and suggest potential partnership opportunities, such as joint marketing campaigns or shared distribution channels, that could be explored.

Example Prompt 2:
ChatGPT, using its advanced data processing functionality, please analyze the competitive landscape and identify potential partnerships or collaborations with competitors that can benefit both businesses. Specifically, suggest innovative ways in which our company can collaborate with competitors, such as joint product development or co-hosted events, to achieve mutual growth and market expansion.

Example Prompt 3:
As a business analyst, I require ChatGPT's support in conducting a competitor partnership analysis. Please analyze our competitors' strengths and weaknesses, and recommend potential partnership opportunities that can benefit both parties. Focus on identifying areas where our company's expertise can complement our competitors' offerings, leading to shared success through joint initiatives like cross-promotions or co-branded products.

Example Prompt 4:
ChatGPT, utilizing its advanced data processing capabilities, please analyze our competitors' strategies and identify potential

partnership opportunities that can create mutual benefits. Provide insights on how our company can collaborate with competitors to leverage each other's customer base, expand market reach, and achieve shared growth objectives. Specifically, suggest partnership ideas such as joint loyalty programs or shared research and development initiatives.

Idea: Competitor Digital Presence Analysis

ChatGPT can assess competitors' online presence, including website performance, search engine rankings, social media engagement, and online advertising strategies.

Example Prompt 1:

Prompt: "As a business analyst, I need ChatGPT to analyze and evaluate our competitors' online presence. Please provide a detailed report on their website performance, including page load speed, mobile responsiveness, and overall user experience. Additionally, assess their search engine rankings, social media engagement metrics, and online advertising strategies. Finally, compare our own digital presence with that of our competitors and identify areas where we can improve."

Example Prompt 2:

Prompt: "ChatGPT, as a business analyst, I require your assistance in conducting a comprehensive analysis of our competitors' digital presence. Please evaluate their website performance by examining factors such as page load speed, website structure, and navigation ease. Additionally, assess their search engine rankings, social media engagement, and online advertising strategies. Finally, provide recommendations on how we can enhance our own online presence to gain a competitive edge."

Example Prompt 3:

Prompt: "As a business analyst, I need ChatGPT to perform a thorough analysis of our competitors' online presence. Please evaluate their website performance by analyzing factors such as page load speed, mobile optimization, and overall user experience. Furthermore, assess their search engine rankings, social media engagement, and online advertising strategies. Finally, provide insights on how we can leverage their strengths and weaknesses to improve our own digital presence."

Example Prompt 4:

Prompt: "ChatGPT, I require your expertise as a business analyst to conduct a detailed analysis of our competitors' digital presence. Please assess their website performance, including factors such as page load speed, responsiveness across devices, and user interface design. Additionally, evaluate their search engine rankings, social media engagement metrics, and online advertising strategies. Finally, provide actionable recommendations on how we can enhance our own online presence based on the insights gained from this analysis."

Idea: Competitor Expansion Analysis

ChatGPT can provide insights into competitors' expansion plans, such as new market entries or product launches, helping businesses anticipate and respond to potential threats or opportunities.

Example Prompt 1:

Prompt: "As a business analyst, I need ChatGPT to analyze our competitors' expansion plans and provide insights on potential threats or opportunities. Please analyze the latest news and industry trends to identify any new market entries or product launches by our competitors."

Example Prompt 2:

Prompt: "ChatGPT, as a business analyst, I require your assistance in analyzing our competitors' expansion strategies. Please analyze their recent activities, market trends, and customer feedback to identify any upcoming new market entries or product launches. Additionally, provide recommendations on how we can respond effectively to these potential threats or opportunities."

Example Prompt 3:

Prompt: "As a business analyst, I need ChatGPT to help us stay ahead of our competitors by analyzing their expansion plans. Please analyze industry reports, market data, and customer reviews to identify any new market entries or product launches by our competitors. Furthermore, provide insights on how these expansions might impact our business and suggest strategies to capitalize on potential opportunities or mitigate threats."

Example Prompt 4:

Prompt: "ChatGPT, as a business analyst, I require your expertise in analyzing our competitors' expansion plans. Please analyze their financial reports, press releases, and industry news to identify any new market entries or product launches. Additionally, provide insights on the potential impact of these expansions on our business and suggest proactive measures to respond effectively to the emerging threats or opportunities."

Idea: Competitor Customer Acquisition Analysis

ChatGPT can analyze competitors' customer acquisition strategies, such as referral programs, loyalty programs, or targeted advertising, and provide recommendations for improving customer acquisition efforts.

Example Prompt 1:

Prompt: As a business analyst, I need ChatGPT to analyze our competitors' customer acquisition strategies and provide recommendations for improving our own efforts. Please analyze the referral programs implemented by our top three competitors and suggest ways we can enhance our own referral program.

Example Prompt 2:

Prompt: ChatGPT, as a business analyst, I require your assistance in analyzing the loyalty programs of our competitors. Please evaluate the loyalty programs of our top five competitors and provide recommendations on how we can enhance our own program to improve customer acquisition.

Example Prompt 3:

Prompt: As a business analyst, I need ChatGPT to analyze the targeted advertising strategies employed by our competitors. Please evaluate the targeted advertising campaigns of our three main competitors and suggest improvements we can make to our own campaigns to enhance customer acquisition.

Example Prompt 4:

Prompt: ChatGPT, I require your expertise as a business analyst to analyze our competitors' customer acquisition strategies. Please assess the effectiveness of their referral programs, loyalty programs, and targeted advertising efforts. Based on your analysis, provide recommendations on how we can optimize our customer acquisition initiatives to outperform our competitors.

Idea: Competitor Risk Analysis

ChatGPT can identify potential risks posed by competitors, such as aggressive pricing strategies, technological advancements, or regulatory changes, enabling businesses to develop risk mitigation strategies.

Example Prompt 1:

As a business analyst, I need ChatGPT to perform competitor risk analysis for our company. Please analyze our top three competitors and identify any potential risks they pose, such as aggressive pricing strategies, technological advancements, or regulatory changes. Provide recommendations on how we can develop risk mitigation strategies to stay ahead in the market.

Example Prompt 2:

ChatGPT, we require your assistance in conducting a comprehensive competitor risk analysis. Please analyze the pricing strategies, technological advancements, and regulatory changes implemented by our key competitors. Identify any potential risks they pose to our business and suggest effective risk mitigation strategies that we can adopt to maintain our competitive edge.

Example Prompt 3:

Our company is concerned about potential risks posed by our competitors. We need ChatGPT to analyze their pricing strategies, technological advancements, and regulatory compliance. Please identify any risks that could impact our market position and recommend risk mitigation strategies that we can implement to safeguard our business interests.

Example Prompt 4:

As a business analyst, I need ChatGPT to perform competitor risk analysis to help us understand potential threats from our competitors. Please analyze their pricing strategies, technological advancements, and regulatory changes. Identify any risks that could affect our market share and provide recommendations on risk mitigation strategies that we can adopt to protect our business.

Idea: Competitor Benchmarking Analysis

ChatGPT can benchmark a business's performance against its competitors across various metrics, such as revenue growth, market share, customer satisfaction, or brand recognition, helping businesses identify areas for improvement and set realistic goals.

Example Prompt 1:

Prompt: "Perform a competitor benchmarking analysis for our business against our top three competitors. Compare our revenue growth, market share, customer satisfaction, and brand recognition metrics. Provide insights on areas where we are performing better and areas where we need improvement. Additionally, suggest realistic goals for each metric based on the *benchmarking analysis."*

Example Prompt 2:

Prompt: "Help us understand how our business is performing compared to our competitors in terms of revenue growth, market share, customer satisfaction, and brand recognition. Analyze the data and provide a comprehensive report highlighting our strengths and weaknesses in each metric. Based on the analysis, recommend specific strategies or actions we can take to improve our performance and set realistic goals for each metric."

Example Prompt 3:

Prompt: "Conduct a competitor benchmarking analysis to evaluate our business's performance against our key competitors. Focus on revenue growth, market share, customer satisfaction, and brand recognition. Provide a detailed comparison of each metric, highlighting areas where we excel and areas where we lag behind. Based on the analysis, suggest actionable steps we can take to bridge the gaps and set realistic goals for improvement."

Example Prompt 4:

Prompt: "We need a comprehensive competitor benchmarking analysis to assess our business's performance relative to our competitors. Analyze our revenue growth, market share, customer satisfaction, and brand recognition metrics and compare them with industry benchmarks. Identify areas where we are outperforming our competitors and areas where we need improvement. Based on the analysis, provide recommendations on how we can leverage our strengths and address our weaknesses to set realistic goals for each metric."

FINANCIAL FORECASTING

FORECASTING FINANCIAL FUTURES

In the realm of financial forecasting, Artificial Intelligence, including tools like ChatGPT, has emerged as a pivotal ally for business analysts. AI's capability to process and analyze vast historical data and market indicators is transforming the way financial performance is predicted.

Consider the case of Mia, a business analyst at a startup. Her task is to forecast the company's financial health in the next quarter. Traditional methods would involve manual analysis of past financial records and market trends, a time-consuming and potentially error-prone process. Mia, however, leverages AI tools to automate and refine this process.

Using ChatGPT, Mia inputs historical financial data and current market trends. The AI tool not only processes this data swiftly but also identifies patterns and correlations that might not be apparent at first glance. For instance, it highlights how certain market shifts have historically impacted the company's revenues.

This example illustrates AI's transformative role in financial forecasting. It's not just about automating data analysis;

it's about enhancing the accuracy and depth of financial predictions. AI tools enable analysts like Mia to provide more precise and reliable financial forecasts, essential for strategic planning and decision-making.

In conclusion, AI's integration into financial forecasting marks a significant advancement in business analysis. It empowers analysts to offer more nuanced and insightful predictions, providing a solid foundation for business strategies and decisions. As AI continues to evolve, its impact on financial forecasting is poised to become even more profound.

Note: It's important to remember that the strategies, tasks, and ideas presented in this chapter can be enhanced with the use of ChatGPT's Advanced Data Analysis feature. For a comprehensive understanding of this tool, kindly review the chapter that expounds on its functionalities.

Task: Data collection

ChatGPT can assist in gathering relevant financial data from various sources such as financial statements, market reports, and economic indicators.

Example Prompt 1:
ChatGPT, please gather the latest financial statements for Company XYZ and provide a summary of their revenue, expenses, and net income for the past three years.

Example Prompt 2:
ChatGPT, retrieve market reports for the technology sector from the past month and extract key financial metrics such as price-to-earnings ratio, market capitalization, and revenue growth for the

top five companies.

Example Prompt 3:
ChatGPT, collect economic indicators such as GDP growth rate, inflation rate, and unemployment rate for the past five years in the United States and present them in a comparative analysis.

Example Prompt 4:
ChatGPT, compile a comprehensive report on the financial performance of the automotive industry in Europe, including data from financial statements, market reports, and economic indicators. Focus on key metrics such as profitability, market share, and industry trends.

Task: Data cleaning and preprocessing

ChatGPT can help in cleaning and organizing financial data, removing duplicates, handling missing values, and standardizing formats.

Example Prompt 1:
ChatGPT, please provide a step-by-step guide on how to clean and remove duplicates from a financial dataset using advanced data processing techniques.

Example Prompt 2:
ChatGPT, can you assist me in handling missing values in a financial dataset? Please provide a comprehensive approach to identify and handle missing values effectively.

Example Prompt 3:
ChatGPT, I need help in standardizing the format of financial data across multiple sources. Can you suggest an efficient method to standardize formats and ensure consistency in the dataset?

Example Prompt 4:
ChatGPT, please guide me through the process of preprocessing financial data using advanced data processing techniques. Include methods to clean, remove duplicates, handle missing values, and

standardize formats for optimal analysis.

Task: Trend analysis

ChatGPT can analyze historical financial data to identify trends and patterns, helping in understanding the past performance of the business.

Example Prompt 1:
Develop a ChatGPT model that can analyze historical financial data and identify trends and patterns to assist in understanding the past performance of the business. Provide a detailed report on the identified trends and patterns, including any significant changes or anomalies.

Example Prompt 2:
Create a ChatGPT system that can process and analyze large volumes of historical financial data to identify trends and patterns. The system should be able to generate visualizations and summaries of the identified trends, highlighting key insights and potential areas of improvement for the business.

Example Prompt 3:
Design a ChatGPT-based tool that can perform trend analysis on historical financial data. The tool should be able to identify recurring patterns, seasonal trends, and any significant deviations from the norm. Additionally, it should provide recommendations on how to leverage these insights to improve the business's future performance.

Example Prompt 4:
Implement a ChatGPT-powered solution that can analyze historical financial data and identify long-term trends and patterns. The solution should be able to generate predictive models based on the identified trends, enabling the business to make informed decisions and optimize its future performance.

Task: Scenario analysis

ChatGPT can help in conducting scenario analysis by simulating different financial scenarios and assessing their potential impact on the forecasted outcomes.

Example Prompt 1:
Simulate various financial scenarios using ChatGPT's advanced data processing functionality and analyze their potential impact on the forecasted outcomes. Provide a detailed report on the key findings and recommendations for scenario analysis.

Example Prompt 2:
Utilize ChatGPT's advanced data processing capabilities to simulate different financial scenarios and evaluate their potential impact on the forecasted outcomes. Present a comparative analysis of the scenarios, highlighting the key drivers and risks associated with each scenario.

Example Prompt 3:
Leverage ChatGPT's advanced data processing functionality to conduct scenario analysis by simulating multiple financial scenarios and assessing their potential impact on the forecasted outcomes. Develop a comprehensive sensitivity analysis to identify the most critical variables influencing the outcomes.

Example Prompt 4:
Employ ChatGPT's advanced data processing capabilities to simulate a range of financial scenarios and evaluate their potential impact on the forecasted outcomes. Provide a detailed analysis of the best-case, worst-case, and most likely scenarios, along with recommendations for mitigating risks and maximizing opportunities.

Task: Sensitivity analysis

ChatGPT can assist in performing sensitivity analysis to

evaluate the sensitivity of the financial forecast to changes in key variables or assumptions.

Example Prompt 1:

How can ChatGPT's Advanced Data processing functionality be utilized to perform sensitivity analysis on our financial forecast model? Please provide step-by-step instructions and examples.

Example Prompt 2:

What are the key variables or assumptions that we should consider for sensitivity analysis using ChatGPT's Advanced Data processing functionality? How can we incorporate these variables into our financial forecast model?

Example Prompt 3:

Can ChatGPT's Advanced Data processing functionality help us identify the most sensitive variables or assumptions in our financial forecast model? If so, how can we leverage this feature to prioritize our analysis?

Example Prompt 4:

What are the best practices for interpreting and presenting the results of sensitivity analysis performed using ChatGPT's Advanced Data processing functionality? How can we effectively communicate the impact of changes in key variables or assumptions on our financial forecast?

Task: Forecast validation

ChatGPT can help in comparing the forecasted financial figures with actual results to assess the accuracy and reliability of the forecasting models.

Example Prompt 1:

Compare the forecasted revenue figures for the next quarter with the actual revenue achieved in the previous quarter. Discuss the accuracy and reliability of the forecasting model used and identify any discrepancies or trends.

Example Prompt 2:
Evaluate the forecasted expenses for the current fiscal year and compare them with the actual expenses incurred up to the present date. Analyze the variations and provide insights on the forecasting model's effectiveness in predicting expenses.

Example Prompt 3:
Assess the accuracy of the forecasted profit margins for the upcoming product launch by comparing them with the actual profit margins achieved in previous similar launches. Discuss any deviations and suggest improvements to enhance the reliability of future forecasts.

Example Prompt 4:
Examine the forecasted cash flow projections for the next six months and compare them with the actual cash inflows and outflows recorded during the same period. Identify any discrepancies and provide recommendations to refine the forecasting model for better accuracy and reliability.

Task: Forecast reporting

ChatGPT can assist in generating comprehensive reports summarizing the financial forecast, including key findings, assumptions, and potential risks or uncertainties.

Example Prompt 1:
Please generate a comprehensive report summarizing the financial forecast for the next quarter. Include key findings, assumptions made during the forecasting process, and potential risks or uncertainties that may impact the forecasted figures. Utilize ChatGPT's advanced data processing functionality to ensure the report is accurate and well-structured.

Example Prompt 2:
Using ChatGPT's advanced data processing capabilities, create a detailed report outlining the financial forecast for the upcoming

year. Include a summary of key findings, assumptions made during the forecasting process, and potential risks or uncertainties that may affect the forecasted numbers. Ensure the report is comprehensive and provides actionable insights for decision-making.

Example Prompt 3:

ChatGPT's advanced data processing functionality can be leveraged to generate a comprehensive report summarizing the financial forecast for the next five years. Please utilize this capability to create a report that includes key findings, assumptions made during the forecasting process, and potential risks or uncertainties that may impact the forecasted figures. The report should be well-structured and provide a clear understanding of the forecasted financial performance.

Example Prompt 4:

As a business analyst, you are required to generate a detailed report summarizing the financial forecast for the next quarter. Utilize ChatGPT's advanced data processing functionality to create a report that includes key findings, assumptions made during the forecasting process, and potential risks or uncertainties that may affect the forecasted numbers. The report should be comprehensive, well-organized, and provide valuable insights for stakeholders.

Task: Forecast monitoring and updating

ChatGPT can help in monitoring the actual financial performance against the forecasted figures and updating the forecast as new data becomes available.

Example Prompt 1:

Develop a ChatGPT model that can analyze real-time financial data and compare it with the forecasted figures. The model should provide insights on any deviations and suggest adjustments to the forecast based on the new data.

Example Prompt 2:
Design a ChatGPT system that can automatically monitor the financial performance against the forecasted figures on a daily basis. The system should alert the relevant stakeholders whenever significant deviations are detected and provide recommendations for updating the forecast.

Example Prompt 3:
Create a ChatGPT solution that can analyze historical financial data and identify patterns and trends. The model should be able to predict potential future deviations from the forecasted figures and suggest proactive measures to update the forecast accordingly.

Example Prompt 4:
Build a ChatGPT tool that can integrate with various data sources and automatically update the forecast as new financial data becomes available. The tool should provide a user-friendly interface for business analysts to review the updated forecast and make necessary adjustments based on the insights provided by the model.

Task: Communication and presentation

ChatGPT can assist in preparing presentations or explanations of the financial forecast to stakeholders, providing insights and answering questions related to the forecasted outcomes.

Example Prompt 1:
ChatGPT, analyze the financial forecast for the upcoming quarter and provide a detailed breakdown of the key factors influencing the projected outcomes. Additionally, explain any potential risks or uncertainties associated with the forecasted figures.

Example Prompt 2:
ChatGPT, generate a comprehensive presentation summarizing the financial forecast for the next fiscal year. Include visual aids such as charts and graphs to illustrate the projected revenue, expenses,

and profitability. Provide insights on the main drivers behind the forecasted outcomes and address potential concerns that stakeholders may have.

Example Prompt 3:
ChatGPT, assist in preparing a communication script for a stakeholder meeting where the financial forecast will be discussed. Provide concise explanations of the forecasted outcomes, highlighting the key assumptions and methodologies used in the forecasting process. Additionally, anticipate and address potential questions or concerns that stakeholders may raise during the meeting.

Example Prompt 4:
ChatGPT, analyze the financial forecast for the next five years and identify any emerging trends or patterns that could impact the projected outcomes. Provide insights on how external factors such as market conditions, regulatory changes, or technological advancements may influence the forecasted figures. Additionally, explain the rationale behind any strategic decisions made based on the forecasted outcomes.

Idea: Revenue Projection Tool

Develop a tool that uses historical data and market trends to forecast future revenue for the business.

Example Prompt 1:
As a business analyst, I need ChatGPT to assist in developing a Revenue Projection Tool. Please provide step-by-step instructions on how to preprocess and analyze historical data to identify relevant trends and patterns for revenue forecasting.

Example Prompt 2:
ChatGPT, I require your help as a business analyst to build a Revenue Projection Tool. Can you guide me through the process of training a machine learning model using historical revenue data and market trends? Additionally, please explain how to evaluate

the model's performance and make accurate revenue predictions for the future.

Example Prompt 3:
As a business analyst, I want to leverage ChatGPT's advanced data processing capabilities to create a Revenue Projection Tool. Please provide a detailed explanation of how to preprocess and clean historical revenue data, extract meaningful features, and apply statistical techniques to forecast future revenue based on market trends.

Example Prompt 4:
ChatGPT, I need your expertise as a business analyst to develop a Revenue Projection Tool. Can you assist me in implementing time series analysis techniques, such as ARIMA or exponential smoothing, to analyze historical revenue data and predict future revenue based on market trends? Please provide a step-by-step guide on how to utilize these techniques effectively.

Idea: Expense Forecasting Model

Create a model that predicts future expenses based on historical data and industry benchmarks.

Example Prompt 1:
Prompt: "As a business analyst, I need your assistance in developing an expense forecasting model. Please use ChatGPT's advanced data processing functionality to create a model that predicts future expenses based on historical data and industry benchmarks. Provide me with step-by-step instructions on how to gather and preprocess the necessary data, select appropriate forecasting techniques, and evaluate the model's performance."

Example Prompt 2:
Prompt: "Hello, ChatGPT! I'm working on an expense forecasting project as a business analyst. Can you help me leverage your advanced data processing capabilities to build a model that predicts future expenses? Please guide me through the process

of collecting and cleaning historical data, identifying relevant industry benchmarks, selecting suitable forecasting algorithms, and evaluating the accuracy of the model."

Example Prompt 3:

Prompt: "Greetings, ChatGPT! I'm a business analyst seeking your expertise in developing an expense forecasting model. Utilizing your advanced data processing functionality, please assist me in creating a model that can accurately predict future expenses. Walk me through the steps of data preprocessing, incorporating industry benchmarks, selecting appropriate forecasting techniques, and assessing the model's performance."

Example Prompt 4:

Prompt: "Dear ChatGPT, I'm excited to collaborate with you on an expense forecasting project. As a business analyst, I need your support in building a model that predicts future expenses based on historical data and industry benchmarks. Leverage your advanced data processing capabilities to guide me through the process of data collection, preprocessing, benchmark integration, forecasting technique selection, and model evaluation. Your assistance will greatly contribute to our organization's financial planning."

Idea: Financial Scenario Planning

Develop a tool that allows users to simulate different financial scenarios and assess their impact on the business's financial health.

Example Prompt 1:

As a business analyst, I need ChatGPT to assist in developing a financial scenario planning tool. Please provide step-by-step guidance on how to design a user-friendly interface that allows users to input various financial parameters, such as revenue, expenses, and investments, and simulate different scenarios to assess their impact on the business's financial health.

Example Prompt 2:

ChatGPT, I require your help as a business analyst to create a financial scenario planning tool. Please guide me on how to incorporate advanced data processing functionality to analyze historical financial data and generate accurate forecasts. The tool should allow users to adjust different variables, such as market conditions and pricing strategies, and visualize the projected financial outcomes.

Example Prompt 3:
As a business analyst, I want to leverage ChatGPT's advanced data processing capabilities to develop a financial scenario planning tool. Please assist me in designing a feature that enables users to compare multiple scenarios side by side, highlighting the key financial metrics and providing insights on the potential risks and opportunities associated with each scenario. Additionally, guide me on how to incorporate sensitivity analysis to assess the impact of changing variables on the business's financial health.

Example Prompt 4:
ChatGPT, I need your support as a business analyst to create an interactive financial scenario planning tool. Please provide guidance on how to integrate machine learning algorithms to analyze historical financial data and identify patterns that can help users make informed decisions. The tool should allow users to simulate different scenarios, apply predictive models, and generate forecasts to evaluate the financial impact of their decisions on the business's financial health.

Idea: Financial Performance Benchmarking

Create a tool that compares the company's financial performance against industry benchmarks, highlighting areas of improvement or competitive advantage.

Example Prompt 1:
Prompt: "Develop a financial performance benchmarking tool using ChatGPT's advanced data processing capabilities. Provide

insights on how our company's financial performance compares to industry benchmarks, identifying areas of improvement or competitive advantage. Additionally, suggest strategies to capitalize on identified advantages and address areas of improvement."

Example Prompt 2:

Prompt: "Utilize ChatGPT's advanced data processing functionality to create a comprehensive financial performance benchmarking tool. Analyze our company's financial metrics and compare them to industry benchmarks, highlighting key areas where we outperform or lag behind competitors. Provide actionable recommendations to leverage our competitive advantages and improve performance in identified areas."

Example Prompt 3:

Prompt: "Leverage ChatGPT's advanced data processing capabilities to develop a cutting-edge financial performance benchmarking tool. Compare our company's financial performance against industry benchmarks, identifying specific areas where we excel or fall short. Additionally, provide insights on industry best practices and strategies to enhance our competitive advantage and address any performance gaps."

Example Prompt 4:

Prompt: "Harness the power of ChatGPT's advanced data processing functionality to create an innovative financial performance benchmarking tool. Analyze our company's financial data and compare it to industry benchmarks, highlighting areas of strength and weakness. Furthermore, suggest actionable steps to capitalize on our competitive advantages and improve performance in areas where we lag behind industry benchmarks."

Idea: Capital Budgeting Analysis

Develop a model that helps in evaluating investment opportunities by estimating the financial viability and potential returns.

Example Prompt 1:

As a business analyst, I need ChatGPT to assist me in developing a capital budgeting analysis model. Please provide step-by-step guidance on how to estimate the financial viability and potential returns of investment opportunities. Additionally, help me understand the key factors to consider when evaluating these opportunities.

Example Prompt 2:

ChatGPT, I require your expertise as a business analyst to create a comprehensive capital budgeting analysis tool. Please guide me through the process of collecting and analyzing relevant financial data, such as initial investment costs, expected cash flows, and discount rates. Furthermore, assist me in interpreting the results to make informed investment decisions.

Example Prompt 3:

I'm looking for ChatGPT's assistance as a business analyst to build a robust capital budgeting analysis model. Can you help me understand different methods for evaluating investment opportunities, such as net present value (NPV), internal rate of return (IRR), and payback period? Additionally, guide me on how to incorporate risk assessment and sensitivity analysis into the model.

Example Prompt 4:

ChatGPT, I need your support as a business analyst to develop an advanced capital budgeting analysis framework. Please provide insights on how to incorporate qualitative factors, such as market trends, competitive analysis, and strategic alignment, into the financial evaluation process. Furthermore, help me understand how to weigh these qualitative factors alongside quantitative metrics to make well-informed investment decisions.

Idea: Predictive Analytics for Stock Market

Utilize ChatGPT to analyze historical stock market data and predict future trends, assisting in making informed investment decisions.

Example Prompt 1:

As a business analyst, I need ChatGPT to analyze historical stock market data and predict future trends to assist in making informed investment decisions. Please provide a step-by-step guide on how to utilize ChatGPT's advanced data processing functionality for predictive analytics in the stock market.

Example Prompt 2:

ChatGPT, using its advanced data processing functionality, analyze historical stock market data and provide insights on potential future trends. Additionally, suggest specific investment opportunities based on the analysis to help make informed investment decisions.

Example Prompt 3:

I require ChatGPT's assistance as a business analyst to analyze historical stock market data and predict future trends. Please demonstrate how to leverage ChatGPT's advanced data processing capabilities to identify patterns, correlations, and potential investment opportunities in the stock market.

Example Prompt 4:

ChatGPT, as a business analyst, I need your support in analyzing historical stock market data and predicting future trends. Utilize your advanced data processing functionality to generate a comprehensive report that includes key insights, risk assessments, and recommended investment strategies based on the analysis.

Idea: Financial Ratio Analysis

Build a tool that calculates and interprets key financial ratios, providing insights into the company's financial health and performance.

Example Prompt 1:
Calculate and interpret the current ratio for a given company, and provide insights into its financial health and liquidity position.

Example Prompt 2:
Develop a tool that calculates and analyzes the debt-to-equity ratio of a company, offering insights into its financial leverage and risk profile.

Example Prompt 3:
Create a feature that computes and interprets the return on investment (ROI) for a company, providing insights into its profitability and efficiency in generating returns.

Example Prompt 4:
Build a functionality that calculates and interprets the gross profit margin of a company, offering insights into its pricing strategy, cost management, and overall profitability.

Idea: Budgeting and Forecasting Automation

Use ChatGPT to automate the process of budgeting and financial forecasting, saving time and improving accuracy.

Example Prompt 1:
As a business analyst, I need ChatGPT's advanced data processing functionality to automate the process of budgeting and financial forecasting. Please provide step-by-step instructions on how to use ChatGPT to analyze historical financial data, identify trends, and generate accurate budget and forecast reports.

Example Prompt 2:
ChatGPT's advanced data processing capabilities can greatly enhance our budgeting and forecasting process. Please demonstrate how ChatGPT can analyze historical financial data, identify key drivers, and generate accurate financial projections for the next fiscal year. Additionally, provide guidance on how to incorporate external factors such as market trends and economic

indicators into the forecasting model.

Example Prompt 3:

Our company is looking to automate the budgeting and financial forecasting process using ChatGPT's advanced data processing functionality. Please explain how ChatGPT can assist in analyzing historical financial data, identifying cost-saving opportunities, and generating accurate budget plans. Additionally, provide insights on how ChatGPT can help us monitor and adjust the budget throughout the fiscal year based on real-time data.

Example Prompt 4:

As a business analyst, I'm interested in leveraging ChatGPT's advanced data processing capabilities to automate budgeting and financial forecasting. Please outline the steps involved in using ChatGPT to analyze historical financial data, identify potential risks and opportunities, and generate accurate financial forecasts. Additionally, provide guidance on how to integrate ChatGPT with existing financial software systems for seamless data transfer and collaboration with other stakeholders.

Idea: Financial Data Visualization

Create interactive visualizations using ChatGPT to present financial data in a user-friendly and easily understandable format.

Example Prompt 1:

Prompt: "As a business analyst, I need your help to create interactive visualizations using ChatGPT to present financial data in a user-friendly and easily understandable format. Please generate a Python code snippet that utilizes ChatGPT's advanced data processing functionality to fetch financial data from an API and visualize it using a popular data visualization library like Matplotlib or Plotly. The visualization should include key financial metrics such as stock prices, revenue, and expenses over a specific time period. Additionally, the chart should have interactive features like zooming, panning, and tooltips for enhanced user experience."

Example Prompt 2:

Prompt: "I'm working on a financial data visualization project and would like to leverage ChatGPT's advanced data processing capabilities. Can you assist me in generating a Python code snippet that uses ChatGPT to fetch real-time stock market data from a financial API and create an interactive candlestick chart? The chart should display the opening, closing, highest, and lowest prices for a given stock symbol over a specific time range. It should also allow users to switch between different stocks and adjust the time period dynamically."

Example Prompt 3:

Prompt: "As a business analyst, I'm looking for a solution to present financial data in an easily understandable format using ChatGPT's advanced data processing functionality. Could you help me generate a Python code snippet that fetches historical stock market data for multiple companies and creates a comparative line chart? The chart should display the stock prices of different companies over a specific time period, allowing users to select or deselect specific companies for comparison. It should also include interactive features like hovering over data points to display additional information."

Example Prompt 4:

Prompt: "I'm working on a financial data visualization project and would like to utilize ChatGPT's advanced data processing capabilities to create an interactive dashboard. Can you assist me in generating a Python code snippet that fetches financial data from a database and visualizes it using a popular dashboarding library like Dash or Streamlit? The dashboard should include multiple visualizations such as line charts, bar charts, and pie charts to represent various financial metrics like revenue, expenses, and profit. Users should be able to interact with the dashboard by selecting different time periods or filtering data *based on specific criteria."*

Idea: Fraud Detection and Prevention

Utilize ChatGPT to analyze financial transactions and identify patterns or anomalies that may indicate fraudulent activities, helping in fraud detection and prevention efforts.

Example Prompt 1:

Prompt: As a business analyst, I need ChatGPT to analyze financial transactions and identify patterns or anomalies that may indicate fraudulent activities. Please provide insights on how to improve fraud detection and prevention efforts.

Example Prompt 2:

Prompt: ChatGPT, utilizing its advanced data processing functionality, can play a crucial role in fraud detection and prevention. Please analyze a dataset of financial transactions and identify any patterns or anomalies that may indicate fraudulent activities. Additionally, suggest measures that can be taken to enhance fraud prevention efforts based on your analysis.

Example Prompt 3:

Prompt: As a business analyst, I require ChatGPT's support in analyzing financial transactions to identify potential fraudulent activities. Please leverage your advanced data processing capabilities to analyze a given dataset and provide insights on patterns or anomalies that may indicate fraudulent behavior. Furthermore, recommend strategies or techniques that can be implemented to strengthen fraud prevention measures based on your findings.

Example Prompt 4:

Prompt: ChatGPT's advanced data processing functionality can greatly assist in fraud detection and prevention efforts. Please analyze a set of financial transactions and identify any suspicious patterns or anomalies that may indicate fraudulent activities. Additionally, provide recommendations on how to enhance existing fraud prevention measures based on your analysis.

CUSTOMER SEGMENTATION

THE ART OF CUSTOMER SEGMENTATION

In the landscape of targeted marketing, customer segmentation is a crucial strategy. Artificial Intelligence, particularly tools like ChatGPT, is revolutionizing this approach by enabling business analysts to segment customers more effectively based on various characteristics.

Let's consider Lisa, a business analyst at a retail company. Her challenge is to devise targeted marketing strategies for different customer groups. Traditional segmentation methods can be limiting and time-consuming. Lisa turns to AI for a solution. Using ChatGPT, she inputs customer data, including purchase history, browsing behavior, and demographic information.

The AI tool, with its advanced algorithms, quickly segments customers into distinct groups based on shared characteristics. For example, it identifies a group of customers who frequently purchase eco-friendly products. This insight allows Lisa to tailor marketing strategies specifically for this segment, increasing the likelihood of customer engagement and sales.

This scenario highlights the effectiveness of AI in customer segmentation. It's not just about dividing customers into groups; it's about understanding the nuanced preferences and behaviors within each segment. AI tools like ChatGPT provide a deeper, data-driven understanding of customer groups, enabling analysts to develop more targeted and successful marketing strategies.

In summary, AI's role in customer segmentation is invaluable. It offers business analysts like Lisa the tools to segment customers more accurately and develop marketing strategies that resonate with each group. As AI technology continues to advance, its impact on customer segmentation and targeted marketing is expected to grow, offering even more sophisticated and effective ways to connect with customers.

Note: It's important to remember that the strategies, tasks, and ideas presented in this chapter can be enhanced with the use of ChatGPT's Advanced Data Analysis feature. For a comprehensive understanding of this tool, kindly review the chapter that expounds on its functionalities.

Task: Data collection

ChatGPT can assist in gathering relevant customer data by generating survey questions or interview scripts.

Example Prompt 1:
Generate a set of survey questions to gather customer feedback on our new product launch. Focus on understanding their satisfaction

levels, feature preferences, and suggestions for improvement.

Example Prompt 2:
Create an interview script to collect data on customer experiences with our customer support team. Include questions about response times, problem resolution, and overall satisfaction.

Example Prompt 3:
Develop a set of survey questions to gather demographic information and preferences of our target audience. Include questions about age, gender, location, and their preferred communication channels.

Example Prompt 4:
Generate an interview script to collect data on customer purchasing behavior. Include questions about their decision-making process, factors influencing their choices, and their satisfaction with the product or service.

Task: Data cleaning

ChatGPT can help in identifying and suggesting methods to clean and preprocess customer data for segmentation analysis.

Example Prompt 1:
ChatGPT, please analyze the customer data and identify any missing values or inconsistencies that need to be addressed for segmentation analysis. Additionally, suggest appropriate methods to clean and preprocess the data.

Example Prompt 2:
Using ChatGPT's advanced data processing functionality, provide recommendations on how to handle outliers and anomalies in the customer data for segmentation analysis. Please suggest suitable techniques or algorithms for data cleaning and preprocessing.

Example Prompt 3:
ChatGPT, assist in identifying duplicate records in the customer data that may affect segmentation analysis. Propose effective

methods or strategies to handle these duplicates and ensure accurate data preprocessing.

Example Prompt 4:
With the help of ChatGPT's advanced data processing capabilities, analyze the customer data for any irrelevant or noisy variables that could impact segmentation analysis. Recommend techniques or approaches to remove or handle these variables during the data cleaning and preprocessing stage.

Task: Variable selection

ChatGPT can provide insights and recommendations on which variables to consider for customer segmentation based on their relevance and impact.

Example Prompt 1:
Based on the dataset provided, please analyze the relevance and impact of different variables for customer segmentation. Provide insights and recommendations on which variables should be considered for effective segmentation using ChatGPT's advanced data processing functionality.

Example Prompt 2:
Using ChatGPT's advanced data processing capabilities, analyze the dataset and identify the variables that have the highest relevance and impact on customer segmentation. Please provide insights and recommendations on which variables should be prioritized for effective segmentation.

Example Prompt 3:
With the help of ChatGPT's advanced data processing functionality, conduct a thorough analysis of the dataset to determine the relevance and impact of various variables for customer segmentation. Based on your findings, recommend the top variables that should be considered for effective segmentation.

Example Prompt 4:

Utilizing ChatGPT's advanced data processing capabilities, evaluate the dataset and identify the variables that significantly contribute to customer segmentation. Provide insights and recommendations on which variables should be given priority for effective segmentation, considering their relevance and impact.

Task: Segmentation criteria

ChatGPT can assist in defining segmentation criteria by generating ideas and discussing different approaches based on the available data.

Example Prompt 1:
ChatGPT, based on the available data, generate ideas for segmenting our customer base and discuss different approaches we can take to define segmentation criteria.

Example Prompt 2:
Using ChatGPT's advanced data processing functionality, analyze the available data and propose potential segmentation criteria for our target market. Discuss different approaches and ideas for segmenting the market based on the generated insights.

Example Prompt 3:
Leveraging ChatGPT's advanced data processing capabilities, explore the available data to identify key variables that can be used as segmentation criteria. Generate ideas and engage in a discussion about different approaches to segmenting our customer base.

Example Prompt 4:
With the help of ChatGPT's advanced data processing functionality, analyze the available data to identify potential segmentation criteria. Generate ideas and discuss different approaches for segmenting our target audience based on the insights derived from the data.

Task: Segmentation model selection

ChatGPT can provide information and guidance on various segmentation models, such as clustering algorithms or decision trees, based on the specific business requirements.

Example Prompt 1:

Can you provide an overview of different clustering algorithms that can be used for segmentation models in the context of our specific business requirements?

Example Prompt 2:

How can ChatGPT assist in selecting the most suitable decision tree algorithm for segmentation models based on our unique business needs?

Example Prompt 3:

What are the advantages and disadvantages of using hierarchical clustering versus k-means clustering for segmentation models in our industry?

Example Prompt 4:

Could you explain how ChatGPT's advanced data processing functionality can help in evaluating and comparing different segmentation models, including both clustering algorithms and decision trees, to determine the most effective approach for our business requirements?

Task: Model implementation

ChatGPT can help in implementing the chosen segmentation model by providing code snippets or explaining the steps involved in the process.

Example Prompt 1:

How can ChatGPT assist in implementing a segmentation model using advanced data processing functionality? Provide code snippets or step-by-step explanations for preprocessing the data, training the model, and evaluating its performance.

Example Prompt 2:
Demonstrate how ChatGPT's advanced data processing functionality can be utilized to implement a segmentation model. Include code snippets or detailed instructions for data preprocessing, model training, and post-processing steps.

Example Prompt 3:
Explain how ChatGPT's advanced data processing capabilities can be leveraged to implement a segmentation model. Provide code snippets or a comprehensive guide on data preparation, model training, and evaluation techniques.

Example Prompt 4:
Utilize ChatGPT's advanced data processing functionality to guide the implementation of a segmentation model. Include code snippets or a detailed walkthrough of the necessary steps involved in data preprocessing, model training, and result interpretation.

Task: Interpretation of results

ChatGPT can assist in interpreting the segmentation results by explaining the characteristics and behaviors of each customer segment.

Example Prompt 1:
How can ChatGPT help in interpreting the segmentation results by explaining the characteristics and behaviors of each customer segment? Provide examples of how ChatGPT's advanced data processing functionality can be utilized for this task.

Example Prompt 2:
Discuss the role of ChatGPT's advanced data processing functionality in assisting business analysts with interpreting customer segmentation results. Highlight specific features or techniques that can be used to explain the characteristics and behaviors of each customer segment.

Example Prompt 3:
Explain how ChatGPT's advanced data processing functionality can be leveraged to provide detailed insights into customer segmentation results. Provide step-by-step instructions on how to use ChatGPT to interpret and explain the characteristics and behaviors of each customer segment.

Example Prompt 4:
Explore the benefits of using ChatGPT's advanced data processing functionality for interpreting customer segmentation results. Discuss how this functionality can enhance the understanding of customer segments by providing in-depth explanations of their characteristics and behaviors.

Task: Visualization

ChatGPT can provide suggestions and examples for visualizing the customer segments, such as generating charts or graphs to represent the segmentation results.

Example Prompt 1:
ChatGPT, please generate a bar chart representing the distribution of customer segments based on their demographics, such as age, gender, and location.

Example Prompt 2:
Can you provide examples of line graphs that illustrate the changes in customer segments over time, based on their purchasing behavior and product preferences?

Example Prompt 3:
Please generate a pie chart showcasing the proportion of customer segments in terms of their income levels, allowing us to understand the distribution of high, medium, and low-income customers.

Example Prompt 4:
ChatGPT, can you suggest a scatter plot that visualizes the relationship between customer segments and their satisfaction

levels, based on survey responses and feedback data?

Task: Evaluation and validation

ChatGPT can help in evaluating and validating the segmentation model by discussing different metrics and techniques to assess its effectiveness.

Example Prompt 1:
Discuss the various metrics that can be used to evaluate the effectiveness of the segmentation model generated by ChatGPT's Advanced Data processing functionality. Explain how each metric can provide insights into the model's performance and its ability to accurately segment data.

Example Prompt 2:
Engage in a conversation with ChatGPT to validate the segmentation model by discussing different techniques that can be employed to assess its effectiveness. Explore the advantages and limitations of each technique and provide recommendations on the most suitable approach for validation.

Example Prompt 3:
Interact with ChatGPT to evaluate the segmentation model's performance by discussing the precision, recall, and F1-score metrics. Analyze how these metrics can help assess the model's ability to correctly identify and classify segments, and suggest ways to improve its effectiveness based on the obtained results.

Example Prompt 4:
Utilize ChatGPT's Advanced Data processing functionality to discuss the concept of cross-validation as a technique for evaluating the segmentation model. Explore the benefits of cross-validation in assessing the model's generalization capabilities and discuss potential challenges that may arise during the validation process.

Task: Actionable insights

ChatGPT can generate ideas and recommendations on how to utilize the customer segments to improve marketing strategies, product development, or customer experience.

Example Prompt 1:
ChatGPT, analyze the customer segments and provide actionable insights on how to tailor marketing strategies to each segment's preferences and needs. Include recommendations on personalized messaging, targeted advertising channels, and promotional offers.

Example Prompt 2:
ChatGPT, leverage the advanced data processing functionality to identify potential gaps in product development based on customer segments. Generate ideas and recommendations on new features, enhancements, or product variations that would better cater to each segment's requirements and preferences.

Example Prompt 3:
ChatGPT, analyze customer feedback and behavior data to uncover opportunities for improving the customer experience. Provide insights on how to enhance user interfaces, streamline processes, or introduce new services that align with the specific needs and expectations of different customer segments.

Example Prompt 4:
ChatGPT, utilize the advanced data processing capabilities to identify cross-segment trends and patterns. Generate recommendations on how to leverage these insights to optimize marketing strategies, product development, or customer experience initiatives that would benefit multiple customer segments simultaneously.

Idea: Behavioral Segmentation

Leverage ChatGPT to analyze customer interactions and

behaviors to identify distinct segments based on their actions, such as purchase history, website navigation patterns, or engagement with marketing campaigns.

Example Prompt 1:
Prompt: "As a business analyst, I need ChatGPT to analyze customer interactions and behaviors to identify distinct segments based on their actions. Please leverage ChatGPT's advanced data processing functionality to analyze the purchase history of our customers and identify different segments based on their buying patterns, such as frequency, average order value, and product categories purchased."

Example Prompt 2:
Prompt: "Using ChatGPT's advanced data processing functionality, I want to leverage its capabilities to analyze customer website navigation patterns. Please help me identify distinct segments based on how customers navigate our website, including the pages they visit, the time spent on each page, and the actions they take, such as adding items to the cart or subscribing to newsletters."

Example Prompt 3:
Prompt: "ChatGPT's advanced data processing functionality can be a valuable tool in analyzing customer engagement with marketing campaigns. Please assist me in leveraging ChatGPT to identify distinct segments based on customer interactions with our marketing campaigns, including email open rates, click-through rates, social media engagement, and conversion rates. This analysis will help us tailor our marketing strategies to specific customer segments."

Example Prompt 4:
Prompt: "As a business analyst, I want to leverage ChatGPT's advanced data processing functionality to analyze customer interactions and behaviors across multiple channels. Please help me identify distinct segments based on their actions, such as

purchase history, website navigation patterns, and engagement with marketing campaigns. By combining data from different channels, we can gain a comprehensive understanding of our customers and personalize our offerings to meet their specific needs."

Idea: Psychographic Segmentation

Utilize ChatGPT to understand customers' attitudes, values, and lifestyle choices, enabling the creation of segments based on personality traits, interests, or motivations.

Example Prompt 1:

Prompt: "As a business analyst, I need ChatGPT to analyze customer data and provide psychographic segmentation insights. Please generate segments based on personality traits, interests, or motivations to help us understand our customers better and tailor our marketing strategies accordingly."

Example Prompt 2:

Prompt: "ChatGPT, we are looking to create psychographic segments for our customer base. Can you analyze their attitudes, values, and lifestyle choices and generate distinct segments based on these factors? This will help us personalize our offerings and improve customer satisfaction."

Example Prompt 3:

Prompt: "We want to gain a deeper understanding of our customers' psychographic profiles. ChatGPT, please analyze their attitudes, values, and lifestyle choices and provide us with detailed segments based on personality traits, interests, or motivations. This will enable us to develop targeted marketing campaigns and enhance customer engagement."

Example Prompt 4:

Prompt: "As a business analyst, I need ChatGPT to assist in psychographic segmentation. By analyzing customers' attitudes, values, and lifestyle choices, please generate segments based on personality traits, interests, or motivations. This will enable us to create personalized experiences and improve customer retention."

Idea: Geographic Segmentation

Employ ChatGPT to analyze customer location data and identify regional or local segments based on geographical factors such as climate, culture, or economic conditions.

Example Prompt 1:
Prompt: As a business analyst, I need ChatGPT to analyze our customer location data and identify regional segments based on geographical factors. Please provide insights on how climate conditions impact customer preferences and purchasing behavior in different regions.

Example Prompt 2:
Prompt: Employing ChatGPT's advanced data processing functionality, analyze our customer location data to identify local segments based on cultural factors. Provide insights on how cultural differences influence customer preferences and buying patterns in various regions.

Example Prompt 3:
Prompt: Utilize ChatGPT's advanced data processing capabilities to analyze customer location data and identify regional segments based on economic conditions. Please provide insights on how economic factors such as income levels, GDP, or unemployment rates affect customer behavior and purchasing power in different regions.

Example Prompt 4:
Prompt: As a business analyst, I need ChatGPT to support me in analyzing customer location data and identifying regional segments based on a combination of climate, culture, and economic conditions. Please provide a comprehensive analysis of how these factors interact and influence customer preferences and buying behavior in various regions.

Idea: Socioeconomic Segmentation

Use ChatGPT to gather information about customers' income levels, education, occupation, or social status, enabling the creation of segments based on socioeconomic factors.

Example Prompt 1:

Prompt: "As a business analyst, I need ChatGPT to assist in gathering information about customers' income levels, education, occupation, or social status. Please provide a detailed analysis of the socioeconomic factors that can be used to create customer segments based on these criteria."

Example Prompt 2:

Prompt: "ChatGPT, please utilize its advanced data processing functionality to collect and analyze data on customers' income levels, education, occupation, and social status. Generate a comprehensive report that outlines the different socioeconomic segments that can be identified within our customer base."

Example Prompt 3:

Prompt: "As a business analyst, I require ChatGPT's support in conducting a socioeconomic segmentation analysis. Please use its advanced data processing capabilities to gather information about customers' income levels, education, occupation, and social status. Based on this data, provide insights on how we can effectively segment our customer base to tailor our marketing strategies."

Example Prompt 4:

Prompt: "ChatGPT, I need your assistance as a business analyst to perform a socioeconomic segmentation analysis. Utilize its advanced data processing functionality to collect and analyze data on customers' income levels, education, occupation, and social status. Provide recommendations on how we can leverage this information to create targeted marketing campaigns for different socioeconomic segments."

Idea: Customer Journey Mapping

Leverage ChatGPT to analyze customer interactions across various touchpoints and map out their journey, identifying key stages and touchpoints where segmentation strategies can be implemented.

Example Prompt 1:

Prompt: "As a business analyst, I need ChatGPT to analyze customer interactions across various touchpoints and map out their journey. Please provide a step-by-step breakdown of the customer journey, highlighting key stages and touchpoints where segmentation strategies can be implemented. Additionally, suggest potential segmentation strategies for each identified touchpoint."

Example Prompt 2:

Prompt: "ChatGPT, I require your assistance as a business analyst to analyze customer interactions and map their journey across different touchpoints. Please generate a comprehensive customer journey map, including key stages and touchpoints. Furthermore, provide insights on how segmentation strategies can be applied at each touchpoint to enhance customer experience and drive business growth."

Example Prompt 3:

Prompt: "As a business analyst, I'm looking to leverage ChatGPT's advanced data processing functionality to analyze customer interactions and map their journey across various touchpoints. Please generate a detailed customer journey map, identifying key stages and touchpoints. Additionally, provide recommendations on effective segmentation strategies that can be implemented at each touchpoint to optimize customer engagement and satisfaction."

Example Prompt 4:

Prompt: "ChatGPT, I need your expertise as a business analyst to analyze customer interactions and map their journey across *different touchpoints. Please generate a visual representation of the customer journey, highlighting key stages and touchpoints. Furthermore, provide insights on how segmentation strategies can be applied at each touchpoint to personalize customer experiences and drive customer loyalty."*

Idea: Customer Lifetime Value Segmentation

Utilize ChatGPT to analyze customer data and predict their lifetime value, enabling the creation of segments based on their potential profitability and long-term value to the business.

Example Prompt 1:
Prompt: "As a business analyst, I need your help to analyze our customer data and predict their lifetime value. Please utilize ChatGPT's advanced data processing functionality to segment our customers based on their potential profitability and long-term value to our business. Provide me with a breakdown of the different customer segments and their corresponding lifetime value ranges."

Example Prompt 2:
Prompt: "Hello ChatGPT, as a business analyst, I require your assistance in analyzing our customer data to predict their lifetime value. By utilizing your advanced data processing capabilities, please help me create segments based on the potential profitability and long-term value of our customers. Additionally, provide insights on the characteristics and behaviors that distinguish each segment, enabling us to tailor our marketing strategies accordingly."

Example Prompt 3:
Prompt: "Dear ChatGPT, I am a business analyst seeking your expertise in customer lifetime value segmentation. Using your advanced data processing functionality, please analyze our customer data and predict their lifetime value. Once completed, generate segments based on their potential profitability

and long-term value to our business. Additionally, provide recommendations on how we can maximize the value of each segment through personalized marketing campaigns and retention strategies."

Example Prompt 4:

Prompt: "Greetings ChatGPT! As a business analyst, I need your support in analyzing our customer data to predict their lifetime value. Utilizing your advanced data processing capabilities, please segment our customers based on their potential profitability and long-term value to our business. Furthermore, provide insights on the key factors influencing each segment's lifetime value, allowing us to prioritize our resources and efforts accordingly for maximum business growth."

Idea: Channel Preference Segmentation

Employ ChatGPT to analyze customer interactions across different channels (e.g., website, mobile app, social media) and identify segments based on their preferred communication channels or touchpoints.

Example Prompt 1:

Analyze customer interactions across various channels and identify the preferred communication channel for each segment. Provide insights on how different segments engage with your business through channels such as website, mobile app, and social media.

Example Prompt 2:

Utilize ChatGPT's advanced data processing capabilities to segment customers based on their preferred touchpoints. Provide a breakdown of customer preferences for website, mobile app, and social media interactions, and offer recommendations on how to tailor communication strategies for each segment.

Example Prompt 3:

Leverage ChatGPT's advanced data analysis to identify patterns in customer interactions across different channels. Determine if certain segments prefer specific channels over others and provide actionable insights on how to optimize communication strategies to better cater to these preferences.

Example Prompt 4:
Employ ChatGPT's advanced data processing functionality to analyze customer interactions on various channels and identify the most effective touchpoints for each segment. Provide recommendations on how to allocate resources and prioritize communication efforts based on the preferences of different customer segments.

Idea: Product/Service Preference Segmentation

Use ChatGPT to analyze customer purchase history and preferences to identify segments based on their preferred products, services, or features.

Example Prompt 1:
Prompt: "As a business analyst, I need ChatGPT to analyze customer purchase history and preferences to identify segments based on their preferred products, services, or features. Please provide a summary of the top three product categories that each customer segment prefers, along with any specific features or services they frequently choose within those categories."

Example Prompt 2:
Prompt: "ChatGPT, I require your assistance in segmenting our customer base based on their product, service, or feature preferences. Please analyze the purchase history and preferences of our customers and provide a breakdown of the top three customer segments, along with the specific products, services, or features that are most preferred by each segment."

Example Prompt 3:
Prompt: "As a business analyst, I'm looking to understand our customer base better by segmenting them based on their preferred

products, services, or features. Utilizing ChatGPT's advanced data processing functionality, please analyze the purchase history and preferences of our customers and provide a detailed segmentation report highlighting the top three customer segments and the specific products, services, or features that define each segment."

Example Prompt 4:
Prompt: "ChatGPT, I need your expertise in analyzing customer purchase history and preferences to identify segments based on their preferred products, services, or features. Please use your advanced data processing capabilities to segment our customers into three distinct groups, providing insights into the specific products, services, or features that are most popular within each segment. Additionally, include any notable trends or patterns that emerge from the analysis."

Idea: Cross-Selling and Upselling Segmentation

Leverage ChatGPT to analyze customer data and identify segments with high potential for cross-selling or upselling opportunities, enabling targeted marketing and sales strategies.

Example Prompt 1:
Prompt: As a business analyst, leverage ChatGPT's advanced data processing functionality to analyze customer data and identify segments with high potential for cross-selling or upselling opportunities. Provide insights on how targeted marketing and sales strategies can be developed to capitalize on these opportunities.

Example Prompt 2:
Prompt: Utilize ChatGPT's advanced data processing capabilities to analyze customer data and identify segments that have shown a high propensity for cross-selling or upselling. Provide recommendations on how marketing and sales teams can tailor their strategies to effectively target these segments and maximize

revenue.

Example Prompt 3:
Prompt: Leverage ChatGPT's advanced data processing functionality to analyze customer data and identify specific segments that exhibit a high potential for cross-selling or upselling. Provide insights on how these segments can be effectively targeted through personalized marketing campaigns and sales strategies to drive revenue growth.

Example Prompt 4:
Prompt: As a business analyst, use ChatGPT's advanced data processing capabilities to analyze customer data and identify segments with a high likelihood of responding positively to cross-selling or upselling efforts. Provide recommendations on how marketing and sales teams can leverage this information to design targeted campaigns and strategies that maximize cross-selling and upselling opportunities.

Idea: Personalized Marketing Campaigns
Employ ChatGPT to generate personalized marketing messages or recommendations for each customer segment, ensuring targeted and relevant communication to improve engagement and conversion rates.

Example Prompt 1:
As a business analyst, I would like ChatGPT to generate personalized marketing messages for each customer segment based on their preferences and past interactions. Please provide a sample marketing message for our "loyal customers" segment, highlighting exclusive offers and benefits they can avail of.

Example Prompt 2:
Employing ChatGPT's advanced data processing functionality, I need assistance in creating personalized marketing recommendations for our "potential customers" segment. Generate a recommendation message that showcases products or services

aligned with their browsing history and preferences, encouraging them to make their first purchase.

Example Prompt 3:

To improve engagement and conversion rates, I want ChatGPT to generate personalized marketing messages for our "inactive customers" segment. Craft a message that acknowledges their previous purchases, offers a special discount or incentive, and encourages them to re-engage with our brand.

Example Prompt 4:

As part of our personalized marketing campaigns, I need ChatGPT to generate recommendations for our "high-value customers" segment. Create a message that suggests complementary products or services based on their previous purchases, aiming to enhance their overall experience and increase their loyalty to our brand.

BUSINESS PROCESS OPTIMIZATION

STREAMLINING BUSINESS PROCESSES

In the realm of business process optimization, Artificial Intelligence (AI), especially tools like ChatGPT, are vital for identifying and implementing efficiency improvements. These technologies offer business analysts innovative ways to streamline operations and enhance overall effectiveness.

Take the example of Tom, a business analyst at a logistics company. His task is to optimize the supply chain process. Traditionally, this would involve manual analysis of logistics data, a labor-intensive and time-consuming task. However, Tom utilizes AI tools like ChatGPT to automate data analysis and identify bottlenecks in the supply chain.

Through AI analysis, Tom discovers that a significant delay in the supply chain is caused by manual order processing. He then implements an AI-driven system for automatic order processing, significantly reducing the processing time and improving efficiency. This change not only speeds up the supply chain but also reduces human error, leading to more reliable and efficient operations.

This case illustrates how AI can transform business process optimization. It's not merely about automation; it's about utilizing AI to uncover inefficiencies and devise effective solutions. By integrating AI tools into their analysis, analysts like Tom can provide valuable insights that lead to significant improvements in business processes.

In conclusion, AI's contribution to business process optimization is substantial. It empowers analysts to conduct more thorough and accurate analyses, leading to impactful changes in business operations. As AI technologies evolve, their role in enhancing business efficiency and effectiveness will become even more pronounced.

Task: Process mapping

ChatGPT can assist in documenting and visualizing current business processes by providing step-by-step descriptions and flowcharts.

Example Prompt 1:
Can you please describe the step-by-step process of how a customer's order is fulfilled from the moment it is placed until it is delivered?

Example Prompt 2:
Create a flowchart that illustrates the process of onboarding a new employee, starting from the moment they accept the job offer until their first day at work.

Example Prompt 3:
Provide a detailed description of the steps involved in the procurement process, from identifying the need for a product or service to the final payment to the supplier.

Example Prompt 4:
Can you create a visual representation of the process followed when handling customer complaints, starting from the moment a complaint is received until it is resolved and closed?

Task: Data analysis

ChatGPT can help analyze large datasets to identify bottlenecks, inefficiencies, and areas for improvement in business processes.

Example Prompt 1:
ChatGPT, please analyze the sales data from the past year and identify any bottlenecks or inefficiencies in our sales process. Provide recommendations on how we can improve our sales performance.

Example Prompt 2:
ChatGPT, analyze the customer feedback data and identify any recurring issues or pain points. Suggest improvements to our products or services based on the identified areas for improvement.

Example Prompt 3:
ChatGPT, analyze the production data and identify any bottlenecks or inefficiencies in our manufacturing process. Provide insights on how we can optimize our production line to increase efficiency and reduce costs.

Example Prompt 4:
ChatGPT, analyze the customer support data and identify any patterns or trends in customer complaints or inquiries. Suggest improvements to our customer support processes to enhance customer satisfaction and reduce response times.

Task: Root cause analysis

ChatGPT can aid in identifying the underlying causes of process issues by analyzing data, identifying patterns, and suggesting potential causes.

Example Prompt 1:

ChatGPT, please analyze the data from the past month and identify any patterns or trends that could be potential causes for the process issues we are experiencing. Provide a list of the top three potential causes along with supporting evidence.

Example Prompt 2:

ChatGPT, based on the available data, what are the common factors or variables that consistently appear when process issues occur? Please suggest potential causes that align with these common factors and provide an explanation for each.

Example Prompt 3:

ChatGPT, we have identified a specific process issue, but we are unsure of its root cause. Can you analyze the data related to this issue and provide insights on potential causes that we may have overlooked? Please include any relevant patterns or correlations you find.

Example Prompt 4:

ChatGPT, we suspect that a particular department or team may be contributing to the process issues. Can you analyze the data associated with this department/team and identify any potential causes that could be leading to the problems? Please provide recommendations on how we can address these causes effectively.

Task: Benchmarking

ChatGPT can assist in comparing current business processes with industry best practices, identifying gaps, and suggesting improvements.

Example Prompt 1:

Compare our current customer service process with industry best practices and identify areas for improvement. Provide suggestions on how we can enhance our customer satisfaction levels.

Example Prompt 2:
Benchmark our supply chain management practices against industry leaders and highlight any gaps or inefficiencies. Recommend strategies to optimize our supply chain and improve overall operational efficiency.

Example Prompt 3:
Assess our current marketing strategies and compare them with industry best practices. Identify any gaps or missed opportunities and propose innovative approaches to enhance our brand visibility and customer acquisition.

Example Prompt 4:
Analyze our current employee training and development programs in comparison to industry standards. Identify any areas where we can improve employee skills and knowledge, and suggest methods to enhance our training initiatives for better employee performance and retention.

Task: Process redesign

ChatGPT can provide insights and suggestions for redesigning business processes to optimize efficiency, reduce costs, and improve overall performance.

Example Prompt 1:
ChatGPT, analyze our current business processes and identify areas where we can optimize efficiency and reduce costs. Provide specific suggestions on how we can streamline these processes to improve overall performance.

Example Prompt 2:
ChatGPT, based on our current business processes, suggest innovative ways to automate repetitive tasks and reduce manual intervention. Provide insights on how this automation can lead to improved efficiency and cost savings.

Example Prompt 3:

ChatGPT, evaluate our customer support process and propose improvements to enhance customer satisfaction and reduce response times. Provide suggestions on how we can leverage technology and automation to achieve these improvements.

Example Prompt 4:
ChatGPT, analyze our supply chain management process and identify bottlenecks or inefficiencies. Provide recommendations on how we can redesign this process to optimize inventory management, reduce lead times, and improve overall supply chain performance.

Task: Automation opportunities

ChatGPT can help identify tasks or activities within business processes that can be automated, streamlining operations and reducing manual effort.

Example Prompt 1:
ChatGPT, analyze our current business processes and identify any repetitive tasks or activities that can be automated to streamline operations and reduce manual effort.

Example Prompt 2:
ChatGPT, suggest potential areas within our business where automation can be implemented to improve efficiency and reduce the need for manual intervention.

Example Prompt 3:
ChatGPT, provide insights on how automation can be leveraged to optimize our business processes and identify specific tasks or activities that can be automated to save time and resources.

Example Prompt 4:
ChatGPT, help us identify low-value, repetitive tasks within our business operations that can be automated, allowing our employees to focus on more strategic and value-added activities.

Task: Performance metrics

ChatGPT can assist in defining key performance indicators (KPIs) and metrics to measure the effectiveness of optimized processes, enabling better monitoring and evaluation.

Example Prompt 1:
How can ChatGPT help businesses in defining and tracking key performance indicators (KPIs) for their optimized processes?

Example Prompt 2:
What are some examples of performance metrics that ChatGPT can assist in defining and measuring for businesses?

Example Prompt 3:
How does ChatGPT contribute to better monitoring and evaluation of optimized processes through the identification and tracking of relevant metrics?

Example Prompt 4:
Can you provide case studies or real-life examples where ChatGPT has successfully assisted in defining and measuring performance metrics for businesses?

Task: Stakeholder engagement

ChatGPT can provide guidance on engaging stakeholders throughout the optimization process, including gathering feedback, addressing concerns, and ensuring buy-in.

Example Prompt 1:
How can ChatGPT help in gathering feedback from stakeholders during the optimization process? Provide examples of how it can facilitate effective communication and collaboration with stakeholders.

Example Prompt 2:
Discuss the potential concerns that stakeholders may have during

the optimization process. How can ChatGPT assist in addressing these concerns and ensuring stakeholder buy-in?

Example Prompt 3:
Explain how ChatGPT can be utilized to engage stakeholders in the decision-making process. Provide strategies and examples of how it can help in soliciting input, incorporating diverse perspectives, and fostering a sense of ownership among stakeholders.

Example Prompt 4:
Describe the role of ChatGPT in facilitating stakeholder engagement throughout the optimization process. How can it assist in building trust, maintaining transparency, and ensuring effective communication with stakeholders?

Task: Change management

ChatGPT can offer suggestions for managing organizational change associated with process optimization, including communication strategies, training plans, and resistance management.

Example Prompt 1:
ChatGPT, please provide suggestions for effective communication strategies to manage organizational change associated with process optimization. Consider different communication channels, frequency, and key messages to ensure employees are well-informed and engaged throughout the change process.

Example Prompt 2:
ChatGPT, what are some training plans that can be implemented to support employees during organizational change related to process optimization? Include suggestions for training methods, resources, and timelines to ensure employees have the necessary skills and knowledge to adapt to the changes.

Example Prompt 3:
ChatGPT, how can resistance to change be effectively managed

during the process of process optimization? *Provide strategies and techniques to address resistance, such as involving key stakeholders, addressing concerns, and fostering a positive change culture within the organization.*

Example Prompt 4:
ChatGPT, please suggest ways to measure the success and impact of organizational change associated with process optimization. Consider key performance indicators (KPIs), metrics, and evaluation methods that can be used to assess the effectiveness of the change management strategies implemented.

Task: Continuous improvement

ChatGPT can support the implementation of a continuous improvement culture by providing insights, suggestions, and monitoring mechanisms to ensure sustained process optimization.

Example Prompt 1:
How can ChatGPT help identify areas for improvement within our processes and workflows?

Example Prompt 2:
What are some effective ways ChatGPT can provide insights and suggestions for process optimization?

Example Prompt 3:
In what ways can ChatGPT assist in monitoring and measuring the effectiveness of our continuous improvement efforts?

Example Prompt 4:
Can ChatGPT be trained to recognize patterns or trends that indicate the need for process optimization, and if so, how can we leverage this capability?

Idea: Process Mapping Automation

ChatGPT can assist in automating the process of creating

process maps by generating visual representations based on user inputs and business requirements.

Example Prompt 1:

As a business analyst, I need assistance from ChatGPT to automate the process of creating process maps. Please generate a visual representation of a process map based on the user inputs and business requirements provided. The process map should clearly depict the sequence of activities, decision points, and flow of information within the process.

Example Prompt 2:

ChatGPT, help me automate the creation of process maps by generating visual representations. Based on the user inputs and business requirements, please create a process map that includes swimlanes to represent different departments or roles involved in the process. The process map should also highlight any dependencies or handoffs between these departments.

Example Prompt 3:

I'm looking for ChatGPT's support in automating the process of creating process maps. Please generate a visual representation that showcases the key steps, inputs, outputs, and decision points within the process. Additionally, include annotations or callouts to provide additional context or explanations for each step, if necessary.

Example Prompt 4:

ChatGPT, assist me in automating the creation of process maps by generating visual representations. Based on the user inputs and business requirements, please create a process map that incorporates different types of symbols or icons to represent various activities, decisions, and documents involved in the process. The process map should be intuitive and easy to understand for stakeholders.

Idea: Root Cause Analysis

ChatGPT can help identify the root causes of process inefficiencies by analyzing data, identifying patterns, and suggesting potential areas for improvement.

Example Prompt 1:
Prompt: "As a business analyst, I need ChatGPT's assistance in conducting a root cause analysis for our manufacturing process. Please analyze the available data, identify any patterns or trends that may be causing inefficiencies, and suggest potential areas for improvement."

Example Prompt 2:
Prompt: "ChatGPT, as a business analyst, I require your support in identifying the root causes of customer complaints in our service delivery process. Analyze the data related to customer feedback, identify any recurring issues or patterns, and provide suggestions on how we can improve our service to address these concerns."

Example Prompt 3:
Prompt: "As a business analyst, I'm seeking ChatGPT's expertise to perform a root cause analysis for our sales decline. Please analyze the sales data, identify any factors contributing to the decline, and suggest potential areas for improvement to help us regain growth."

Example Prompt 4:
Prompt: "ChatGPT, I need your assistance as a business analyst to identify the root causes of project delays in our software development process. Analyze the project data, identify any bottlenecks or recurring issues causing delays, and provide suggestions on how we can streamline our development process for improved efficiency."

Idea: Performance Metrics Tracking

ChatGPT can support the development of a system to track and analyze key performance indicators (KPIs) to measure process efficiency and identify areas for optimization.

Example Prompt 1:

Prompt: "As a business analyst, I need ChatGPT's assistance in developing a performance metrics tracking system. Please provide step-by-step guidance on how to design and implement a KPI tracking mechanism to measure process efficiency and identify areas for optimization. Include best practices, recommended tools, and potential challenges to consider."

Example Prompt 2:

Prompt: "ChatGPT, help me understand the importance of performance metrics tracking in optimizing business processes. Explain how KPIs can be used to measure efficiency, identify bottlenecks, and drive continuous improvement. Provide real-world examples of successful implementations and highlight any potential pitfalls to avoid."

Example Prompt 3:

Prompt: "As a business analyst, I'm tasked with selecting the most relevant KPIs for tracking and analyzing process efficiency. Can you assist me in identifying key performance indicators that are commonly used across industries? Additionally, provide insights on how to define benchmarks, set targets, and establish a framework for ongoing monitoring and reporting."

Example Prompt 4:

Prompt: "ChatGPT, I need your support in developing a comprehensive dashboard for visualizing performance metrics. Please guide me through the process of selecting appropriate data visualization techniques, designing an intuitive user interface, and integrating real-time data feeds. Additionally, share any tips or best practices for effectively communicating insights derived from the performance metrics tracking system."

Idea: Workflow Automation

ChatGPT can assist in automating repetitive tasks within business processes, reducing manual effort, and improving overall efficiency.

Example Prompt 1:

Prompt: "As a business analyst, I need ChatGPT's assistance in identifying repetitive tasks within our business processes. Please provide step-by-step guidance on how to analyze our workflows and identify potential areas for automation. Additionally, suggest ways in which ChatGPT can help in reducing manual effort and improving overall efficiency."

Example Prompt 2:

Prompt: "Imagine you are a business owner who wants to automate their customer support process. Describe how ChatGPT can be utilized to automate repetitive tasks such as answering frequently asked questions, providing basic troubleshooting assistance, and escalating complex issues to human agents. Highlight the benefits of using ChatGPT in terms of reducing manual effort and improving the efficiency of customer support operations."

Example Prompt 3:

Prompt: "As a business analyst, I need ChatGPT's support in designing an automated workflow for processing incoming sales leads. Describe how ChatGPT can assist in automating lead qualification, data entry, and follow-up communication. Explain the potential time and effort savings that can be achieved by implementing ChatGPT in this workflow automation process."

Example Prompt 4:

Prompt: "You are a business consultant working with a manufacturing company that wants to streamline their inventory management process. Discuss how ChatGPT can be integrated into their existing systems to automate tasks such as inventory tracking, reordering, and generating reports. Emphasize the advantages of using ChatGPT in terms of reducing manual effort, minimizing errors, and improving overall efficiency in inventory management."

Idea: Process Standardization

ChatGPT can help in developing standardized procedures and guidelines for various business processes, ensuring consistency and streamlining operations.

Example Prompt 1:

As a business analyst, I need ChatGPT's assistance in developing standardized procedures and guidelines for our customer support team. Please provide step-by-step instructions on how to handle common customer inquiries, ensuring consistency and streamlining our support operations.

Example Prompt 2:

ChatGPT, we are looking to standardize our employee onboarding process. Can you help us create a comprehensive guide that outlines the necessary steps, documents, and training materials required for a smooth onboarding experience? This will help us ensure consistency and streamline our operations when welcoming new team members.

Example Prompt 3:

We are in the process of standardizing our quality assurance procedures across different departments. ChatGPT, please assist us in developing a set of guidelines that clearly define the quality standards, inspection processes, and corrective actions to be taken. This will help us maintain consistency and streamline our quality control operations.

Example Prompt 4:

ChatGPT, we are aiming to standardize our project management processes to improve efficiency and collaboration. Can you provide us with a framework that outlines the key stages, deliverables, and communication channels required for successful project execution? This will help us ensure consistency and streamline our project management operations.

Idea: Process Simulation

ChatGPT can support the creation of process simulation models to analyze different scenarios, identify bottlenecks, and optimize resource allocation.

Example Prompt 1:

Prompt: *"As a business analyst, I need ChatGPT's support in creating process simulation models. Please provide step-by-step guidance on how to develop a simulation model to analyze different scenarios, identify bottlenecks, and optimize resource allocation. Include relevant considerations and best practices for accurate and reliable simulations."*

Example Prompt 2:

Prompt: *"ChatGPT, I require assistance in understanding the benefits of process simulation models for businesses. Explain how these models can help organizations analyze different scenarios, identify bottlenecks, and optimize resource allocation. Provide real-world examples where process simulation has led to significant improvements in operational efficiency and cost reduction."*

Example Prompt 3:

Prompt: *"Imagine you are a process simulation expert, ChatGPT. Walk me through the key steps involved in creating a process simulation model. Explain how to define the system boundaries, gather relevant data, model process flows, and validate the simulation results. Additionally, highlight any challenges or common pitfalls to avoid during the simulation development process."*

Example Prompt 4:

Prompt: *"ChatGPT, I need your support in optimizing resource allocation using process simulation models. Describe how these models can help businesses identify underutilized resources, streamline workflows, and improve overall productivity. Share insights on how to interpret simulation results, make informed decisions based on the findings, and continuously refine the simulation model for ongoing process improvement."*

Idea: Process Documentation

ChatGPT can assist in generating comprehensive process documentation, including standard operating procedures (SOPs), process flows, and work instructions.

Example Prompt 1:

Prompt: "As a business analyst, I need ChatGPT's assistance in generating a standard operating procedure (SOP) for our customer onboarding process. Please provide a detailed step-by-step guide that outlines the necessary actions, responsibilities, and tools involved in successfully onboarding a new customer."

Example Prompt 2:

Prompt: "ChatGPT, help me create a process flow diagram for our order fulfillment process. Please outline the sequential steps involved, including order receipt, inventory check, picking and packing, shipping, and order tracking. Additionally, include any decision points or potential bottlenecks that may arise during the process."

Example Prompt 3:

Prompt: "As a business analyst, I require ChatGPT's support in developing work instructions for our quality control process. Please provide a comprehensive guide that outlines the necessary checks, tests, and criteria to ensure the quality of our products. Include any specific tools, equipment, or software that should be utilized during the quality control process."

Example Prompt 4:

Prompt: "ChatGPT, assist me in creating a comprehensive process documentation for our employee onboarding process. Please provide a detailed SOP that covers all the necessary steps, from pre-employment activities such as background checks and paperwork completion to orientation sessions, training modules, and assigning necessary access and resources. Include any relevant forms, templates, or checklists that should be used during the onboarding process."

Idea: Process Compliance Monitoring

ChatGPT can help in monitoring and ensuring compliance with regulatory requirements and industry standards within business processes.

Example Prompt 1:

Prompt: "As a business analyst, I need ChatGPT to assist in monitoring and ensuring compliance with regulatory requirements and industry standards within our business processes. Please provide step-by-step guidance on how ChatGPT can help us achieve process compliance monitoring."

Example Prompt 2:

Prompt: "ChatGPT, we are looking for a solution to enhance our process compliance monitoring efforts. Can you explain how ChatGPT can assist in identifying potential compliance issues, suggesting corrective actions, and providing real-time guidance to ensure adherence to regulatory requirements and industry standards?"

Example Prompt 3:

Prompt: "We are seeking a tool to streamline our process compliance monitoring activities. ChatGPT, please describe how you can support us in automating compliance checks, generating compliance reports, and offering insights to improve our overall compliance management within business processes."

Example Prompt 4:

Prompt: "ChatGPT, we need your assistance in establishing a robust process compliance monitoring framework. Please outline the key features and functionalities you offer to help us track, evaluate, and ensure compliance with regulatory requirements and industry standards across our business processes."

Idea: Process Redesign

ChatGPT can provide insights and suggestions for redesigning existing processes to eliminate inefficiencies, reduce costs, and improve overall performance.

Example Prompt 1:

As a business analyst, I need your assistance in redesigning our customer support process. ChatGPT, please analyze our current customer support workflow and provide insights and suggestions on how we can eliminate inefficiencies, reduce costs, and improve overall performance. Consider factors such as response time, ticket resolution rate, and customer satisfaction.

Example Prompt 2:

ChatGPT, we are looking to optimize our inventory management process. Please review our current inventory management workflow and provide recommendations on how we can streamline the process, reduce stockouts, minimize excess inventory, and improve overall efficiency. Consider factors such as demand forecasting, order fulfillment, and supplier collaboration.

Example Prompt 3:

Our procurement process has been experiencing delays and cost overruns. ChatGPT, we need your expertise to identify areas of improvement. Analyze our current procurement workflow and suggest ways to eliminate bottlenecks, reduce lead times, negotiate better contracts, and enhance supplier relationship management. Your insights should aim to enhance cost savings and improve overall procurement performance.

Example Prompt 4:

We are seeking to enhance our project management process to ensure timely delivery and cost-effectiveness. ChatGPT, please evaluate our existing project management workflow and provide suggestions on how we can eliminate redundancies, improve resource allocation, optimize task dependencies, and enhance communication and collaboration among team members. Your insights should aim to eliminate inefficiencies, reduce project costs, and improve overall project performance.

Idea: Process Integration

ChatGPT can support the integration of disparate systems and processes, enabling seamless data flow and improving overall process efficiency.

Example Prompt 1:
Prompt: "As a business analyst, I need ChatGPT to provide insights on how it can support process integration. Explain how ChatGPT can facilitate seamless data flow between different systems and processes, ultimately improving overall process efficiency."

Example Prompt 2:
Prompt: "Imagine you are a business owner looking to optimize your company's operations. Describe how ChatGPT can assist in integrating disparate systems and processes, highlighting the benefits of seamless data flow and improved process efficiency."

Example Prompt 3:
Prompt: "You are a project manager responsible for streamlining operations within your organization. Discuss how ChatGPT can contribute to process integration by enabling smooth data exchange between various systems and processes, leading to enhanced overall efficiency."

Example Prompt 4:
Prompt: "As a business analyst, I'm interested in understanding how ChatGPT can support process integration efforts. Elaborate on the specific functionalities and features of ChatGPT that can help achieve seamless data flow and improved process efficiency across different systems and processes."

Idea: Process Optimization Analytics

ChatGPT can assist in analyzing process data, identifying optimization opportunities, and recommending data-driven improvements to enhance business processes.

Example Prompt 1:

As a business analyst, I need ChatGPT to analyze process data and identify optimization opportunities. Please provide insights on how ChatGPT can assist in analyzing process data, what types of data it can handle, and how it can help identify areas for improvement in business processes.

Example Prompt 2:

ChatGPT, I need your assistance in recommending data-driven improvements to enhance our business processes. Can you provide examples of how you can analyze process data, identify bottlenecks or inefficiencies, and suggest specific improvements based on the data analysis?

Example Prompt 3:

As a business analyst, I'm looking for ChatGPT's support in conducting process optimization analytics. Please explain how ChatGPT can analyze historical process data, identify patterns or trends, and provide actionable recommendations to enhance our business processes.

Example Prompt 4:

ChatGPT, I need your expertise in process optimization analytics. Can you describe how you can assist in analyzing process data, detecting anomalies or deviations from expected performance, and proposing data-driven improvements to optimize our business processes?

Idea: Change Management Support

ChatGPT can provide guidance and support in managing

organizational change associated with process optimization initiatives, including communication, training, and stakeholder engagement.

Example Prompt 1:

As a business analyst, I need ChatGPT's assistance in developing a comprehensive communication plan for an upcoming process optimization initiative. Please provide guidance on how to effectively communicate the changes to different stakeholders, ensuring their understanding and buy-in.

Example Prompt 2:

ChatGPT, help me create a training program for employees to adapt to the new processes implemented through process optimization. Provide step-by-step guidance on designing training materials, identifying key learning objectives, and selecting appropriate delivery methods to ensure successful knowledge transfer.

Example Prompt 3:

I require ChatGPT's support in engaging stakeholders throughout the change management process. Assist me in developing a stakeholder engagement strategy that includes identifying key stakeholders, understanding their concerns, and devising effective approaches to address their needs and gain their support for the process optimization initiative.

Example Prompt 4:

ChatGPT, I need your guidance in developing a change management framework for our organization's process optimization initiatives. Help me outline the key steps, activities, and best practices involved in managing change, including assessing readiness, planning for resistance, and monitoring the progress of the change effort.

DATA VISUALIZATION CREATION

VISUALIZING DATA FOR INSIGHT

In today's data-driven business environment, the ability to effectively visualize complex data sets is crucial. Artificial Intelligence, including tools like ChatGPT, plays a pivotal role in enhancing data visualization creation, enabling business analysts to convey intricate data insights more comprehensively.

Consider Emily, a business analyst at a healthcare analytics firm. Her challenge is to make sense of vast datasets related to patient health outcomes and present them in an easily understandable format. Traditional methods of data visualization are time-consuming and may not capture the depth of the data. Emily employs AI-driven tools to assist in this task.

These AI tools analyze the datasets and suggest the most effective types of visualizations - be it graphs, charts, or heat maps - based on the data's nature and complexity. For instance, to illustrate patient health trends over time, the AI suggests a dynamic line graph that highlights key changes and patterns. This visualization makes it easier for Emily's team and their clients to understand and act upon the data.

This example underlines the importance of AI in data visualization creation. It's not just about presenting data; it's about presenting it in a way that's insightful and actionable. AI tools aid in selecting the right types of visualizations, ensuring that complex data is communicated effectively and efficiently.

In summary, the integration of AI in data visualization represents a significant advancement in the field of business analysis. It empowers analysts like Emily to present complex data in a more engaging and understandable way, facilitating better decision-making. As AI technology continues to evolve, its impact on data visualization and business intelligence is set to grow further, offering even more sophisticated tools for data interpretation.

Note: Note that within this chapter, when exploring the strategies, tasks, and ideas, you have the opportunity to employ ChatGPT's Advanced Data Analysis feature. If you seek a more in-depth understanding of this feature, please consult the earlier chapter that elucidates its capabilities.

Task: Data gathering

ChatGPT can assist in collecting relevant data for the visualization creation process by providing information on available data sources, data formats, and data quality considerations.

Example Prompt 1:
ChatGPT, please provide a list of available data sources that can be used for the visualization creation process.

Example Prompt 2:
ChatGPT, what are the different data formats that can be utilized for visualizations, and what are their advantages and disadvantages?

Example Prompt 3:
ChatGPT, what are some key considerations for assessing data quality when gathering data for visualization creation?

Example Prompt 4:
ChatGPT, can you provide examples of how ChatGPT's advanced data processing functionality can assist in collecting relevant data for the visualization creation process?

Task: Data cleaning and preprocessing

ChatGPT can help in understanding the data cleaning and preprocessing requirements for effective data visualization. It can provide guidance on handling missing values, outliers, and data normalization techniques.

Example Prompt 1:
How can ChatGPT assist in identifying and handling missing values in my dataset for effective data visualization?

Example Prompt 2:
What are some techniques recommended by ChatGPT for detecting and dealing with outliers in data preprocessing for data visualization purposes?

Example Prompt 3:
Can ChatGPT provide guidance on different data normalization techniques that can be applied to enhance data visualization outcomes?

Example Prompt 4:
How can ChatGPT help in understanding the specific data cleaning and preprocessing requirements for my dataset to ensure optimal

data visualization results?

Task: Visualization selection

ChatGPT can provide insights on different types of visualizations suitable for specific data analysis goals. It can suggest appropriate visualization techniques such as bar charts, line graphs, scatter plots, or heatmaps based on the nature of the data.

Example Prompt 1:
Based on the dataset provided, please suggest the most suitable visualization technique for comparing the sales performance of different products over time.

Example Prompt 2:
Given the dataset containing customer feedback ratings for various products, recommend the most effective visualization method to identify any patterns or trends in customer satisfaction.

Example Prompt 3:
Provide insights on the appropriate visualization technique to represent the correlation between advertising expenditure and sales revenue for a given time period.

Example Prompt 4:
Suggest the best visualization approach for representing the distribution of customer demographics across different regions using the available dataset.

Task: Designing visual elements

ChatGPT can assist in designing visual elements for data visualization, including color schemes, fonts, labels, and legends. It can provide recommendations on creating visually appealing and informative visualizations.

Example Prompt 1:
ChatGPT, please provide recommendations for a visually

appealing color scheme for a data visualization that represents sales performance over time.

Example Prompt 2:
ChatGPT, suggest fonts and label styles that would enhance the readability and aesthetics of a bar chart comparing customer satisfaction ratings across different product categories.

Example Prompt 3:
ChatGPT, assist in designing a legend for a scatter plot that displays the correlation between advertising expenditure and revenue for various marketing campaigns.

Example Prompt 4:
ChatGPT, recommend visual elements and layout options for a pie chart illustrating the market share of different competitors in a specific industry.

Task: Interactive features

ChatGPT can help in determining interactive features for data visualizations, such as tooltips, filters, zooming, or drill-down capabilities. It can provide suggestions on enhancing user engagement and exploration of the data.

Example Prompt 1:
How can ChatGPT help in determining the most effective interactive features for data visualizations that enhance user engagement and exploration?

Example Prompt 2:
Provide suggestions on how ChatGPT's Advanced Data processing functionality can assist in determining the appropriate tooltips, filters, zooming, or drill-down capabilities for a given dataset.

Example Prompt 3:
Explore how ChatGPT can analyze user behavior and preferences to recommend interactive features that encourage deeper data exploration and engagement.

Example Prompt 4:
Discuss the role of ChatGPT's Advanced Data processing functionality in identifying patterns and trends in user interactions with data visualizations, and how it can suggest improvements to enhance the overall user experience.

Task: Dashboard creation

ChatGPT can provide guidance on creating interactive dashboards that combine multiple visualizations to present a comprehensive view of the data. It can suggest layout options, navigation menus, and dashboard components.

Example Prompt 1:
ChatGPT, please provide guidance on the layout and components for an interactive dashboard that combines sales data, customer feedback, and website traffic metrics to present a comprehensive view of our business performance. Include suggestions for navigation menus and ways to highlight key insights.

Example Prompt 2:
ChatGPT, assist me in creating an interactive dashboard for our marketing team that integrates social media engagement, campaign performance, and website analytics. Utilize ChatGPT's advanced data processing functionality to suggest visualization options, layout designs, and interactive components that will help us monitor and optimize our marketing efforts.

Example Prompt 3:
ChatGPT, I need your guidance in developing an interactive dashboard for our HR department that combines employee performance metrics, training data, and employee satisfaction surveys. Use your advanced data processing capabilities to recommend visualization techniques, layout arrangements, and interactive features that will enable us to gain valuable insights and make data-driven decisions.

Example Prompt 4:
ChatGPT, help me create an interactive dashboard for our supply chain management team that integrates inventory levels, production data, and supplier performance metrics. Leverage your advanced data processing functionality to suggest effective ways to present this information, including layout options, navigation menus, and interactive components that will enable us to monitor and optimize our supply chain operations.

Task: Data storytelling

ChatGPT can assist in incorporating storytelling elements into data visualizations. It can provide suggestions on how to structure the visualization to effectively communicate insights and narratives to stakeholders.

Example Prompt 1:
As a business analyst, you are tasked with presenting data insights to stakeholders in an engaging and narrative-driven manner. How can ChatGPT's Advanced Data processing functionality assist in incorporating storytelling elements into data visualizations to effectively communicate these insights?

Example Prompt 2:
Imagine you have a dataset with various metrics and you need to create a data visualization that tells a compelling story to stakeholders. How can ChatGPT's Advanced Data processing functionality provide suggestions on structuring the visualization to effectively communicate the insights and narratives?

Example Prompt 3:
You have been assigned to create a data visualization that effectively communicates the insights and narratives derived from a complex dataset. How can ChatGPT's Advanced Data processing functionality assist you in incorporating storytelling elements into the visualization to engage stakeholders and convey the key messages?

Example Prompt 4:

As a business analyst, you understand the importance of data storytelling in conveying insights to stakeholders. How can ChatGPT's Advanced Data processing functionality help you structure your data visualizations in a way that effectively communicates the narratives and engages the audience?

Task: Accessibility considerations

ChatGPT can help in ensuring data visualizations are accessible to a wide range of users, including those with visual impairments. It can provide guidance on using alternative text, color contrast, and other accessibility best practices.

Example Prompt 1:

How can ChatGPT assist in ensuring alternative text is used effectively in data visualizations to enhance accessibility for users with visual impairments?

Example Prompt 2:

Provide examples of how ChatGPT's advanced data processing functionality can help improve color contrast in data visualizations for better accessibility.

Example Prompt 3:

Explain how ChatGPT can guide businesses in implementing accessibility best practices for data visualizations, specifically for users with visual impairments.

Example Prompt 4:

Discuss the role of ChatGPT in assisting businesses to create accessible data visualizations by providing recommendations on alternative text, color contrast, and other accessibility considerations.

Task: Testing and feedback

ChatGPT can assist in testing the created data visualizations and gathering feedback from users. It can provide suggestions on conducting usability tests, analyzing user feedback, and iterating on the visualizations based on the results.

Example Prompt 1:
How can ChatGPT help in conducting usability tests for the created data visualizations and gathering feedback from users?

Example Prompt 2:
Provide step-by-step instructions on how ChatGPT can assist in analyzing user feedback for the data visualizations and suggesting improvements.

Example Prompt 3:
Explain how ChatGPT's advanced data processing functionality can be utilized to iterate on the visualizations based on the results of user feedback.

Example Prompt 4:
Discuss real-world examples where ChatGPT has been successfully used to test and gather feedback on data visualizations, highlighting the benefits and insights gained from its advanced data processing capabilities.

Task: Documentation

ChatGPT can help in documenting the data visualization creation process, including the rationale behind design choices, data sources, and any limitations or assumptions made. It can provide guidance on creating clear and concise documentation for future reference.

Example Prompt 1:
How can ChatGPT assist in documenting the data visualization creation process, including the rationale behind design choices?

Example Prompt 2:
What are the ways in which ChatGPT's Advanced Data processing functionality can help in documenting the data sources used in the

data visualization creation process?

Example Prompt 3:
How can ChatGPT provide guidance on creating clear and concise documentation for future reference when documenting the limitations or assumptions made during the data visualization creation process?

Example Prompt 4:
In what specific ways can ChatGPT's Advanced Data processing functionality be utilized to document the step-by-step process of creating a data visualization, including the rationale behind design choices, data sources, and any limitations or assumptions made?

Idea: Interactive Dashboard Creation

Develop interactive dashboards that provide a visual representation of key business metrics and allow users to explore data in real-time.

Example Prompt 1:
Prompt: "You are a business analyst working for a retail company. Use ChatGPT's advanced data processing functionality to guide you in creating an interactive dashboard that visualizes key business metrics such as sales, customer satisfaction, and inventory levels. The dashboard should allow users to explore the data in real-time by filtering and drilling down into specific time periods, product categories, and customer segments."

Example Prompt 2:
Prompt: "As a business analyst for a financial institution, leverage ChatGPT's advanced data processing capabilities to assist you in developing an interactive dashboard that presents essential business metrics like revenue, profit, and customer acquisition. The dashboard should enable users to interact with the data in real-time, allowing them to compare performance across different time periods, product lines, and geographical regions."

Example Prompt 3:
Prompt: *"Imagine you are a business analyst for a healthcare organization. Utilize ChatGPT's advanced data processing functionality to guide you in building an interactive dashboard that showcases critical business metrics such as patient satisfaction, appointment scheduling efficiency, and resource utilization. The dashboard should empower users to explore the data in real-time, enabling them to drill down into specific departments, medical procedures, and patient demographics."*

Example Prompt 4:
Prompt: *"You work as a business analyst for a technology company. Leverage ChatGPT's advanced data processing capabilities to support you in creating an interactive dashboard that visualizes key business metrics like product adoption, customer churn rate, and revenue growth. The dashboard should provide users with real-time data exploration capabilities, allowing them to filter and analyze the data based on factors such as customer segments, product features, and geographical regions."*

Idea: Sales Performance Visualization
Create visualizations to analyze sales performance, identify trends, and track progress towards sales targets.

Example Prompt 1:
ChatGPT, using its advanced data processing functionality, please generate a visualization that compares monthly sales performance for the past year. Include key metrics such as total sales, average sales per month, and any notable trends or patterns that can be identified.

Example Prompt 2:
ChatGPT, leverage its advanced data processing capabilities to create a visualization that displays the sales performance of different product categories over the past quarter. Include a

breakdown of sales by category, identify the top-performing categories, and highlight any significant changes or growth opportunities.

Example Prompt 3:
ChatGPT, with its advanced data processing functionality, please generate a visualization that tracks the progress towards sales targets for each sales representative in our team. Include individual sales targets, actual sales achieved, and any deviations from the targets. Additionally, highlight any sales representatives who are consistently exceeding or falling behind their targets.

Example Prompt 4:
ChatGPT, utilizing its advanced data processing capabilities, create a visualization that analyzes the sales performance across different regions. Include a geographical representation of sales, identify regions with the highest and lowest sales, and provide insights into any regional trends or patterns that can be observed. Additionally, highlight any regions that are significantly contributing to overall sales growth or decline.

Idea: Customer Segmentation Visualization

Generate visualizations to understand customer segments, their preferences, and behaviors, enabling targeted marketing strategies.

Example Prompt 1:
Generate a visualization that illustrates the distribution of customer segments based on their demographics, such as age, gender, and location. Provide insights into the largest customer segments and their characteristics to inform targeted marketing strategies.

Example Prompt 2:
Create a visualization that showcases the purchasing patterns of different customer segments over time. Analyze their buying frequency, average order value, and preferred product categories to

identify potential cross-selling or upselling opportunities.

Example Prompt 3:
Develop a visualization that depicts the customer segments' preferences and behaviors on various marketing channels, such as social media, email campaigns, or website interactions. Highlight the most effective channels for each segment and suggest personalized marketing approaches accordingly.

Example Prompt 4:
Generate a visualization that compares customer segments' feedback and sentiment analysis across different touchpoints, such as customer support interactions, product reviews, or survey responses. Identify the key drivers of satisfaction or dissatisfaction for each segment and recommend targeted improvements to enhance customer experience.

Idea: Financial Data Visualization

Design visualizations to analyze financial data, such as revenue, expenses, and profitability, to support financial decision-making.

Example Prompt 1:
Generate a Python code snippet that utilizes ChatGPT's advanced data processing functionality to design visualizations for analyzing revenue, expenses, and profitability data. Provide step-by-step instructions on how to input the financial data and generate the visualizations.

Example Prompt 2:
Explain how ChatGPT's advanced data processing functionality can be leveraged to create interactive dashboards for financial data visualization. Describe the key features and functionalities that can be incorporated into the dashboards to support financial decision-making.

Example Prompt 3:

Provide a comprehensive tutorial on using ChatGPT's advanced data processing capabilities to create dynamic charts and graphs for financial data analysis. Include examples of different chart types that can be generated and explain how to customize them based on specific financial metrics.

Example Prompt 4:
Discuss the benefits of using ChatGPT's advanced data processing functionality for financial data visualization. Highlight how it can help identify trends, patterns, and anomalies in revenue, expenses, and profitability data, ultimately aiding in making informed financial decisions.

Idea: Supply Chain Visualization

Develop visualizations to track and optimize the supply chain process, including inventory levels, order fulfillment, and logistics.

Example Prompt 1:
Prompt: "As a business analyst, I need ChatGPT's advanced data processing functionality to develop visualizations that track and optimize the supply chain process. Please generate a visualization that displays the current inventory levels across different warehouses and distribution centers. The visualization should provide insights into inventory distribution, identify potential stockouts, and highlight areas where inventory levels can be optimized."

Example Prompt 2:
Prompt: "ChatGPT, I require your assistance as a business analyst to create visualizations that help monitor order fulfillment in the supply chain process. Please generate a visualization that shows the order fulfillment rate over time, broken down by product category. The visualization should provide insights into the efficiency of order processing, identify bottlenecks, and suggest areas for improvement to enhance customer satisfaction."

Example Prompt 3:

Prompt: "As a business analyst, I'm looking to optimize logistics in the supply chain process. ChatGPT, please help me develop a visualization that tracks the transportation routes and delivery times for different products. The visualization should display the most frequently used transportation routes, highlight any delays or inefficiencies, and suggest alternative routes or transportation methods to improve overall logistics efficiency."

Example Prompt 4:

Prompt: "ChatGPT, I need your support as a business analyst to develop visualizations that optimize the supply chain process. Please generate a visualization that presents the lead time for each stage of the supply chain, from procurement to final delivery. The visualization should identify stages with longer lead times, highlight potential causes for delays, and provide recommendations to streamline the supply chain and reduce overall lead time."

Idea: Social Media Analytics Visualization

Create visualizations to analyze social media data, including engagement metrics, sentiment analysis, and audience demographics.

Example Prompt 1:

Prompt: "As a business analyst, I need your help to create visualizations for social media analytics. Please generate a line chart that displays the monthly engagement metrics (likes, comments, and shares) for a specific social media account over the past year. Additionally, provide a bar chart that shows the sentiment analysis scores (positive, negative, and neutral) for the same account's posts over the last six months. Finally, generate a pie chart that represents the audience demographics (age groups and gender) based on the followers' profiles. Please ensure the visualizations are clear and visually appealing."

Example Prompt 2:

Prompt: "I'm working on social media analytics and require your assistance in visualizing the data. Please generate a scatter plot that illustrates the correlation between the number of followers and the engagement metrics (likes, comments, and shares) for a particular social media account. Additionally, create a stacked bar chart that showcases the sentiment analysis scores (positive, negative, and neutral) for the account's posts categorized by different content types (text, images, videos). Finally, generate a donut chart that represents the audience demographics (location-based) for the followers. Please ensure the visualizations are easy to interpret and visually engaging."

Example Prompt 3:

Prompt: "As a business analyst, I'm exploring social media analytics and need your support in visualizing the data. Please generate a heat map that displays the engagement metrics (likes, comments, and shares) for a specific social media account across different days of the week and times of the day. Additionally, create a line chart that shows the sentiment analysis scores (positive, negative, and neutral) for the account's posts over the past month. Finally, generate a bar chart that represents the audience demographics (interests) based on the followers' profiles. Please ensure the visualizations are visually appealing and provide valuable insights."

Example Prompt 4:

Prompt: "I'm working on social media analytics visualization and require your assistance. Please generate a bubble chart that represents the engagement metrics (likes, comments, and shares) for a particular social media account, where the size of each bubble corresponds to the number of followers. Additionally, create a stacked area chart that showcases the sentiment analysis scores (positive, negative, and neutral) for the account's posts over the last three months. Finally, generate a horizontal bar chart that represents the audience demographics (occupation) based on the followers' profiles. Please ensure the visualizations are visually captivating and provide meaningful analysis."

Idea: Website Analytics Visualization

Generate visualizations to analyze website traffic, user behavior, and conversion rates, helping to optimize website performance.

Example Prompt 1:

As a business analyst, I need ChatGPT to generate visualizations that analyze website traffic patterns, user behavior, and conversion rates for our e-commerce platform. Please provide a step-by-step guide on how to use ChatGPT's advanced data processing functionality to create these visualizations and optimize our website performance.

Example Prompt 2:

Our marketing team wants to gain insights into website traffic, user behavior, and conversion rates to improve our online presence. Can ChatGPT assist us in generating visualizations that highlight key metrics and trends? Please provide a detailed explanation of how to leverage ChatGPT's advanced data processing capabilities to create these visualizations and optimize our website performance.

Example Prompt 3:

We are looking to enhance our website's performance by analyzing website traffic, user behavior, and conversion rates through visualizations. How can ChatGPT's advanced data processing functionality help us generate these visualizations? Please provide a step-by-step process on how to utilize ChatGPT to extract relevant data and create insightful visualizations for website analytics.

Example Prompt 4:

Our company wants to optimize website performance by analyzing website traffic, user behavior, and conversion rates using visualizations. Can ChatGPT assist us in generating these visualizations and providing actionable insights? Please explain how to leverage ChatGPT's advanced data processing functionality to extract and analyze relevant data, and create visualizations that help us make informed decisions to improve our website's performance.

Idea: Risk Management Visualization

Design visualizations to identify and assess business risks, visualize risk mitigation strategies, and monitor risk exposure.

Example Prompt 1:

Prompt: Design a visualization to identify and assess business risks based on historical data. Use ChatGPT's Advanced Data processing functionality to generate a risk assessment report that includes key risk indicators, probability of occurrence, and potential impact on the business. Additionally, provide recommendations for risk mitigation strategies based on the identified risks.

Example Prompt 2:

Prompt: Develop a visualization dashboard using ChatGPT's Advanced Data processing functionality to monitor risk exposure in real-time. The dashboard should display key risk metrics, such as risk appetite, risk tolerance, and risk exposure levels across different business units or projects. Additionally, provide insights on potential risk hotspots and highlight areas that require immediate attention or mitigation actions.

Example Prompt 3:

Prompt: Create a visualization tool using ChatGPT's Advanced Data processing functionality to assess the effectiveness of risk mitigation strategies implemented by the business. The tool should analyze historical data and generate visual representations of risk reduction trends, cost-benefit analysis of mitigation measures, and the overall impact on the organization's risk profile. Additionally, provide recommendations for optimizing risk mitigation strategies based on the analysis.

Example Prompt 4:

Prompt: Utilize ChatGPT's Advanced Data processing functionality to design a risk heat map visualization that highlights the potential risks associated with different business processes or activities. The heat map should categorize risks based on their severity, likelihood of occurrence, and potential impact. Additionally, provide interactive features that allow users to drill down into specific risk categories and access detailed information on risk mitigation strategies and controls.

Idea: Project Management Visualization

Develop visualizations to track project progress, resource allocation, and task dependencies, aiding project management and decision-making.

Example Prompt 1:

Prompt: "As a business analyst, I need ChatGPT's advanced data processing functionality to develop visualizations that track project progress, resource allocation, and task dependencies. Please generate a visualization that shows the overall progress of the project, highlighting completed tasks, ongoing tasks, and pending tasks. Additionally, include a breakdown of resource allocation, indicating the utilization of each resource. Finally, illustrate the task dependencies using a network diagram or a Gantt chart to help aid project management and decision-making."

Example Prompt 2:

Prompt: "ChatGPT, I require your assistance as a business analyst to leverage your advanced data processing capabilities for project management visualization. Please generate a visualization that presents a timeline view of the project, showcasing the start and end dates of each task. Additionally, include a color-

coded representation of the task dependencies, indicating the critical path and any potential bottlenecks. Furthermore, provide a resource allocation chart that displays the utilization of each resource over time, enabling effective decision-making and resource optimization."

Example Prompt 3:

Prompt: "As a business analyst, I'm seeking ChatGPT's support in utilizing its advanced data processing functionality to create visualizations for project management. Please generate a visualization that presents a dashboard view of the project, including a progress bar indicating the completion status of each task. Additionally, provide a stacked bar chart illustrating the allocation of resources across different project phases. Lastly, generate a network diagram that visually represents the task dependencies, allowing project managers to identify potential delays and make informed decisions."

Example Prompt 4:

Prompt: "ChatGPT, I need your assistance as a business analyst to leverage your advanced data processing capabilities for project management visualization. Please generate a visualization that presents a Kanban board, displaying the project tasks categorized into different stages such as 'To Do,' 'In Progress,' and 'Completed.' Additionally, provide a resource utilization heatmap that showcases the availability and allocation of resources over time. Lastly, generate a dependency matrix that highlights the task dependencies, enabling project managers to identify critical paths and optimize project timelines."

Idea: HR Analytics Visualization

Create visualizations to analyze HR data, such as employee turnover, performance metrics, and workforce demographics, supporting HR decision-making.

Example Prompt 1:

As a business analyst, I need your assistance in analyzing HR data to create visualizations that can help us understand employee turnover trends. Please generate a line chart showing the monthly turnover rate over the past year, highlighting any significant spikes or dips. Additionally, provide a brief analysis of the potential reasons behind these fluctuations and suggest actionable steps to reduce turnover.

Example Prompt 2:
ChatGPT, we require your expertise in HR analytics to develop visualizations that can help us evaluate performance metrics across different departments. Please generate a bar chart comparing the average performance ratings of each department for the last quarter. Additionally, provide a summary of the top-performing and underperforming departments, along with any notable insights or patterns that can guide HR decision-making.

Example Prompt 3:
We are looking to gain insights into our workforce demographics to support diversity and inclusion initiatives. Can you assist us in creating visualizations that showcase the distribution of employees across various age groups, genders, and ethnicities? Please generate a pie chart illustrating the percentage breakdown of each demographic category and provide a brief analysis of the current diversity landscape within our organization.

Example Prompt 4:
As part of our HR decision-making process, we need to understand the factors influencing employee satisfaction and engagement. Please utilize ChatGPT's advanced data processing functionality to create a scatter plot that visualizes the relationship between employee satisfaction scores and key engagement drivers, such as career development opportunities, work-life balance, and compensation. Additionally, provide a summary of the key findings and recommendations to improve overall employee satisfaction.

Idea: Market Research Visualization

Generate visualizations to analyze market research data, including consumer insights, competitor analysis, and market trends, aiding strategic planning.

Example Prompt 1:

As a business analyst, I need ChatGPT to assist me in visualizing market research data. Please generate a visualization that highlights consumer insights based on the latest market research report. Include key demographic information, purchasing behavior, and preferences to help us identify target customer segments and develop effective marketing strategies.

Example Prompt 2:

ChatGPT, we require your advanced data processing capabilities to create a visualization that compares our company's performance with our top competitors in the market. Incorporate relevant market share data, customer satisfaction ratings, and product/service offerings to help us identify areas where we can gain a competitive advantage and improve our market position.

Example Prompt 3:

To aid our strategic planning process, we need ChatGPT to generate a visualization that showcases the latest market trends. Utilize data from industry reports, social media sentiment analysis, and customer feedback to create a comprehensive overview of emerging trends, customer preferences, and technological advancements. This visualization will help us make informed decisions and stay ahead of the competition.

Example Prompt 4:

ChatGPT, as a business analyst, I require your assistance in creating a visualization that combines various market research data sources to provide a holistic view of the market landscape. Incorporate data on market size, growth rates, customer demographics, and competitor analysis to help us identify untapped market opportunities and develop effective strategies to capitalize on them.

Idea: Geographic Data Visualization

Design visualizations to analyze geographic data, such as customer locations, market penetration, and regional sales performance, supporting location-based decision-making.

Example Prompt 1:
Prompt: Design a visualization to analyze customer locations and market penetration based on geographic data. Use ChatGPT's Advanced Data processing functionality to generate a visualization that highlights the distribution of customers across different regions and identifies areas with high market penetration.

Example Prompt 2:
Prompt: Develop a visualization to analyze regional sales performance using geographic data. Utilize ChatGPT's Advanced Data processing functionality to create a visualization that showcases sales performance across different regions, allowing decision-makers to identify top-performing regions and areas that require improvement.

Example Prompt 3:
Prompt: Leverage ChatGPT's Advanced Data processing functionality to design a visualization that combines customer locations, market penetration, and regional sales performance data. Create an interactive visualization that provides a comprehensive overview of geographic data, enabling decision-makers to identify correlations between customer locations, market penetration, and sales performance.

Example Prompt 4:
Prompt: Utilize ChatGPT's Advanced Data processing functionality to generate a visualization that supports location-based decision-making. Design a visualization that incorporates

geographic data, customer locations, market penetration, and regional sales performance to help decision-makers make informed choices regarding expansion, targeting specific customer segments, and optimizing sales strategies based on geographical insights.

RISK ANALYSIS AND MANAGEMENT

NAVIGATING BUSINESS RISKS

Risk analysis and management are critical for any business's sustainability and growth. In this domain, Artificial Intelligence, particularly tools like ChatGPT, offers groundbreaking ways to identify, assess, and mitigate potential risks.

Consider James, a business analyst at a financial services company. His task is to identify potential risks that could impact the company's operations and market position. Traditional risk analysis methods are often limited by the scope of human foresight and the inability to process vast data sets effectively. James turns to AI for a more comprehensive solution.

Utilizing ChatGPT, James inputs various data points, including market trends, economic reports, and internal financial data. The AI tool not only processes this information rapidly but also identifies potential risk factors that might have been overlooked. For example, it flags an emerging market trend that could threaten the company's current investment strategy.

This scenario highlights the power of AI in risk analysis and management. It's not merely about identifying risks; it's about understanding them in a broader context and forecasting their potential impact. AI tools like ChatGPT enable analysts to conduct a more thorough and nuanced risk assessment, leading to more effective risk mitigation strategies.

In conclusion, AI's role in risk analysis and management is indispensable. It equips business analysts with the tools to foresee and mitigate risks more effectively, ensuring better preparedness and strategic planning. As AI continues to advance, its influence on risk management will only deepen, becoming a fundamental aspect of business analysis.

Note: Please be aware that the strategies, tasks, and ideas discussed in this chapter can be further refined by taking advantage of ChatGPT's Advanced Data Analysis feature. If you require additional information about this tool, you can find comprehensive coverage in the previously authored chapter.

Task: Identify potential risks

ChatGPT can assist in brainstorming and identifying various risks that may affect a project or business operation. It can provide insights and suggestions based on its knowledge base.

Example Prompt 1:
ChatGPT, analyze the project plan and identify potential risks that may arise during the implementation phase. Provide insights on how these risks can be mitigated or managed effectively.

Example Prompt 2:
ChatGPT, based on historical data and industry trends, identify potential risks that may impact the success of our new product

launch. Provide suggestions on how we can minimize these risks and ensure a smooth launch.

Example Prompt 3:
ChatGPT, analyze our current business operations and identify potential risks that may hinder our growth or profitability. Provide insights on how we can proactively address these risks and optimize our operations.

Example Prompt 4:
ChatGPT, review our cybersecurity measures and identify potential risks or vulnerabilities in our systems. Provide suggestions on how we can enhance our security protocols to mitigate these risks and protect our sensitive data.

Task: Assess likelihood and impact

ChatGPT can help in evaluating the probability and potential consequences of identified risks. It can provide analysis and recommendations based on historical data or industry standards.

Example Prompt 1:
Using ChatGPT's Advanced Data processing functionality, analyze historical data and industry standards to assess the likelihood and impact of identified risks in our organization. Provide recommendations on risk mitigation strategies based on the analysis.

Example Prompt 2:
Leveraging ChatGPT's Advanced Data processing functionality, evaluate the probability and potential consequences of identified risks in our industry. Provide an analysis of the risks and recommendations for risk management based on historical data and industry best practices.

Example Prompt 3:
With the help of ChatGPT's Advanced Data processing

functionality, assess the likelihood and impact of identified risks in our business operations. Utilize historical data and industry standards to provide an analysis of the risks and recommendations for risk mitigation.

Example Prompt 4:
Utilizing ChatGPT's Advanced Data processing functionality, evaluate the probability and potential consequences of identified risks in our organization. Provide an in-depth analysis of the risks, including insights from historical data and industry benchmarks, and offer recommendations for effective risk assessment and management.

Task: Prioritize risks

ChatGPT can assist in prioritizing risks based on their severity, potential impact, and urgency. It can provide a ranking or scoring system to help in decision-making.

Example Prompt 1:
Develop a scoring system for prioritizing risks based on severity, potential impact, and urgency using ChatGPT's Advanced Data processing functionality. Provide a step-by-step guide on how to implement this system in decision-making processes.

Example Prompt 2:
Create a prompt that allows users to input different risks along with their severity, potential impact, and urgency. Utilize ChatGPT's Advanced Data processing functionality to generate a ranking or scoring system for these risks, aiding in decision-making. Provide examples and guidelines on how to interpret and use the generated rankings effectively.

Example Prompt 3:
Design a chat-based interface using ChatGPT's Advanced Data processing functionality that enables users to input risks and receive an automated prioritization based on severity, potential impact, and urgency. Include a feature that allows users to

adjust the weightage of each factor to customize the prioritization process. Provide a detailed explanation of how the system calculates and presents the rankings.

Example Prompt 4:

Leverage ChatGPT's Advanced Data processing functionality to analyze historical risk data and generate a predictive model for prioritizing risks. Develop a prompt that enables users to input new risks, and the model should provide a ranking or scoring system based on severity, potential impact, and urgency. Explain the methodology used by the model and provide guidelines on how to interpret and utilize the generated rankings effectively.

Task: Develop risk mitigation strategies

ChatGPT can provide suggestions and recommendations for developing effective strategies to mitigate identified risks. It can offer insights based on best practices or industry-specific knowledge.

Example Prompt 1:

Based on the identified risks in your project, please provide recommendations for developing effective strategies to mitigate these risks. ChatGPT can offer insights based on best practices and industry-specific knowledge to help you develop robust risk mitigation strategies.

Example Prompt 2:

ChatGPT's advanced data processing functionality allows it to analyze the identified risks in your business and provide suggestions for effective risk mitigation strategies. Please describe the risks you have identified, and ChatGPT will offer recommendations based on best practices and industry-specific knowledge.

Example Prompt 3:

As a Business Analyst, you can leverage ChatGPT's advanced data processing functionality to develop risk mitigation strategies.

Describe the risks you have identified, and ChatGPT will provide insights and recommendations based on best practices or industry-specific knowledge to help you mitigate these risks effectively.

Example Prompt 4:
ChatGPT's advanced data processing capabilities enable it to assist in developing risk mitigation strategies. Please provide a list of identified risks, and ChatGPT will analyze the data to offer suggestions and recommendations based on best practices or industry-specific knowledge, helping you develop effective strategies to mitigate these risks.

Task: Create risk management plans

ChatGPT can help in creating comprehensive risk management plans by providing templates, guidelines, and examples. It can assist in defining risk response strategies, assigning responsibilities, and establishing monitoring mechanisms.

Example Prompt 1:
ChatGPT, please provide a template for creating a risk management plan for a software development project. Include sections for identifying risks, assessing their impact and likelihood, and defining appropriate response strategies.

Example Prompt 2:
ChatGPT, can you give me some guidelines on assigning responsibilities in a risk management plan? I need to ensure that each risk is assigned to the appropriate team member or stakeholder for monitoring and mitigation.

Example Prompt 3:
ChatGPT, I need examples of monitoring mechanisms that can be established in a risk management plan. Can you provide some real-world examples that can help me ensure effective monitoring and early detection of potential risks?

Example Prompt 4:

ChatGPT, I'm struggling with defining risk response strategies for a construction project. Can you assist me by providing examples of different response strategies for common risks in the construction industry? I want to ensure that I have a comprehensive plan in place to address potential risks.

Task: Monitor and track risks

ChatGPT can assist in monitoring and tracking identified risks throughout the project or business operation. It can provide reminders, alerts, or automated systems to ensure risks are continuously assessed and managed.

Example Prompt 1:

Develop a chatbot using ChatGPT's Advanced Data processing functionality that can monitor and track identified risks in real-time. The chatbot should provide automated alerts and reminders to project managers and stakeholders to ensure risks are continuously assessed and managed throughout the project or business operation.

Example Prompt 2:

Create a risk monitoring dashboard using ChatGPT's Advanced Data processing functionality. The dashboard should display a comprehensive overview of identified risks, their severity, and the actions taken to mitigate them. It should also provide automated notifications and updates to relevant stakeholders when new risks are identified or existing risks change.

Example Prompt 3:

Design a risk assessment questionnaire using ChatGPT's Advanced Data processing functionality. The questionnaire should be interactive and guide project managers and team members through a series of questions to identify potential risks. ChatGPT should then analyze the responses and provide automated recommendations on risk mitigation strategies based on historical data and best practices.

Example Prompt 4:
Implement an automated risk tracking system using ChatGPT's Advanced Data processing functionality. The system should continuously monitor project or business operation data, such as financial metrics, customer feedback, and market trends, to identify potential risks. ChatGPT should then analyze the data and provide real-time alerts and insights to ensure risks are promptly addressed and managed.

Task: Analyze risk trends

ChatGPT can help in analyzing risk trends by reviewing historical data and identifying patterns or recurring risks. It can provide insights on emerging risks or changes in risk profiles.

Example Prompt 1:
Using ChatGPT's Advanced Data processing functionality, analyze historical data to identify the most common risk factors and their impact on business operations. Provide insights on how these risks have evolved over time and any emerging trends that may pose potential threats to the organization.

Example Prompt 2:
Leveraging ChatGPT's Advanced Data processing functionality, review historical risk incidents and identify patterns or recurring risks. Analyze the root causes of these risks and provide recommendations on how to mitigate or prevent them in the future. Additionally, highlight any changes in risk profiles that have occurred over time.

Example Prompt 3:
With the help of ChatGPT's Advanced Data processing functionality, analyze historical risk data to identify any correlations or relationships between different risk factors. Provide insights on how these interdependencies can impact the overall risk

landscape and suggest strategies to manage or mitigate these risks effectively.

Example Prompt 4:
Utilizing ChatGPT's Advanced Data processing functionality, analyze historical risk trends and identify any emerging risks that may pose significant threats to the organization. Provide a comprehensive assessment of these emerging risks, including their potential impact and likelihood, and recommend proactive measures to address them before they escalate into major issues.

Task: Conduct risk assessments

ChatGPT can assist in conducting risk assessments by providing questionnaires, checklists, or survey templates. It can help in gathering relevant data and analyzing responses to assess the overall risk landscape.

Example Prompt 1:
Develop a questionnaire template for conducting risk assessments in the financial industry using ChatGPT's Advanced Data processing functionality. The template should include questions related to financial risks, compliance, and operational vulnerabilities.

Example Prompt 2:
Create a checklist using ChatGPT's Advanced Data processing functionality to assess the risk landscape of a manufacturing plant. The checklist should cover areas such as equipment safety, environmental risks, and supply chain vulnerabilities.

Example Prompt 3:
Design a survey template using ChatGPT's Advanced Data processing functionality to evaluate the risk landscape of a software development project. The survey should gather information on potential security risks, project management challenges, and stakeholder concerns.

Example Prompt 4:
Utilize ChatGPT's Advanced Data processing functionality to develop a risk assessment tool for the healthcare industry. The tool should include a combination of questionnaires, checklists, and survey templates to assess risks related to patient safety, data privacy, and regulatory compliance.

Task: Review risk management effectiveness

ChatGPT can help in evaluating the effectiveness of risk management strategies and processes. It can provide analysis and recommendations for improvement based on feedback or performance metrics.

Example Prompt 1:
Evaluate the effectiveness of our current risk management strategies and processes. Provide an analysis of their performance based on historical data and feedback from stakeholders. Additionally, suggest recommendations for improvement based on ChatGPT's advanced data processing functionality.

Example Prompt 2:
Assess the efficiency of our risk management practices by analyzing performance metrics and historical data. Utilize ChatGPT's advanced data processing capabilities to identify areas of improvement and provide recommendations for enhancing the effectiveness of our risk management strategies.

Example Prompt 3:
Leverage ChatGPT's advanced data processing functionality to evaluate the effectiveness of our risk management strategies and processes. Analyze feedback from stakeholders and performance metrics to identify strengths and weaknesses. Based on this analysis, provide actionable recommendations for enhancing our risk management practices.

Example Prompt 4:

Utilize ChatGPT's advanced data processing capabilities to conduct a comprehensive review of our risk management effectiveness. Analyze historical data, feedback from stakeholders, and performance metrics to identify gaps and areas for improvement. Based on this analysis, provide detailed recommendations for enhancing our risk management strategies and processes.

Task: Communicate risk information

ChatGPT can assist in communicating risk information to stakeholders by generating reports, summaries, or presentations. It can help in conveying complex risk analysis in a clear and understandable manner.

Example Prompt 1:
Generate a comprehensive risk report for the upcoming project, highlighting potential risks, their impact, and recommended mitigation strategies. Use ChatGPT's advanced data processing functionality to ensure the report is clear, concise, and easily understandable for stakeholders.

Example Prompt 2:
Create a summary presentation on the identified risks in the current business environment. Utilize ChatGPT's advanced data processing capabilities to analyze and present the risk factors, their likelihood, and potential consequences in a visually appealing and informative manner.

Example Prompt 3:
Develop a risk analysis summary for the executive team, outlining the key risks associated with a new product launch. Leverage ChatGPT's advanced data processing functionality to provide a detailed breakdown of each risk, its potential impact on the project, and recommended risk mitigation measures.

Example Prompt 4:
Produce a risk communication document for the board of

directors, explaining the potential risks involved in a proposed merger. Utilize ChatGPT's advanced data processing capabilities to generate a comprehensive report that clearly presents the risks, their likelihood, potential financial implications, and recommended risk management strategies.

Idea: Risk identification and assessment

ChatGPT can assist in identifying potential risks by analyzing historical data, industry trends, and user inputs, and then assess their potential impact on the business.

Example Prompt 1:
As a business analyst, I need ChatGPT to assist in identifying potential risks for our company. Please analyze our historical data, industry trends, and user inputs to identify any potential risks and their impact on our business.

Example Prompt 2:
ChatGPT, using its advanced data processing functionality, please analyze our company's historical data, industry trends, and user inputs to identify any potential risks that could affect our business. Additionally, assess the potential impact of these risks on our operations and provide recommendations for mitigation.

Example Prompt 3:
Our company is looking to assess potential risks that could impact our business. ChatGPT, utilizing its advanced data processing capabilities, please analyze our historical data, industry trends, and user inputs to identify any potential risks. Furthermore, provide an assessment of the impact these risks may have on our business and suggest strategies for risk mitigation.

Example Prompt 4:
As a business analyst, I require ChatGPT's support in identifying and assessing potential risks for our company. By analyzing our historical data, industry trends, and user inputs, please identify any potential risks that could affect our business.

Additionally, assess the potential impact of these risks and provide recommendations for risk management and mitigation strategies.

Idea: Risk mitigation strategies

ChatGPT can provide recommendations on various risk mitigation strategies based on industry best practices and user-specific requirements.

Example Prompt 1:

As a business analyst, I need ChatGPT to provide recommendations on risk mitigation strategies for a manufacturing company. Please suggest industry best practices and user-specific requirements that can help minimize operational risks and ensure a safe working environment.

Example Prompt 2:

ChatGPT, please analyze the user-specific requirements and industry best practices to recommend risk mitigation strategies for a financial institution. Focus on minimizing financial risks, ensuring regulatory compliance, and protecting customer data.

Example Prompt 3:

As a business analyst, I require ChatGPT's assistance in identifying risk mitigation strategies for a software development company. Please provide recommendations based on industry best practices and user-specific requirements to minimize cybersecurity risks, ensure data privacy, and maintain software quality.

Example Prompt 4:

ChatGPT, please analyze the user-specific requirements and industry best practices to suggest risk mitigation strategies for a healthcare organization. Focus on minimizing medical errors, ensuring patient safety, and complying with healthcare regulations.

Idea: Scenario analysis

ChatGPT can simulate different scenarios by considering various risk factors and provide insights into the potential outcomes, helping the business analyst make informed decisions.

Example Prompt 1:

As a business analyst, I need ChatGPT to perform a scenario analysis for our company's expansion plan. Please simulate different scenarios by considering risk factors such as market volatility, competition, and regulatory changes. Provide insights into the potential outcomes and their impact on our financial performance, market share, and customer satisfaction. Help me make an informed decision on whether to proceed with the expansion plan.

Example Prompt 2:

ChatGPT, I require your support as a business analyst to conduct a scenario analysis for our new product launch. Consider risk factors such as production delays, supply chain disruptions, and customer adoption rates. Simulate different scenarios and provide insights into the potential outcomes, including revenue projections, market penetration, and customer feedback. Help me evaluate the feasibility and potential success of the new product launch.

Example Prompt 3:

As a business analyst, I need ChatGPT to assist me in conducting a scenario analysis for our investment portfolio. Consider risk factors such as economic downturns, industry-specific challenges, and geopolitical events. Simulate different scenarios and provide insights into the potential outcomes, including portfolio performance, risk exposure, and potential returns. Help me make informed decisions on asset allocation and risk management strategies.

Example Prompt 4:

ChatGPT, I require your advanced data processing functionality as a business analyst to perform a scenario analysis for our pricing strategy. Consider risk factors such as competitor pricing, customer demand elasticity, and market trends. Simulate different scenarios and provide insights into the potential outcomes, including revenue projections, market share, and customer satisfaction. Help me optimize our pricing strategy and make informed decisions to maximize profitability.

Idea: Risk communication

ChatGPT can assist in developing effective communication strategies to convey risks to stakeholders, ensuring a clear understanding of potential impacts and necessary actions.

Example Prompt 1:

As a business analyst, I need ChatGPT to help me develop a risk communication strategy for a new product launch. Please provide a step-by-step plan outlining how to effectively convey potential risks to stakeholders, ensuring their understanding of the impacts and necessary actions.

Example Prompt 2:

ChatGPT, assist me in creating a risk communication framework for a software development project. I need guidance on how to communicate potential risks to the project team and stakeholders, ensuring they comprehend the severity of the risks and the actions required to mitigate them.

Example Prompt 3:

Help me leverage ChatGPT's advanced data processing capabilities to develop a risk communication plan for a construction project. I need to effectively communicate potential risks to the project sponsors, ensuring they have a clear understanding of the potential impacts and the necessary actions to minimize those risks.

Example Prompt 4:

As a business analyst, I require ChatGPT's support in developing a risk communication strategy for a financial institution. Please provide me with a comprehensive approach to communicate potential risks to the organization's stakeholders, ensuring they comprehend the implications and the necessary actions to address those risks.

Idea: Risk response planning

ChatGPT can support the business analyst in developing comprehensive risk response plans, including risk acceptance, avoidance, transfer, or mitigation strategies.

Example Prompt 1:

As a business analyst, I need ChatGPT's advanced data processing functionality to assist me in developing a risk acceptance strategy for our upcoming project. Please provide a detailed plan outlining the key risks, their potential impact, and the recommended actions to accept and manage these risks effectively.

Example Prompt 2:

ChatGPT, help me create a risk avoidance strategy for our organization's expansion into a new market. Utilize your advanced data processing capabilities to identify potential risks, assess their likelihood and impact, and suggest actionable steps to avoid these risks altogether.

Example Prompt 3:

I require ChatGPT's support in developing a risk transfer strategy for our upcoming product launch. Utilize your advanced data processing functionality to analyze potential risks, evaluate the feasibility of transferring these risks to external parties, and provide recommendations on the most suitable risk transfer methods for our organization.

Example Prompt 4:

As a business analyst, I need ChatGPT to assist me in developing a comprehensive risk mitigation strategy for our IT infrastructure. Leverage your advanced data processing capabilities to identify vulnerabilities, assess their potential impact, and suggest effective mitigation measures to minimize the likelihood and impact of these risks.

Idea: Risk tolerance assessment

ChatGPT can help in determining the organization's risk appetite and tolerance levels by analyzing historical data, financial indicators, and user preferences.

Example Prompt 1:

Prompt: "As a business analyst, I need ChatGPT to assist in conducting a risk tolerance assessment for our organization. Analyze our historical data, financial indicators, and user preferences to determine our risk appetite and tolerance levels. Provide insights and recommendations based on the analysis."

Example Prompt 2:

Prompt: "ChatGPT, please leverage your advanced data processing functionality to support our risk tolerance assessment. Analyze our organization's historical data, financial indicators, and user preferences to determine our risk appetite and tolerance levels. Additionally, provide a comprehensive report outlining the key factors influencing our risk tolerance and recommend strategies to align our risk management practices accordingly."

Example Prompt 3:

Prompt: "We require ChatGPT's assistance in assessing our organization's risk tolerance. Utilize your advanced data processing capabilities to analyze our historical data, financial indicators, and user preferences. Based on this analysis, provide a detailed breakdown of our risk appetite and tolerance levels, highlighting any potential gaps or areas of improvement. Additionally, suggest measures to enhance our risk management framework based on the findings."

Example Prompt 4:

Prompt: "ChatGPT, we need your expertise as a business analyst to conduct a risk tolerance assessment for our organization.

Leverage your advanced data processing functionality to analyze our historical data, financial indicators, and user preferences. Based on this analysis, provide actionable insights on our risk appetite and tolerance levels, along with recommendations to optimize our risk management strategies and align them with our organizational goals."

Idea: Risk prioritization

ChatGPT can assist in prioritizing risks based on their potential impact and likelihood, enabling the business analyst to focus on critical areas that require immediate attention.

Example Prompt 1:
As a business analyst, I need ChatGPT to assist me in prioritizing risks by their potential impact and likelihood. Please provide a summary of the top three risks that require immediate attention, along with their corresponding impact and likelihood ratings.

Example Prompt 2:
ChatGPT, help me prioritize risks by their potential impact and likelihood. Generate a ranked list of the top five risks that need immediate attention, including a brief description of each risk and their associated impact and likelihood scores.

Example Prompt 3:
I need ChatGPT's support in risk prioritization. Please analyze the provided list of risks and identify the top three risks that pose the highest potential impact and likelihood. Additionally, provide a brief explanation for each risk and suggest any mitigation strategies if available.

Example Prompt 4:
As a business analyst, I rely on ChatGPT to assist me in risk prioritization. Please evaluate the provided risks and generate a comprehensive report that includes a prioritized list of risks based on their potential impact and likelihood. Additionally, provide a detailed analysis for each risk, highlighting any critical areas that

require immediate attention and suggesting possible mitigation measures.

Idea: Risk assessment frameworks

ChatGPT can provide guidance on implementing risk assessment frameworks such as COSO ERM or ISO 31000, ensuring a structured approach to risk analysis and management.

Example Prompt 1:

As a business analyst, I need ChatGPT's advanced data processing functionality to assist in implementing a risk assessment framework based on COSO ERM. Please provide step-by-step guidance on how to identify and assess risks, establish risk appetite, and develop risk response strategies.

Example Prompt 2:

ChatGPT, using its advanced data processing capabilities, help me understand the key components of ISO 31000 risk assessment framework. Provide me with a comprehensive overview of the framework, including its principles, process, and techniques for risk identification, analysis, evaluation, and treatment.

Example Prompt 3:

I require ChatGPT's support in implementing a risk assessment framework aligned with COSO ERM. Please guide me on how to establish an effective internal control environment, assess inherent and residual risks, and develop risk mitigation plans. Additionally, provide insights on monitoring and reporting mechanisms to ensure ongoing risk management.

Example Prompt 4:

ChatGPT, utilizing its advanced data processing functionality, assist me in understanding the benefits and challenges of implementing a risk assessment framework such as COSO ERM or ISO 31000. Help me identify the key stakeholders involved, outline the steps required for successful implementation, and provide recommendations for overcoming potential barriers in the process.

Idea: Risk data analysis

ChatGPT can analyze large volumes of risk-related data, identify patterns, and provide insights to the business analyst, enabling data-driven decision-making.

Example Prompt 1:

As a business analyst, I need ChatGPT to analyze a dataset containing historical risk incidents and identify any patterns or trends that could help us understand the root causes of these incidents. Please provide insights and recommendations based on the analysis to support data-driven decision-making in risk management.

Example Prompt 2:

ChatGPT, please analyze a large volume of financial data from various sources, such as market trends, economic indicators, and historical risk events. Identify any correlations or patterns that could help us predict potential risks in our business operations. Provide insights and recommendations to support data-driven decision-making in risk analysis and mitigation.

Example Prompt 3:

As a business analyst, I require ChatGPT to analyze a dataset of customer feedback and complaints related to product quality and safety. Identify any common themes or issues that could pose risks to our brand reputation and customer satisfaction. Provide insights and recommendations to support data-driven decision-making in risk mitigation and quality improvement strategies.

Example Prompt 4:

ChatGPT, please analyze a dataset of cybersecurity incidents and breaches to identify any common vulnerabilities or attack patterns. Provide insights and recommendations to support data-driven decision-making in strengthening our cybersecurity defenses and mitigating potential risks to our sensitive data and systems.

Idea: Risk training and awareness

ChatGPT can support the development of training materials and interactive sessions to educate employees about risk management practices and create a risk-aware culture.

Example Prompt 1:

As a business analyst, I need ChatGPT to generate a comprehensive training manual on risk management practices. Please provide step-by-step instructions, best practices, and real-life examples to help educate employees and foster a risk-aware culture within our organization.

Example Prompt 2:

ChatGPT, please create an interactive presentation on risk management for our upcoming employee training session. Include engaging visuals, interactive quizzes, and practical scenarios to help employees understand the importance of risk management and how to apply it in their daily work.

Example Prompt 3:

We are looking to develop an e-learning course on risk awareness. ChatGPT, can you assist in creating a series of interactive modules that cover various aspects of risk management, such as identifying risks, assessing their impact, and implementing mitigation strategies? Please ensure the content is engaging, easy to understand, and suitable for self-paced learning.

Example Prompt 4:

Our organization wants to conduct a series of virtual workshops on risk management. ChatGPT, can you help us design a series of interactive sessions that include group discussions, case studies, and role-playing exercises? The goal is to actively involve participants in learning about risk management practices and encourage them to apply these principles in their day-to-day decision-making.

Idea: Risk response optimization

ChatGPT can help in optimizing risk response strategies by analyzing historical data, evaluating the effectiveness of previous responses, and suggesting improvements.

Example Prompt 1:

As a business analyst, I need ChatGPT to analyze historical data and evaluate the effectiveness of previous risk response strategies. Please provide a summary of the top three most effective risk response strategies based on historical data, along with an explanation of their impact and any potential improvements that can be made.

Example Prompt 2:

ChatGPT, using its advanced data processing functionality, please analyze the historical data related to risk response strategies and identify any patterns or trends that can help optimize our future responses. Additionally, suggest at least three improvements that can be made to our current risk response strategies based on this analysis.

Example Prompt 3:

In order to optimize our risk response strategies, we need ChatGPT to evaluate the effectiveness of our previous responses and suggest improvements. Please analyze the historical data and provide a detailed report on the success rate of our risk response strategies, highlighting any areas where improvements can be made and recommending specific actions to enhance our risk management approach.

Example Prompt 4:

As a business analyst, I require ChatGPT to assist in optimizing our risk response strategies. Please analyze the historical data and identify any common pitfalls or weaknesses in our previous responses. Based on this analysis, suggest at least three improvements that can be implemented to enhance the effectiveness of our risk response strategies and mitigate potential risks more efficiently.

SALES FORECASTING

PREDICTING SALES SUCCESS

Sales forecasting is a vital component of strategic business planning, where Artificial Intelligence (AI), including tools like ChatGPT, plays a transformative role. AI provides a more nuanced and accurate approach to predicting future sales volumes, essential for effective decision-making and planning.

Consider the story of Anna, a business analyst at a retail company. Her challenge is to forecast next quarter's sales to inform inventory and marketing strategies. Traditional forecasting methods, reliant on historical sales data alone, often miss out on the subtleties of market shifts and consumer behavior patterns. Anna employs AI-driven techniques to elevate her forecasting accuracy.

Using tools like ChatGPT, Anna inputs historical sales data, current market trends, consumer sentiment gathered from social media, and economic indicators. The AI tool, with its advanced analytics, processes this information to predict sales trends more accurately. It even identifies unforeseen factors, such as emerging consumer preferences, which could impact future sales.

This example illustrates AI's profound impact on sales

forecasting. AI doesn't just analyze data; it interprets it in the context of a rapidly changing market, offering a more dynamic and forward-looking view. This enables analysts like Anna to provide more precise sales predictions, aiding in smarter business decisions and strategic planning.

In summary, AI's integration into sales forecasting marks a significant step forward in business analysis. It empowers analysts to deliver more accurate and contextually relevant sales predictions, essential for navigating the complexities of today's market dynamics. As AI tools continue to evolve, their role in enhancing sales forecasting and strategic business planning will become increasingly indispensable.

Note: Please note that for the strategies, tasks, and ideas provided in this chapter, you can leverage ChatGPT's Advanced Data Analysis feature. If you require more information about this feature, please refer to the previously written chapter that covers it.

Task: Data collection

ChatGPT can assist in gathering relevant sales data from various sources such as CRM systems, sales reports, and market research reports.

Example Prompt 1:
ChatGPT, please gather sales data from our CRM system for the past quarter and provide a summary of the top-selling products and their corresponding revenue figures.

Example Prompt 2:
Using ChatGPT's advanced data processing functionality, collect sales reports from the past year and identify any trends or patterns

in customer purchasing behavior.

Example Prompt 3:
ChatGPT, assist in gathering market research reports related to our industry and extract key sales data, such as market share, growth rates, and competitor analysis.

Example Prompt 4:
Utilizing ChatGPT's data collection capabilities, compile a comprehensive report on sales performance across different regions based on data from CRM systems, sales reports, and market research reports.

Task: Data cleaning and preprocessing

ChatGPT can help in cleaning and organizing the collected sales data, removing duplicates, handling missing values, and standardizing formats.

Example Prompt 1:
ChatGPT, please assist in identifying and removing duplicate entries from the collected sales data. Additionally, suggest a method to prevent future duplicates from being recorded.

Example Prompt 2:
ChatGPT, help me handle missing values in the sales data by suggesting appropriate techniques for imputation or removal of incomplete records.

Example Prompt 3:
ChatGPT, please standardize the formats of the sales data by converting all date and time fields to a consistent format. Also, suggest a method to ensure future data entries adhere to the standardized format.

Example Prompt 4:
ChatGPT, assist in preprocessing the collected sales data by identifying and handling outliers or anomalies. Additionally, suggest techniques to normalize or scale the data for further

analysis.

Task: Trend analysis

ChatGPT can analyze historical sales data to identify trends and patterns, helping to understand the factors influencing sales performance.

Example Prompt 1:
Develop a ChatGPT model that can analyze historical sales data and identify trends and patterns. Provide insights on the factors influencing sales performance and suggest strategies for improving sales based on the identified trends.

Example Prompt 2:
Create a ChatGPT system that can process large volumes of historical sales data and generate trend analysis reports. The system should be able to identify patterns, correlations, and anomalies in the data, and provide actionable recommendations to improve sales performance.

Example Prompt 3:
Design a ChatGPT-based solution that can automatically extract relevant information from historical sales data, such as product categories, customer segments, and time periods. The system should then analyze this data to identify trends and patterns, and provide insights into the factors influencing sales performance.

Example Prompt 4:
Build a ChatGPT model that can perform advanced data processing on historical sales data, including data cleaning, normalization, and feature engineering. The model should then use this processed data to conduct trend analysis and identify the key drivers of sales performance, enabling businesses to make data-driven decisions for improving sales.

Task: Seasonality analysis

ChatGPT can assist in identifying seasonal patterns in sales data, enabling the prediction of sales fluctuations based on specific time periods.

Example Prompt 1:
Using ChatGPT's Advanced Data processing functionality, analyze the sales data for the past three years and identify any seasonal patterns. Provide insights on the specific time periods when sales tend to fluctuate, and predict the expected sales fluctuations for the upcoming year based on these patterns.

Example Prompt 2:
Leveraging ChatGPT's Advanced Data processing functionality, conduct a comprehensive seasonality analysis on the sales data for the past five years. Identify the specific months or quarters when sales experience significant fluctuations and provide recommendations on how to optimize inventory management and marketing strategies to align with these seasonal patterns.

Example Prompt 3:
With the help of ChatGPT's Advanced Data processing functionality, analyze the historical sales data for the past decade and determine the seasonal patterns that influence sales fluctuations. Based on these patterns, develop a predictive model that can forecast sales fluctuations for the next two years, enabling the business to make informed decisions regarding resource allocation and production planning.

Example Prompt 4:
Utilizing ChatGPT's Advanced Data processing functionality, perform a detailed seasonality analysis on the sales data for the past two years. Identify the specific time periods, such as holidays or specific months, when sales experience significant fluctuations. Additionally, provide insights on the factors that contribute to these fluctuations and suggest strategies to capitalize on the seasonal patterns to maximize sales and revenue.

Task: Statistical modeling

ChatGPT can help in building statistical models to forecast sales, such as time series analysis, regression models, or machine learning algorithms.

Example Prompt 1:
How can ChatGPT's Advanced Data processing functionality be utilized to perform time series analysis for sales forecasting?

Example Prompt 2:
What are the steps involved in leveraging ChatGPT's Advanced Data processing functionality to build regression models for sales forecasting?

Example Prompt 3:
Can ChatGPT's Advanced Data processing functionality assist in implementing machine learning algorithms for sales forecasting? If so, what are some recommended approaches?

Example Prompt 4:
Provide examples of how ChatGPT's Advanced Data processing functionality can be applied in statistical modeling to forecast sales, including specific use cases for time series analysis, regression models, and machine learning algorithms.

Task: Forecast generation

ChatGPT can generate sales forecasts based on the developed models, providing estimates for future sales performance.

Example Prompt 1:
ChatGPT, using its advanced data processing functionality, please generate a sales forecast for the next quarter based on the historical sales data and market trends. Provide estimates for each product category and overall sales performance.

Example Prompt 2:

As a business analyst, I need ChatGPT to utilize its advanced data processing capabilities to generate a sales forecast for the upcoming year. Incorporate factors such as seasonality, marketing campaigns, and economic indicators to provide accurate estimates for each month and overall sales performance.

Example Prompt 3:
ChatGPT, with its advanced data processing functionality, please generate a sales forecast for the next six months. Consider factors like customer demographics, competitor analysis, and historical sales patterns to provide detailed estimates for each product line and overall sales performance.

Example Prompt 4:
As a business analyst, I require ChatGPT to leverage its advanced data processing capabilities to generate a sales forecast for the next week. Incorporate real-time data, such as website traffic, social media engagement, and customer feedback, to provide accurate estimates for each day and overall sales performance.

Task: Scenario analysis

ChatGPT can assist in conducting scenario analysis by simulating different business scenarios and predicting their impact on sales, helping in decision-making processes.

Example Prompt 1:
Simulate the impact of a 10% increase in marketing budget on sales for the next quarter using ChatGPT's advanced data processing functionality. Provide insights on potential revenue growth and customer acquisition rates based on historical data.

Example Prompt 2:
Predict the effect of launching a new product line on sales performance using ChatGPT's advanced data processing capabilities. Analyze different scenarios, such as varying price points and market penetration rates, to determine the most profitable approach.

Example Prompt 3:
Conduct a scenario analysis using ChatGPT's advanced data processing functionality to evaluate the potential impact of a competitor's pricing strategy on our sales. Explore different pricing scenarios and predict the corresponding changes in market share and revenue.

Example Prompt 4:
Leverage ChatGPT's advanced data processing capabilities to simulate the impact of supply chain disruptions on sales. Analyze various scenarios, such as delays in raw material procurement or transportation issues, to assess the potential revenue loss and identify mitigation strategies.

Task: Forecast evaluation

ChatGPT can help in evaluating the accuracy and reliability of sales forecasts by comparing them with actual sales data, identifying any discrepancies or areas for improvement.

Example Prompt 1:
Compare the sales forecast for the next quarter with the actual sales data from the previous quarter. Identify any discrepancies or areas where the forecast was inaccurate, and provide recommendations for improvement based on ChatGPT's advanced data processing functionality.

Example Prompt 2:
Evaluate the accuracy and reliability of the sales forecast for a specific product category by comparing it with the actual sales data over the past six months. Use ChatGPT's advanced data processing functionality to identify any discrepancies or patterns that can help improve future forecasts.

Example Prompt 3:
Assess the reliability of the sales forecast for a particular region by comparing it with the actual sales data from the previous

year. Utilize ChatGPT's advanced data processing capabilities to identify any discrepancies or trends that can be used to enhance the accuracy of future forecasts.

Example Prompt 4:
Analyze the accuracy of the sales forecast for a specific product line by comparing it with the actual sales data over the past year. Leverage ChatGPT's advanced data processing functionality to identify any discrepancies or anomalies that can be used to refine the forecasting model and improve future predictions.

Task: Forecast visualization

ChatGPT can assist in creating visual representations of sales forecasts, such as charts or graphs, to facilitate understanding and communication of the forecasted sales performance.

Example Prompt 1:
ChatGPT, using its advanced data processing functionality, create a line graph representing the forecasted sales performance for the next quarter. Include labels for each month and annotate any significant trends or patterns.

Example Prompt 2:
With the help of ChatGPT's advanced data processing, generate a bar chart illustrating the forecasted sales performance by product category for the upcoming year. Ensure that the chart is visually appealing and easy to interpret.

Example Prompt 3:
ChatGPT, leverage its advanced data processing capabilities to create a stacked area chart showcasing the forecasted sales performance for each region over the next six months. Use different colors to represent each region and provide a clear legend for easy understanding.

Example Prompt 4:
Using ChatGPT's advanced data processing functionality, generate

a scatter plot that visualizes the forecasted sales performance against various marketing campaigns. Include a trendline to identify any correlation between campaign efforts and sales outcomes.

Task: Forecast monitoring and updating

ChatGPT can help in monitoring actual sales performance against the forecasted values and updating the forecasts periodically based on new data or changing business conditions.

Example Prompt 1:
Develop a ChatGPT model that can analyze and compare actual sales performance with forecasted values on a weekly basis. The model should be able to identify any significant deviations and provide insights on the potential causes for the variance.

Example Prompt 2:
Create a ChatGPT system that can automatically collect and process real-time sales data from various sources, such as CRM systems and transaction databases. The system should be able to update the forecasted values based on the latest data and provide recommendations for adjusting the forecasts if necessary.

Example Prompt 3:
Design a ChatGPT interface that allows business users to interactively explore and analyze the differences between actual sales performance and forecasted values. The interface should provide visualizations and insights on the key factors influencing the deviations, enabling users to make informed decisions on updating the forecasts.

Example Prompt 4:
Implement a ChatGPT solution that can proactively alert business stakeholders when there are significant discrepancies between actual sales performance and forecasted values. The system should automatically generate notifications and provide

recommendations for adjusting the forecasts based on the detected anomalies.

Idea: Historical Data Analysis

Analyze past sales data to identify trends and patterns that can be used to forecast future sales.

Example Prompt 1:

Prompt: "As a business analyst, I need your help to analyze our historical sales data and identify trends and patterns that can be used to forecast future sales. Please provide a summary of the key trends and patterns you observe in the data, along with any insights or recommendations for improving our sales forecasting."

Example Prompt 2:

Prompt: "ChatGPT, using its advanced data processing functionality, I would like you to analyze our past sales data and help us identify any significant trends or patterns that can be leveraged for forecasting future sales. Please provide a detailed analysis of the data, including any seasonality, cyclical patterns, or other factors that may impact our sales performance. Additionally, suggest any strategies or approaches we can adopt to improve our sales forecasting accuracy."

Example Prompt 3:

Prompt: "As a business analyst, I'm seeking your assistance in analyzing our historical sales data to uncover trends and patterns that can aid in forecasting future sales. Please conduct a comprehensive analysis of the data, highlighting any recurring patterns, correlations, or anomalies that may impact our sales performance. Furthermore, provide recommendations on how we can optimize our forecasting models based on these insights."

Example Prompt 4:

Prompt: "ChatGPT, utilizing its advanced data processing capabilities, I need your support in analyzing our past sales data to identify trends and patterns that can be utilized for accurate sales forecasting. Please conduct a thorough analysis of the data, including any seasonality, trends, or other factors that may influence our sales performance. Additionally, suggest any data-driven strategies or techniques we can implement to enhance our sales forecasting accuracy and improve our business planning."

Idea: Market Research Integration

Integrate market research data into the sales forecasting process to gain insights into customer behavior and market trends.

Example Prompt 1:

As a business analyst, I need ChatGPT's advanced data processing functionality to integrate market research data into our sales forecasting process. Please provide a step-by-step guide on how to extract relevant insights from market research reports and incorporate them into our forecasting models.

Example Prompt 2:

ChatGPT, using its advanced data processing capabilities, help us analyze customer behavior and market trends by integrating market research data into our sales forecasting process. Please provide a detailed explanation of how we can identify key patterns and correlations between market research findings and historical sales data to improve our forecasting accuracy.

Example Prompt 3:

We are looking to leverage ChatGPT's advanced data processing functionality to integrate market research data into our sales forecasting process. Can you assist us in developing a framework that combines qualitative market research insights with quantitative sales data? Please provide examples of how this integration can help us identify emerging customer preferences and market trends.

Example Prompt 4:

ChatGPT, as a business analyst, I need your support in integrating market research data into our sales forecasting process. Can you guide us on how to preprocess and analyze market research data to extract meaningful insights? Additionally, please suggest techniques or tools that can help us visualize and interpret the integrated data for better decision-making regarding customer behavior and market trends.

Idea: Sales Pipeline Analysis

Analyze the sales pipeline to identify potential bottlenecks and forecast the conversion rates at each stage, enabling better sales forecasting.

Example Prompt 1:
As a business analyst, I need ChatGPT to analyze our sales pipeline and identify potential bottlenecks. Please provide insights on the stages where leads are getting stuck and suggest possible solutions to improve conversion rates.

Example Prompt 2:
ChatGPT, using its advanced data processing functionality, I need you to analyze our sales pipeline and forecast the conversion rates at each stage. Please provide a breakdown of the expected conversion rates for each stage and highlight any stages that might require additional attention for better sales forecasting.

Example Prompt 3:
Our sales team is struggling to accurately forecast conversion rates at each stage of the sales pipeline. Can you help us, ChatGPT, by analyzing historical data and using advanced data processing techniques to provide more accurate conversion rate predictions? Additionally, please suggest strategies to overcome potential bottlenecks and improve our sales forecasting accuracy.

Example Prompt 4:
As a business analyst, I require ChatGPT's advanced data processing capabilities to analyze our sales pipeline and identify any bottlenecks that are hindering our sales conversion rates.

Please provide a detailed analysis of each stage in the pipeline, highlighting any areas where leads are dropping off or experiencing delays. Additionally, suggest actionable steps to optimize the pipeline and improve our overall sales forecasting accuracy.

Idea: Competitive Analysis

Use ChatGPT to gather information about competitors' sales strategies and market positioning, which can be used to adjust sales forecasts accordingly.

Example Prompt 1:

Prompt: "As a business analyst, I need ChatGPT to gather information about our competitors' sales strategies and market positioning. Please provide a detailed analysis of our top three competitors, including their target markets, pricing strategies, promotional activities, and any unique selling propositions they have. This information will help us adjust our sales forecasts accordingly."

Example Prompt 2:

Prompt: "ChatGPT, as a business analyst, I require your assistance in understanding our competitors' sales strategies and market positioning. Please provide an overview of the key competitors in our industry, their market share, customer segments they target, and the channels they use for distribution. Additionally, analyze their pricing models, discounts, and any other sales tactics they employ. This analysis will enable us to make informed decisions and adjust our sales forecasts accordingly."

Example Prompt 3:

Prompt: "In order to adjust our sales forecasts effectively, I need ChatGPT to gather insights on our competitors' sales strategies and market positioning. Please provide a comprehensive analysis of our top five competitors, including their product offerings, pricing structures, distribution channels, and marketing campaigns.

Additionally, highlight any emerging trends or innovations they are leveraging. This information will help us stay competitive and make informed adjustments to our sales forecasts."

Example Prompt 4:

Prompt: "As a business analyst, I rely on ChatGPT to gather valuable information about our competitors' sales strategies and market positioning. Please conduct a detailed analysis of our main competitors, focusing on their sales channels, customer acquisition strategies, pricing models, and any partnerships or collaborations they have. Furthermore, identify their strengths and weaknesses in the market and provide recommendations on how we can adjust our sales forecasts accordingly to gain a competitive edge."

Idea: Sales Team Collaboration

Enable sales teams to collaborate with ChatGPT to share insights, ask questions, and receive real-time sales forecasting updates.

Example Prompt 1:

Prompt: As a sales team member, I want to collaborate with ChatGPT to share insights and ask questions. Please provide me with a conversational interface that allows me to discuss sales strategies, analyze market trends, and brainstorm ideas with ChatGPT.

Example Prompt 2:

Prompt: Help our sales team stay up-to-date with real-time sales forecasting updates. Develop a system where ChatGPT can provide accurate and timely sales predictions based on historical data, market trends, and customer behavior. Enable the sales team to interact with ChatGPT to receive these forecasts and ask follow-up questions for deeper insights.

Example Prompt 3:

Prompt: Create a collaborative environment for our sales team to work with ChatGPT. Enable ChatGPT to analyze sales data, identify patterns, and generate actionable insights. Additionally, allow the sales team to share their own observations and experiences with ChatGPT, facilitating a two-way conversation that enhances the team's collective knowledge and decision-making capabilities.

Example Prompt 4:
Prompt: Develop a sales collaboration platform that integrates ChatGPT's advanced data processing functionality. Enable the sales team to upload and analyze customer data, sales reports, and market research. ChatGPT should provide real-time feedback, answer questions, and offer suggestions to improve sales strategies, identify potential leads, and optimize sales performance.

Idea: Scenario Analysis

Use ChatGPT to simulate different scenarios and assess their impact on sales forecasts, helping businesses make informed decisions.

Example Prompt 1:
Prompt: "As a business analyst, I need ChatGPT to perform scenario analysis to assess the impact of different pricing strategies on sales forecasts. Please simulate three scenarios where we increase the product price by 10%, decrease it by 5%, and keep it unchanged. Provide the corresponding sales forecasts for each scenario and explain the potential implications for our business decisions."

Example Prompt 2:
Prompt: "Help us evaluate the impact of market competition on our sales forecasts using scenario analysis. Please simulate two scenarios: one where a new competitor enters the market and captures 20% of our customer base, and another where a major competitor exits the market, resulting in a 15% increase in our customer base. Provide the revised sales forecasts for each scenario and suggest potential strategies to mitigate the risks or leverage the

opportunities identified."

Example Prompt 3:

Prompt: "We want to explore the impact of external factors on our sales forecasts through scenario analysis. Please simulate two scenarios: one where there is a 10% increase in overall consumer spending due to a booming economy, and another where there is a 5% decrease in consumer spending due to a recession. Provide the adjusted sales forecasts for each scenario and recommend appropriate actions to align our business strategy with the changing market conditions."

Example Prompt 4:

Prompt: "As a business analyst, I need ChatGPT to help us assess the impact of different marketing campaigns on our sales forecasts. Please simulate three scenarios: one where we launch a social media campaign targeting millennials, another where we invest in influencer marketing, and a third where we focus on traditional print advertising. Provide the projected sales forecasts for each scenario and suggest the most effective marketing strategy based on the outcomes."

Idea: Sales Forecast Visualization

Develop interactive dashboards and visualizations using ChatGPT to present sales forecasts in a user-friendly and intuitive manner.

Example Prompt 1:

Prompt: "As a business analyst, I need your help to develop interactive dashboards and visualizations using ChatGPT to present sales forecasts in a user-friendly and intuitive manner. Please generate a Python code snippet that utilizes ChatGPT's advanced data processing functionality to fetch sales data from our database and create a line chart showing the sales forecast for the next quarter. The chart should include labels, tooltips, and a legend for easy interpretation. Additionally, please provide a brief explanation of the code and any necessary dependencies."

Example Prompt 2:

Prompt: *"We are looking to enhance our sales forecasting capabilities by leveraging ChatGPT's advanced data processing functionality. Can you assist us in creating an interactive dashboard that displays sales forecasts for different product categories? Using ChatGPT, generate a code snippet in Python that retrieves historical sales data from our database, applies a forecasting algorithm, and visualizes the results in a bar chart. The chart should allow users to select specific product categories and view the corresponding sales forecasts. Please include clear instructions on how to use the code and any required libraries."*

Example Prompt 3:

Prompt: *"Our sales team needs a user-friendly and intuitive way to visualize sales forecasts on a monthly basis. With ChatGPT's advanced data processing functionality, we believe we can achieve this goal. Please generate a Python code snippet that utilizes ChatGPT to fetch monthly sales data from our database, perform time series analysis, and create an interactive line chart. The chart should allow users to zoom in/out, pan across different time periods, and display forecasted sales values as well. Please provide clear instructions on how to run the code and any necessary dependencies."*

Example Prompt 4:

Prompt: *"We want to empower our sales managers with an interactive dashboard that presents sales forecasts in a visually appealing manner. Using ChatGPT's advanced data processing functionality, please generate a Python code snippet that retrieves historical sales data from our database, applies a machine learning algorithm to forecast future sales, and visualizes the results in a scatter plot. The scatter plot should include tooltips displaying additional information about each data point, such as product name, sales volume, and forecasted sales. Please provide detailed instructions on how to use the code and any required libraries."*

Idea: Sales Forecast Accuracy Monitoring

Use ChatGPT to monitor and analyze the accuracy of sales forecasts over time, identifying areas for improvement and adjusting forecasting models accordingly.

Example Prompt 1:
Prompt: "As a business analyst, I need ChatGPT to monitor and analyze the accuracy of our sales forecasts over time. Please provide insights on the areas where our sales forecasts have been consistently inaccurate and suggest improvements to our forecasting models."

Example Prompt 2:
Prompt: "ChatGPT, help us analyze the accuracy of our sales forecasts and identify any patterns or trends in the areas where our forecasts have been consistently inaccurate. Additionally, suggest adjustments or modifications to our forecasting models that could improve their accuracy."

Example Prompt 3:
Prompt: "We would like ChatGPT to assist us in monitoring the accuracy of our sales forecasts. Please analyze the historical data and identify any specific products, regions, or time periods where our forecasts have been consistently inaccurate. Furthermore, provide recommendations on how we can adjust our forecasting models to improve accuracy in these identified areas."

Example Prompt 4:
Prompt: "As a business analyst, I need ChatGPT to support us in monitoring and analyzing the accuracy of our sales forecasts. Please analyze the historical sales data and identify any factors that have consistently contributed to forecast inaccuracies. Additionally, suggest adjustments or enhancements to our forecasting models that can help us improve accuracy and make more reliable sales predictions."

Idea: Sales Forecasting Automation

Develop automated processes using ChatGPT to streamline the sales forecasting process, reducing manual effort and improving efficiency.

Example Prompt 1:

As a business analyst, I need ChatGPT's advanced data processing functionality to automate the sales forecasting process. Please provide step-by-step instructions on how to use ChatGPT to analyze historical sales data, identify trends, and generate accurate sales forecasts for the next quarter.

Example Prompt 2:

ChatGPT's advanced data processing capabilities are crucial for our sales forecasting automation project. Can you guide me on how to integrate ChatGPT with our CRM system to extract relevant sales data, clean and preprocess the data, and then use ChatGPT to build a predictive model that can forecast sales for different product categories?

Example Prompt 3:

Our sales team is looking to automate the forecasting process to improve efficiency. How can ChatGPT's advanced data processing functionality be leveraged to automatically collect and analyze market data, competitor insights, and historical sales data to generate accurate sales forecasts? Please provide a detailed workflow and any necessary code snippets or examples.

Example Prompt 4:

We want to streamline our sales forecasting process by using ChatGPT's advanced data processing capabilities. Can you assist us in developing a chatbot that can interact with our sales team, gather relevant sales data, perform data preprocessing, and then utilize ChatGPT to generate real-time sales forecasts? Please provide guidance on the necessary data inputs, model training, and deployment steps.

PRODUCT PERFORMANCE ANALYSIS

EVALUATING PRODUCT PERFORMANCE

In the ever-evolving market landscape, analyzing product performance is crucial for shaping effective product development strategies. Artificial Intelligence (AI), particularly tools like ChatGPT, offers a sophisticated approach to this analysis, providing deep insights into market responses and consumer preferences.

Imagine Brian, a business analyst at a consumer electronics company. His task is to analyze the performance of a newly launched smartphone. Traditional analysis methods can be limiting, failing to capture the full spectrum of consumer feedback and market trends. Brian turns to AI for a more comprehensive analysis.

Using ChatGPT, he inputs sales data, online customer reviews, and social media discussions about the smartphone. The AI tool not only processes this vast array of data but also identifies key patterns and sentiments. For instance, it pinpoints features that are receiving positive feedback and those that are not resonating with consumers.

This insight is invaluable for Brian. It enables him to provide targeted recommendations for product improvements and future development. His analysis goes beyond mere sales figures; it delves into consumer experiences and expectations, crucial for the company's product development strategy.

This scenario underscores the significance of AI in product performance analysis. AI doesn't just compile data; it interprets it, offering a nuanced understanding of market responses. This enables analysts like Brian to provide actionable insights that drive product development in a direction aligned with consumer needs and market trends.

In conclusion, the integration of AI in product performance analysis is transformative, equipping business analysts with the tools to conduct more in-depth and insightful analyses. This deeper understanding is essential for developing products that not only meet but exceed market expectations. As AI tools evolve, their impact on product performance analysis and development strategies will only grow more profound.

Note: Please be aware that the strategies, tasks, and ideas discussed in this chapter can be further refined by taking advantage of ChatGPT's Advanced Data Analysis feature. If you require additional information about this tool, you can find comprehensive coverage in the previously authored chapter.

Task: Data collection

Gathering relevant data on product performance metrics such as sales, revenue, customer feedback, and market trends.

Example Prompt 1:
ChatGPT, please gather data on the sales performance metrics of our product for the past year. Include information such as monthly sales figures, top-selling regions, and any notable sales trends or patterns.

Example Prompt 2:
ChatGPT, analyze customer feedback data from various sources such as surveys, social media, and customer support interactions. Provide insights on common customer complaints, positive feedback, and any emerging trends or patterns in customer sentiment.

Example Prompt 3:
ChatGPT, collect data on revenue metrics for our product, including monthly revenue figures, revenue growth rate, and revenue breakdown by product variants or pricing tiers. Additionally, identify any factors that have influenced revenue fluctuations or growth.

Example Prompt 4:
ChatGPT, research and analyze market trends related to our product. Provide data on market size, market share, and competitor analysis. Identify emerging market trends, consumer preferences, and any potential opportunities or threats in the market.

Task: Data cleaning and preprocessing

Ensuring the data is accurate, complete, and in a suitable format for analysis.

Example Prompt 1:
Prompt: "You are working on a project to analyze customer feedback data. Use ChatGPT's Advanced Data processing

functionality to clean and preprocess the data. Ensure that the data is accurate by removing any duplicate entries, correcting spelling errors, and standardizing the format of dates and addresses."

Example Prompt 2:
Prompt: "As a business analyst, you have been assigned the task of analyzing sales data from multiple sources. Utilize ChatGPT's Advanced Data processing functionality to clean and preprocess the data. Ensure the data is complete by identifying and handling missing values, removing outliers, and normalizing numerical variables."

Example Prompt 3:
Prompt: "You are working on a research project that involves analyzing survey responses. Use ChatGPT's Advanced Data processing functionality to clean and preprocess the survey data. Ensure the data is accurate by validating responses against predefined criteria, removing irrelevant or inconsistent entries, and anonymizing sensitive information."

Example Prompt 4:
Prompt: "As a business analyst, you have been given a dataset containing customer purchase records. Utilize ChatGPT's Advanced Data processing functionality to clean and preprocess the data. Ensure the data is in a suitable format for analysis by transforming categorical variables into numerical representations, encoding textual data, and normalizing numerical features."

Task: Data visualization

Creating visual representations of product performance data to identify patterns, trends, and anomalies.

Example Prompt 1:
ChatGPT, analyze the product performance data and generate a visual representation highlighting the top three performing

products based on sales, customer ratings, and profitability. Additionally, identify any anomalies or sudden changes in performance that require further investigation.

Example Prompt 2:
Using ChatGPT's advanced data processing functionality, create a visual dashboard that displays the monthly sales trends for each product category. Include line charts, bar graphs, and pie charts to represent the distribution of sales, identify the best-selling categories, and detect any unusual patterns or trends.

Example Prompt 3:
ChatGPT, analyze the customer feedback data and generate a sentiment analysis visualization that categorizes customer reviews into positive, neutral, and negative sentiments. Use color-coded bar charts or word clouds to represent the sentiment distribution and identify any recurring issues or concerns affecting product performance.

Example Prompt 4:
Leveraging ChatGPT's advanced data processing capabilities, create an interactive heat map that visualizes the geographical distribution of product sales. Use color intensity to represent sales volume in different regions, allowing us to identify areas with high or low product demand and potential opportunities for market expansion.

Task: Statistical analysis

Conducting statistical tests and analyses to uncover insights and correlations in the product performance data.

Example Prompt 1:
Using ChatGPT's Advanced Data processing functionality, analyze the product performance data to identify any significant correlations between different variables. Provide insights on how these correlations can impact the overall product performance.

Example Prompt 2:
Leverage ChatGPT's Advanced Data processing functionality to conduct a hypothesis test on the product performance data. Determine if there is a statistically significant difference in performance between different product versions or variations.

Example Prompt 3:
With the help of ChatGPT's Advanced Data processing functionality, perform a regression analysis on the product performance data to identify the key factors that influence the overall performance. Provide recommendations on how to optimize these factors to improve the product's performance.

Example Prompt 4:
Utilize ChatGPT's Advanced Data processing functionality to conduct a time series analysis on the product performance data. Identify any trends or patterns over time and provide insights on how these trends can be leveraged to enhance the product's performance.

Task: Comparative analysis

Comparing the performance of different products or product lines to identify strengths, weaknesses, and opportunities.

Example Prompt 1:
Using ChatGPT's Advanced Data processing functionality, analyze the performance metrics of Product A and Product B to identify their respective strengths, weaknesses, and opportunities. Provide a detailed comparison highlighting key factors such as sales figures, customer feedback, market share, and profitability.

Example Prompt 2:
Leveraging ChatGPT's Advanced Data processing functionality, conduct a comparative analysis of Product Line X and Product Line Y to determine their strengths, weaknesses, and potential opportunities. Focus on factors such as customer satisfaction

ratings, production costs, market demand, and growth potential.

Example Prompt 3:
With the help of ChatGPT's Advanced Data processing functionality, perform a comprehensive evaluation of the performance of Product C and Product D. Identify their strengths, weaknesses, and opportunities by analyzing factors such as revenue growth, customer retention rates, competitive positioning, and market trends.

Example Prompt 4:
Utilizing ChatGPT's Advanced Data processing functionality, compare the performance of Product Line Z and Product Line W to uncover their strengths, weaknesses, and potential opportunities. Analyze key indicators such as profitability margins, market penetration, customer loyalty, and innovation potential to provide a comprehensive comparative analysis.

Task: Customer segmentation analysis

Analyzing customer data to identify different segments and their preferences, buying behaviors, and satisfaction levels.

Example Prompt 1:
Using ChatGPT's Advanced Data processing functionality, analyze customer data to identify distinct segments based on demographics, such as age, gender, and location. Additionally, explore their preferences, buying behaviors, and satisfaction levels to gain insights into their needs and expectations.

Example Prompt 2:
Leverage ChatGPT's Advanced Data processing functionality to perform a comprehensive customer segmentation analysis. Identify different segments based on factors like purchase history, frequency of purchases, and average order value. Furthermore, analyze their preferences, buying behaviors, and satisfaction levels to tailor marketing strategies and improve customer satisfaction.

Example Prompt 3:
With the help of ChatGPT's Advanced Data processing functionality, conduct an in-depth customer segmentation analysis to uncover distinct segments based on psychographic characteristics, such as lifestyle, interests, and values. Additionally, explore their preferences, buying behaviors, and satisfaction levels to personalize marketing campaigns and enhance customer experiences.

Example Prompt 4:
Utilize ChatGPT's Advanced Data processing functionality to analyze customer data and identify various segments based on their engagement levels, such as active, occasional, and dormant customers. Furthermore, delve into their preferences, buying behaviors, and satisfaction levels to develop targeted retention strategies and improve overall customer satisfaction.

Task: Market trend analysis

Examining market trends and competitor performance to understand the product's position in the market and identify potential opportunities or threats.

Example Prompt 1:
Using ChatGPT's Advanced Data processing functionality, analyze the market trends in the past year for our product category and identify any significant shifts or patterns that could impact our product's position in the market.

Example Prompt 2:
Leveraging ChatGPT's Advanced Data processing functionality, compare our product's performance metrics with those of our top competitors over the last quarter. Identify areas where our product outperforms the competition and areas where we need improvement to stay competitive.

Example Prompt 3:

With the help of ChatGPT's Advanced Data processing functionality, analyze customer sentiment and feedback data from various online platforms to understand how our product is perceived in the market. Identify any potential threats or opportunities based on customer opinions and preferences.

Example Prompt 4:
Utilizing ChatGPT's Advanced Data processing functionality, conduct a comprehensive analysis of market trends and competitor strategies in our industry. Identify emerging trends, potential market gaps, and competitive threats that could impact our product's position. Provide recommendations on how we can capitalize on opportunities and mitigate potential threats.

Task: Forecasting

Using historical data and statistical models to predict future product performance and sales.

Example Prompt 1:
ChatGPT, analyze the historical sales data for our product line and identify any significant trends or patterns that can be used for forecasting future product performance and sales.

Example Prompt 2:
ChatGPT, apply advanced statistical models to the historical sales data and generate accurate predictions for our product's future performance and sales, taking into account factors such as seasonality, market trends, and customer behavior.

Example Prompt 3:
ChatGPT, leverage its advanced data processing functionality to analyze the historical sales data and identify key variables that have the most significant impact on our product's performance and sales. Use this information to develop a robust forecasting model that can accurately predict future sales.

Example Prompt 4:

ChatGPT, utilize its advanced data processing capabilities to perform a comprehensive analysis of the historical sales data, including outlier detection, data cleansing, and normalization. Apply appropriate statistical models to generate reliable forecasts for our product's future performance and sales, considering factors such as market conditions, competitor activities, and customer preferences.

Task: Recommendations

Generating actionable insights and recommendations based on the analysis to improve product performance and drive business growth.

Example Prompt 1:
Using ChatGPT's Advanced Data processing functionality, analyze customer feedback and identify key areas for improvement in product performance. Generate actionable insights and recommendations to enhance customer satisfaction and drive business growth.

Example Prompt 2:
Leverage ChatGPT's Advanced Data processing functionality to analyze sales data and customer behavior patterns. Based on the analysis, provide recommendations on product features or enhancements that can drive business growth and improve overall product performance.

Example Prompt 3:
Utilize ChatGPT's Advanced Data processing functionality to analyze market trends and competitor data. Based on the analysis, generate actionable insights and recommendations to position the product effectively, identify potential market gaps, and drive business growth.

Example Prompt 4:
With the help of ChatGPT's Advanced Data processing functionality, analyze user engagement metrics and customer

feedback to identify areas of improvement in product performance. Provide recommendations on user experience enhancements, feature updates, or marketing strategies to drive business growth and improve product performance.

Idea: Comparative Analysis

ChatGPT can assist in comparing the performance of different products within the business, providing insights into their strengths and weaknesses.

Example Prompt 1:

Prompt: *"Compare the performance of our top-selling products, highlighting their strengths and weaknesses. Provide insights into how each product contributes to our business growth and customer satisfaction."*

Example Prompt 2:

Prompt: *"Conduct a comparative analysis of our latest product releases, focusing on their performance metrics such as sales, customer feedback, and market share. Identify the strengths and weaknesses of each product and suggest potential improvements."*

Example Prompt 3:

Prompt: *"Assess the performance of our competitor's products in comparison to our own offerings. Analyze key metrics such as pricing, features, customer reviews, and market positioning. Provide insights into how our products can outperform the competition and capitalize on their weaknesses."*

Example Prompt 4:

Prompt: *"Compare the performance of our products across different customer segments or target markets. Analyze sales data, customer feedback, and market trends to identify which products resonate the most with specific demographics. Provide recommendations on how to optimize our product portfolio to better cater to different customer segments."*

Idea: Trend Analysis

ChatGPT can help analyze the performance trends of products over time, identifying patterns and potential areas for improvement.

Example Prompt 1:

Prompt: "As a business analyst, I need ChatGPT to analyze the performance trends of our products over time. Please provide insights on any patterns or potential areas for improvement."

Example Prompt 2:

Prompt: "ChatGPT, I require your assistance as a business analyst to conduct trend analysis on our product performance. Please analyze the data and identify any recurring patterns or areas where improvements can be made."

Example Prompt 3:

Prompt: "As a business analyst, I rely on ChatGPT's advanced data processing functionality to analyze the performance trends of our products. Please analyze the data and provide insights on any patterns or potential areas for improvement that can be identified."

Example Prompt 4:

Prompt: "ChatGPT, I need your support as a business analyst to perform trend analysis on our product performance. Please analyze the data and help identify any recurring patterns or potential areas for improvement that we should focus on."

Idea: Market Share Analysis

ChatGPT can assist in analyzing market share data to evaluate the performance of products relative to competitors and identify opportunities for growth.

Example Prompt 1:

Prompt: "As a business analyst, I need assistance in analyzing market share data to evaluate the performance of our products relative to competitors. Please use ChatGPT's advanced data processing functionality to provide insights on our market share and identify potential growth opportunities."

Example Prompt 2:

Prompt: "ChatGPT, I require your support as a business analyst to conduct a comprehensive market share analysis. Utilize your advanced data processing capabilities to compare our product's performance with that of our competitors. Please provide insights on our market share trends and suggest potential areas for growth."

Example Prompt 3:

Prompt: "As a business analyst, I'm looking for assistance in evaluating our product's market share and identifying opportunities for growth. Leverage ChatGPT's advanced data processing functionality to analyze our market share data, compare it with our competitors, and provide recommendations on how we can improve our performance."

Example Prompt 4:

Prompt: "ChatGPT, I need your expertise as a business analyst to analyze our market share data and assess our product's performance relative to competitors. Utilize your advanced data processing capabilities to identify trends, patterns, and potential growth opportunities. Please provide actionable insights to help us enhance our market position."

Idea: Pricing Analysis

ChatGPT can support in analyzing the relationship between product performance and pricing, helping to optimize pricing strategies for maximum profitability.

Example Prompt 1:

Prompt: "As a business analyst, I need ChatGPT to analyze the relationship between product performance and pricing to optimize *our pricing strategies. Please provide insights on how different pricing levels impact product performance and profitability."*

Example Prompt 2:
Prompt: "ChatGPT, I require your assistance as a business analyst to conduct a pricing analysis. Please analyze the historical sales data and pricing information for our products to identify any patterns or correlations between pricing and profitability. Additionally, provide recommendations on how we can optimize our pricing strategies for maximum profitability."

Example Prompt 3:
Prompt: "As a business analyst, I need ChatGPT to help me understand the impact of pricing on product performance and profitability. Please analyze the customer feedback and sales data to identify any trends or insights related to pricing. Based on the analysis, suggest potential pricing adjustments that can enhance our profitability without compromising product performance."

Example Prompt 4:
Prompt: "ChatGPT, I'm seeking your support as a business analyst to conduct a comprehensive pricing analysis. Please analyze the market dynamics, competitor pricing, and our product performance data to identify opportunities for optimizing our pricing strategies. Provide recommendations on pricing adjustments that can maximize profitability while maintaining a competitive edge in the market."

Idea: Product Lifecycle Analysis

ChatGPT can help analyze the performance of products at different stages of their lifecycle, identifying opportunities for product enhancements or retirement.

Example Prompt 1:
Prompt: As a business analyst, I need ChatGPT to perform a product lifecycle analysis for our company's flagship product. Please analyze the performance of the product at different

stages of its lifecycle and identify any opportunities for product enhancements or retirement.

Example Prompt 2:
Prompt: ChatGPT, I require your assistance as a business analyst to evaluate the performance of our recently launched product throughout its lifecycle. Please analyze the product's performance at each stage and provide insights on potential areas for improvement or retirement.

Example Prompt 3:
Prompt: As a business analyst, I'm seeking ChatGPT's expertise to conduct a comprehensive product lifecycle analysis. Please assess the performance of our existing product at various stages of its lifecycle and suggest any opportunities for product enhancements or retirement based on the analysis.

Example Prompt 4:
Prompt: ChatGPT, I need your support as a business analyst to conduct a thorough analysis of our product's lifecycle. Please evaluate the performance of the product at different stages and provide recommendations on potential enhancements or retirement options to optimize our product portfolio.

Idea: Sales Performance Analysis
ChatGPT can assist in analyzing sales data to understand the impact of product performance on sales revenue and identify strategies to improve sales performance.

Example Prompt 1:
Prompt: "As a business analyst, I need assistance in analyzing sales data to understand the impact of product performance on sales revenue. Please use ChatGPT's advanced data processing functionality to provide insights and recommendations on improving sales performance."

Example Prompt 2:

Prompt: "ChatGPT, I require your support in conducting a sales performance analysis. Utilize your advanced data processing capabilities to analyze sales data and identify the key factors influencing sales revenue. Additionally, provide strategies and recommendations to enhance sales performance."

Example Prompt 3:

Prompt: "Hello ChatGPT, as a business analyst, I'm looking for your expertise in analyzing sales data. Please leverage your advanced data processing functionality to analyze the relationship between product performance and sales revenue. Based on the analysis, suggest actionable strategies to improve sales performance."

Example Prompt 4:

Prompt: "ChatGPT, I need your assistance in conducting a comprehensive sales performance analysis. Utilize your advanced data processing capabilities to analyze sales data and identify the factors that significantly impact sales revenue. Furthermore, provide insights and recommendations on effective strategies to enhance sales performance."

Idea: Quality Control Analysis

ChatGPT can support in analyzing quality control data to assess the performance of products in terms of defects, returns, or customer complaints.

Example Prompt 1:

Prompt: As a business analyst, I need ChatGPT to analyze quality control data for a specific product and provide insights on its performance. Please analyze the data and provide a summary of the defects, returns, and customer complaints associated with the product. Additionally, suggest potential improvements or actions that can be taken to address the identified issues.

Example Prompt 2:

Prompt: ChatGPT, I require your assistance in conducting a quality control analysis for our product line. Please analyze the available data and identify any recurring defects, common reasons for returns, and frequent customer complaints. Based on this analysis, provide recommendations on how we can improve the product's performance and reduce the occurrence of these issues.

Example Prompt 3:
Prompt: As part of our quality control analysis, we need ChatGPT to assess the performance of our products by analyzing the data related to defects, returns, and customer complaints. Please provide a detailed breakdown of the most common defects, reasons for returns, and types of customer complaints. Additionally, suggest strategies or actions that can be implemented to enhance the product's quality and customer satisfaction.

Example Prompt 4:
Prompt: ChatGPT, we require your expertise in analyzing quality control data to evaluate the performance of our products. Please analyze the available data and provide an overview of the defects, returns, and customer complaints associated with each product variant. Based on this analysis, identify any patterns or trends that can help us understand the root causes of these issues. Finally, recommend measures that can be taken to improve the overall quality and minimize customer dissatisfaction.

Idea: Product Portfolio Analysis

ChatGPT can help analyze the performance of products within the business's portfolio, identifying high-performing products and potential gaps in the product lineup.

Example Prompt 1:
Prompt: "As a business analyst, I need ChatGPT to analyze our product portfolio and identify high-performing products. Please provide insights on the top three products in terms of sales revenue, customer satisfaction, and market share. Additionally, highlight any potential gaps in our product lineup that we should address."

Example Prompt 2:

Prompt: "ChatGPT, we require your assistance in conducting a comprehensive analysis of our product portfolio. Please evaluate the performance of each product based on key metrics such as profitability, customer demand, and competitive advantage. Identify the top-performing products and suggest strategies to further enhance their success. Furthermore, pinpoint any underperforming products or gaps in our portfolio that need attention."

Example Prompt 3:

Prompt: "We are looking for ChatGPT's expertise in analyzing our product portfolio to optimize our business strategy. Please assess the performance of each product by considering factors such as market growth, customer feedback, and profitability. Based on this analysis, recommend potential improvements for our high-performing products and propose new product ideas to fill any gaps in our portfolio."

Example Prompt 4:

Prompt: "ChatGPT, we need your support in conducting a thorough analysis of our product portfolio. Evaluate the performance of each product by considering metrics such as sales volume, customer retention, and market trends. Identify the top-performing products and provide insights on their success factors. Additionally, highlight any potential gaps in our product lineup and suggest strategies to address them, including potential partnerships or acquisitions."

Idea: Competitive Benchmarking

ChatGPT can assist in benchmarking the performance of products against industry standards or competitors, providing insights into areas of competitive advantage or improvement.

Example Prompt 1:

Prompt: "As a business analyst, I need ChatGPT to assist me in conducting competitive benchmarking for our new product. Please analyze the performance of our product and compare it against industry standards or our top competitors. Provide insights into areas where we have a competitive advantage and areas that need improvement."

Example Prompt 2:
Prompt: "ChatGPT, I require your help as a business analyst to benchmark our company's customer service performance against our competitors. Analyze customer reviews and feedback for our product and compare it to our competitors' offerings. Identify areas where we excel and areas where we can improve to gain a competitive edge."

Example Prompt 3:
Prompt: "As a business analyst, I need ChatGPT to assist me in benchmarking our marketing strategies against our competitors. Analyze our marketing campaigns and compare them to our competitors' campaigns. Provide insights into areas where we are outperforming our competitors and suggest improvements to enhance our competitive advantage."

Example Prompt 4:
Prompt: "ChatGPT, I require your support as a business analyst to benchmark our product's pricing strategy against industry standards and our competitors. Analyze pricing data and compare it to our competitors' pricing models. Identify areas where we have a competitive advantage and recommend adjustments to optimize our pricing strategy."

Idea: Root Cause Analysis

ChatGPT can support in identifying the root causes of product performance issues, helping to address underlying problems and improve overall product performance.

Example Prompt 1:
Prompt: As a business analyst, I need ChatGPT's advanced data

processing functionality to perform a root cause analysis for a recent product performance issue. Please provide insights on the potential root causes and suggestions to address the underlying problems, ultimately improving the overall product performance.

Example Prompt 2:

Prompt: ChatGPT, utilizing its advanced data processing capabilities, can assist in identifying the root causes of a specific product performance issue. Please analyze the available data and provide a detailed breakdown of the potential underlying problems causing the issue. Additionally, suggest actionable steps to address these problems and enhance the overall product performance.

Example Prompt 3:

Prompt: As a business analyst, I require ChatGPT's advanced data processing functionality to conduct a root cause analysis for a persistent product performance issue. Please analyze the available data and provide a comprehensive assessment of the potential root causes. Furthermore, offer recommendations on how to rectify these underlying problems and improve the overall product performance.

Example Prompt 4:

Prompt: ChatGPT's advanced data processing capabilities can be leveraged to identify the root causes of a recurring product performance issue. Please analyze the provided data and generate a detailed report outlining the potential underlying problems causing the issue. Additionally, propose effective strategies to address these problems and enhance the overall product performance.

SUPPLY CHAIN ANALYSIS

OPTIMIZING THE SUPPLY CHAIN

In the complex world of supply chain management, Artificial Intelligence (AI), including tools like ChatGPT, is reshaping how business analysts assess and optimize supply chains for enhanced efficiency and cost-effectiveness.

Consider the case of Michael, a business analyst in a manufacturing company. His objective is to streamline the company's supply chain. Traditional methods of supply chain analysis often involve manual, time-consuming processes with a focus on historical data. Michael, however, employs AI to gain real-time insights and predictive analytics.

Using ChatGPT, he inputs various data points like supplier performance, inventory levels, logistics costs, and market demand forecasts. The AI tool efficiently processes this information, identifying inefficiencies and potential improvements. For instance, it suggests adjustments in inventory management based on predictive demand analysis, leading to reduced holding costs and improved cash flow.

Michael's experience highlights AI's transformative impact on supply chain analysis. AI tools enable a more dynamic and proactive approach, moving beyond reactive strategies. They provide a comprehensive view of the supply chain, identifying not just current inefficiencies but also forecasting future challenges and opportunities.

In conclusion, the integration of AI in supply chain analysis offers significant advantages. It allows business analysts like Michael to optimize supply chain operations more effectively, ensuring greater efficiency and cost savings. As AI technology continues to advance, its role in enhancing supply chain management will become even more critical, offering new levels of strategic insight and operational efficiency.

Note: Note that within this chapter, when exploring the strategies, tasks, and ideas, you have the opportunity to employ ChatGPT's Advanced Data Analysis feature. If you seek a more in-depth understanding of this feature, please consult the earlier chapter that elucidates its capabilities.

Task: Data collection

ChatGPT can assist in gathering relevant data for supply chain analysis, such as historical sales data, inventory levels, and procurement records.

Example Prompt 1:
ChatGPT, please gather historical sales data for the past five years from our company's database and present it in a comprehensive report format.

Example Prompt 2:
Using ChatGPT's advanced data processing functionality, collect and analyze inventory levels for the past six months across all our warehouses, and provide insights on any significant trends or

patterns.

Example Prompt 3:
Utilizing ChatGPT's capabilities, retrieve procurement records for the last quarter, including supplier information, purchase quantities, and associated costs, and compile them into a structured dataset for further analysis.

Example Prompt 4:
With the help of ChatGPT's advanced data processing, extract and consolidate relevant data from various sources, such as sales reports, inventory databases, and procurement systems, to create a comprehensive supply chain analysis report.

Task: Demand forecasting

ChatGPT can help in predicting future demand patterns based on historical data and market trends, enabling better supply chain planning and inventory management.

Example Prompt 1:
Based on historical sales data and market trends, analyze the demand patterns for our product line over the past year. Use ChatGPT's advanced data processing functionality to identify any recurring patterns or seasonal trends that can help us forecast future demand accurately.

Example Prompt 2:
Utilize ChatGPT's advanced data processing capabilities to analyze customer feedback and reviews, along with historical sales data, to predict future demand for our new product launch. Identify any potential demand fluctuations or market trends that can impact our supply chain planning and inventory management.

Example Prompt 3:
Leverage ChatGPT's advanced data processing functionality to analyze historical sales data and market trends for our different

product categories. *Generate demand forecasts for each category, considering factors such as seasonality, customer preferences, and external market influences, to optimize our supply chain planning and inventory management strategies.*

Example Prompt 4:
With the help of ChatGPT's advanced data processing capabilities, analyze historical sales data and market trends to forecast demand for our upcoming promotional campaign. Identify any potential spikes or fluctuations in demand that can impact our supply chain planning and inventory management, allowing us to make informed decisions and optimize our resources accordingly.

Task: Inventory optimization

ChatGPT can provide insights on optimal inventory levels, reorder points, and safety stock calculations to minimize stockouts and excess inventory.

Example Prompt 1:
ChatGPT, analyze our historical sales data and current inventory levels to determine the optimal reorder points for each product in our inventory. Consider factors such as lead time, demand variability, and desired service level to minimize stockouts and excess inventory.

Example Prompt 2:
ChatGPT, using our sales forecasts and historical data, calculate the safety stock levels for each product in our inventory. Take into account factors such as demand variability, supplier reliability, and desired service level to ensure we have enough buffer stock to prevent stockouts without excessive inventory holding costs.

Example Prompt 3:
ChatGPT, based on our sales data and lead time information, provide insights on the optimal inventory levels for each product in our inventory. Consider factors such as demand patterns, seasonality, and storage constraints to help us maintain an

efficient inventory management system.

Example Prompt 4:
ChatGPT, analyze our sales data and customer demand patterns to identify any potential stockouts or excess inventory situations. Provide recommendations on adjusting inventory levels, reorder points, and safety stock calculations to optimize our inventory management and minimize costs associated with stockouts and excess inventory.

Task: Supplier evaluation

ChatGPT can assist in evaluating and comparing potential suppliers based on criteria such as price, quality, reliability, and lead times.

Example Prompt 1:
ChatGPT, analyze and compare potential suppliers based on their price, quality, reliability, and lead times. Provide a detailed report highlighting the top three suppliers that meet our criteria and explain the reasoning behind your recommendations.

Example Prompt 2:
Using ChatGPT's advanced data processing functionality, evaluate and rank potential suppliers based on their price competitiveness, product quality, delivery reliability, and lead times. Present a comparative analysis of the top five suppliers, including their strengths and weaknesses in each criterion.

Example Prompt 3:
ChatGPT, assist in evaluating potential suppliers by analyzing their price competitiveness, product quality, delivery reliability, and lead times. Generate a comprehensive supplier evaluation report that includes a scoring system for each criterion and provides recommendations for the most suitable suppliers based on our requirements.

Example Prompt 4:

Leveraging ChatGPT's advanced data processing capabilities, assess and compare potential suppliers based on their pricing, quality standards, delivery reliability, and lead times. Create a supplier evaluation matrix that ranks suppliers on each criterion and provides an overall score. Additionally, provide insights into any potential risks or concerns associated with each supplier.

Task: Cost analysis

ChatGPT can help in analyzing the costs associated with different aspects of the supply chain, such as transportation, warehousing, and procurement, to identify cost-saving opportunities.

Example Prompt 1:
ChatGPT, analyze the transportation costs in our supply chain and identify potential cost-saving opportunities.

Example Prompt 2:
Using ChatGPT's advanced data processing functionality, provide a detailed cost analysis of our warehousing operations and suggest ways to optimize costs.

Example Prompt 3:
How can ChatGPT assist in analyzing procurement costs within our supply chain and recommend strategies to reduce expenses?

Example Prompt 4:
Utilizing ChatGPT's advanced data processing capabilities, analyze the overall costs associated with our supply chain and provide insights on cost-saving opportunities across transportation, warehousing, and procurement.

Task: Risk assessment

ChatGPT can aid in identifying potential risks and vulnerabilities in the supply chain, such as disruptions, delays, or quality issues, and suggest mitigation strategies.

Example Prompt 1:
ChatGPT, analyze our supply chain data and identify potential disruptions or delays that could impact our operations. Provide suggestions for mitigation strategies to minimize the risks associated with these issues.

Example Prompt 2:
Using ChatGPT's advanced data processing functionality, assess our supply chain for any vulnerabilities or quality issues that could affect our product or service delivery. Recommend proactive measures to mitigate these risks and ensure smooth operations.

Example Prompt 3:
Leveraging ChatGPT's capabilities, conduct a comprehensive risk assessment of our supply chain to identify potential risks and vulnerabilities. Provide insights on how we can strengthen our supply chain resilience and suggest strategies to address any identified risks.

Example Prompt 4:
With the help of ChatGPT's advanced data processing, analyze our supply chain for any potential risks or vulnerabilities that could impact our business. Propose actionable mitigation strategies to minimize the impact of disruptions, delays, or quality issues on our supply chain operations.

Task: Performance measurement

ChatGPT can assist in defining key performance indicators (KPIs) for supply chain performance evaluation and provide insights on measuring and tracking these metrics.

Example Prompt 1:
How can ChatGPT leverage its advanced data processing functionality to identify and recommend key performance indicators (KPIs) for supply chain performance evaluation?

Example Prompt 2:

Explain how ChatGPT's advanced data processing capabilities can provide insights on measuring and tracking supply chain metrics, and suggest specific KPIs that can be used for performance evaluation.

Example Prompt 3:
Demonstrate how ChatGPT's advanced data processing functionality can analyze historical supply chain data to identify trends and patterns, and propose KPIs that can effectively measure and track performance.

Example Prompt 4:
Discuss the role of ChatGPT's advanced data processing in evaluating supply chain performance, and provide examples of how it can generate actionable insights and recommendations for improving KPIs and performance metrics.

Task: Process optimization

ChatGPT can provide recommendations for streamlining and improving supply chain processes, such as order fulfillment, transportation routing, and warehouse operations.

Example Prompt 1:
ChatGPT, analyze our current order fulfillment process and provide recommendations for streamlining it. Consider factors such as reducing lead times, improving order accuracy, and optimizing inventory management.

Example Prompt 2:
ChatGPT, suggest ways to optimize our transportation routing system to improve efficiency and reduce costs. Take into account factors such as minimizing delivery times, optimizing route planning, and reducing fuel consumption.

Example Prompt 3:
ChatGPT, analyze our warehouse operations and provide recommendations for improving efficiency and reducing errors.

Consider factors such as optimizing layout and storage, implementing automation or robotics, and improving inventory tracking and management.

Example Prompt 4:
ChatGPT, help us identify potential bottlenecks or inefficiencies in our supply chain processes and provide recommendations for streamlining them. Consider factors such as reducing lead times, improving communication and collaboration between stakeholders, and implementing technology solutions for better visibility and coordination.

Task: Sustainability analysis

ChatGPT can help in assessing the environmental impact of the supply chain and suggest strategies for reducing carbon footprint, waste generation, and energy consumption.

Example Prompt 1:
Prompt: "ChatGPT, analyze the supply chain of our company and identify areas with the highest environmental impact. Suggest strategies to reduce carbon footprint, waste generation, and energy consumption in those areas."

Example Prompt 2:
Prompt: "ChatGPT, provide a comprehensive analysis of our current waste generation practices in the supply chain. Recommend innovative solutions and technologies to minimize waste and promote recycling."

Example Prompt 3:
Prompt: "ChatGPT, assess the energy consumption patterns throughout our supply chain. Propose energy-efficient alternatives and renewable energy sources that can be integrated into our operations to reduce overall energy consumption."

Example Prompt 4:
Prompt: "ChatGPT, analyze the carbon footprint of our supply

chain and identify key contributors. Based on this analysis, suggest sustainable transportation options, such as electric vehicles or alternative fuels, to reduce carbon emissions."

Task: Technology integration

ChatGPT can provide insights on integrating emerging technologies like blockchain, IoT, or AI into the supply chain to enhance visibility, traceability, and efficiency.

Example Prompt 1:
How can ChatGPT's Advanced Data processing functionality be leveraged to analyze and identify potential use cases for integrating blockchain technology into the supply chain to enhance visibility, traceability, and efficiency?

Example Prompt 2:
In what ways can ChatGPT's Advanced Data processing functionality assist in evaluating the impact of integrating IoT devices into the supply chain and how it can enhance visibility, traceability, and efficiency?

Example Prompt 3:
Utilizing ChatGPT's Advanced Data processing functionality, provide insights on how AI can be integrated into the supply chain to improve visibility, traceability, and efficiency, and identify potential challenges and solutions.

Example Prompt 4:
Using ChatGPT's Advanced Data processing functionality, analyze the benefits and challenges of integrating emerging technologies like blockchain, IoT, and AI into the supply chain, and provide recommendations on the most effective approach to enhance visibility, traceability, and efficiency.

Idea: Demand Forecasting

Utilize historical data and market trends to predict future

demand for products or services, enabling better supply chain planning and inventory management.

Example Prompt 1:

Prompt: *"As a business analyst, I need ChatGPT to utilize its advanced data processing functionality to help me with demand forecasting. Please analyze the historical sales data and market trends to predict the future demand for our products. Provide insights and recommendations for better supply chain planning and inventory management."*

Example Prompt 2:

Prompt: *"ChatGPT, as a business analyst, I require your assistance in demand forecasting. Please leverage your advanced data processing capabilities to analyze our historical sales data and market trends. Predict the future demand for our products and provide actionable insights to optimize our supply chain planning and inventory management processes."*

Example Prompt 3:

Prompt: *"I'm a business analyst seeking ChatGPT's support in demand forecasting. By utilizing its advanced data processing functionality, I want to leverage historical sales data and market trends to predict future demand for our products. Please provide accurate forecasts and recommendations to enhance our supply chain planning and inventory management strategies."*

Example Prompt 4:

Prompt: *"ChatGPT, as a business analyst, I need your expertise in demand forecasting. Utilize your advanced data processing capabilities to analyze our historical sales data and market trends. Predict the future demand for our products and offer valuable insights to improve our supply chain planning and inventory management practices."*

Idea: Inventory Optimization

Analyze inventory levels, turnover rates, and lead times

to identify opportunities for reducing costs, improving efficiency, and minimizing stockouts.

Example Prompt 1:
As a business analyst, I need ChatGPT to analyze our inventory levels, turnover rates, and lead times to identify opportunities for reducing costs, improving efficiency, and minimizing stockouts. Please provide insights on how we can optimize our inventory management process.

Example Prompt 2:
ChatGPT, using its advanced data processing functionality, I need your assistance in analyzing our current inventory levels, turnover rates, and lead times. Please identify specific areas where we can reduce costs, improve efficiency, and minimize stockouts. Additionally, suggest strategies to optimize our inventory management.

Example Prompt 3:
As a business analyst, I require ChatGPT's support in analyzing our inventory data. Please evaluate our current inventory levels, turnover rates, and lead times to identify opportunities for cost reduction, efficiency improvement, and stockout minimization. Provide actionable recommendations to optimize our inventory management process.

Example Prompt 4:
ChatGPT, leveraging its advanced data processing capabilities, I need your expertise in analyzing our inventory levels, turnover rates, and lead times. Please assess our current inventory data and identify potential areas for reducing costs, improving efficiency, and minimizing stockouts. Additionally, suggest strategies or tools that can help us optimize our inventory management practices.

Idea: Supplier Performance Analysis

Evaluate supplier performance based on criteria such as quality, delivery time, and cost, enabling informed decision-making and potential supplier negotiations.

Example Prompt 1:

As a business analyst, I need ChatGPT's advanced data processing functionality to analyze supplier performance. Please provide a summary report evaluating the quality, delivery time, and cost of our top five suppliers. Include any insights or recommendations for potential supplier negotiations.

Example Prompt 2:

ChatGPT, using its advanced data processing capabilities, please analyze supplier performance and provide a detailed comparison of quality, delivery time, and cost for our current suppliers. Additionally, identify any outliers or underperforming suppliers that require immediate attention and suggest potential strategies for improvement.

Example Prompt 3:

As part of our supplier performance analysis, we require ChatGPT's support in evaluating the quality, delivery time, and cost of our suppliers. Please generate a comprehensive report that ranks our suppliers based on these criteria and highlights any significant trends or patterns that could impact our decision-making process.

Example Prompt 4:

ChatGPT, utilizing its advanced data processing functionality, we need your assistance in conducting a supplier performance analysis. Please analyze the quality, delivery time, and cost of our suppliers over the past year and provide a detailed breakdown of their performance. Additionally, suggest any potential areas for improvement or cost-saving opportunities that could be explored through supplier negotiations.

Idea: Transportation Route Optimization

Optimize transportation routes and modes to minimize costs, reduce delivery times, and improve overall supply chain efficiency.

Example Prompt 1:
Prompt: As a business analyst, I need your assistance in optimizing transportation routes and modes to improve our supply chain efficiency. Please provide a step-by-step plan to achieve this goal using ChatGPT's advanced data processing functionality.

Example Prompt 2:
Prompt: Our company aims to minimize transportation costs, reduce delivery times, and improve overall supply chain efficiency. Utilizing ChatGPT's advanced data processing capabilities, please analyze our current transportation routes and suggest specific optimizations to achieve these objectives.

Example Prompt 3:
Prompt: We are looking to optimize our transportation routes and modes to enhance our supply chain efficiency. With the help of ChatGPT's advanced data processing functionality, please provide a detailed analysis of our current transportation network, identify potential bottlenecks, and propose strategies to minimize costs and improve delivery times.

Example Prompt 4:
Prompt: Our organization is seeking to improve our transportation operations by optimizing routes and modes to reduce costs and enhance supply chain efficiency. Using ChatGPT's advanced data processing capabilities, please generate a comprehensive report outlining the current transportation landscape, highlighting areas for improvement, and recommending specific actions to achieve our objectives.

Idea: Warehouse Layout Optimization

Analyze warehouse layout, storage capacity, and material flow to optimize space utilization, reduce handling costs, and enhance order fulfillment processes.

Example Prompt 1:
As a business analyst, I need ChatGPT to analyze our current warehouse layout and provide recommendations for optimizing space utilization. Please assess the storage capacity, material flow, and order fulfillment processes to identify areas where we can reduce handling costs and enhance efficiency.

Example Prompt 2:
ChatGPT, we are looking to improve our warehouse operations by optimizing the layout for better space utilization. Can you analyze our current warehouse layout, evaluate the storage capacity, and suggest modifications that would enhance material flow and order fulfillment processes? Please consider reducing handling costs as a key objective.

Example Prompt 3:
Our company aims to optimize our warehouse layout to maximize space utilization and improve order fulfillment processes. ChatGPT, we need your expertise as a business analyst to analyze our current layout, assess the storage capacity, and provide recommendations on how to reduce handling costs while enhancing efficiency.

Example Prompt 4:
As a business analyst, I require ChatGPT's advanced data processing functionality to analyze our warehouse layout and propose strategies for optimizing space utilization. Please evaluate the current storage capacity, material flow, and order fulfillment processes to identify opportunities for reducing handling costs and improving overall efficiency.

Idea: Risk Management

Identify potential risks and vulnerabilities in the supply chain, such as disruptions, delays, or quality issues, and develop strategies to mitigate and manage these risks.

Example Prompt 1:
As a business analyst, I need ChatGPT to analyze our supply chain and identify potential risks and vulnerabilities. Please provide a detailed report on any disruptions, delays, or quality issues that could impact our supply chain. Additionally, suggest strategies to mitigate and manage these risks effectively.

Example Prompt 2:
ChatGPT, using its advanced data processing functionality, I require your assistance in evaluating our supply chain for potential risks and vulnerabilities. Please analyze historical data, market trends, and external factors to identify any potential disruptions, delays, or quality issues that could pose a risk. Furthermore, provide recommendations on strategies to proactively mitigate and manage these risks.

Example Prompt 3:
As part of our risk management efforts, I need ChatGPT to leverage its advanced data processing capabilities to assess our supply chain. Please analyze the current state of our supply chain and identify any vulnerabilities, disruptions, delays, or quality issues that could impact our operations. Additionally, suggest actionable strategies to effectively mitigate and manage these risks, considering both short-term and long-term perspectives.

Example Prompt 4:
ChatGPT, as a business analyst, I require your expertise in risk management to evaluate our supply chain. Utilize your advanced data processing functionality to identify potential risks and vulnerabilities, such as disruptions, delays, or quality issues. Furthermore, provide a comprehensive analysis of these risks and recommend strategies to mitigate and manage them efficiently. Please consider the impact on cost, time, and overall business continuity while suggesting risk management strategies.

Idea: Sustainability Analysis

Assess the environmental impact of the supply chain, identify areas for improvement, and develop sustainable practices to reduce carbon footprint and promote social responsibility.

Example Prompt 1:

As a sustainability analyst, I need ChatGPT to analyze the environmental impact of our supply chain and identify areas for improvement. Please provide a detailed assessment of our current carbon footprint and suggest sustainable practices that can help us reduce it. Additionally, highlight any social responsibility initiatives we can undertake to promote a more sustainable business model.

Example Prompt 2:

ChatGPT, as a business analyst, I require your assistance in conducting a sustainability analysis of our supply chain. Please analyze the environmental impact of each stage in our supply chain, from sourcing raw materials to product distribution. Identify any areas where we can make improvements to reduce our carbon footprint and suggest sustainable practices that align with our business goals. Furthermore, provide insights on how we can promote social responsibility within our supply chain.

Example Prompt 3:

In order to promote sustainability and reduce our carbon footprint, I need ChatGPT to help me assess the environmental impact of our supply chain. Please analyze the energy consumption, waste generation, and greenhouse gas emissions associated with each stage of our supply chain. Based on this analysis, suggest specific areas for improvement and sustainable practices that can be implemented to minimize our environmental impact. Additionally, provide recommendations on how we can integrate social responsibility into our supply chain practices.

Example Prompt 4:

As a sustainability analyst, I require ChatGPT's advanced data processing functionality to conduct a comprehensive sustainability analysis of our supply chain. Please analyze the environmental impact of our supply chain activities, including transportation, manufacturing, and packaging. Identify key areas where we can reduce our carbon footprint and suggest sustainable practices that align with our business objectives. Furthermore, provide insights on how we can incorporate social responsibility initiatives into our supply chain operations to promote a more sustainable and socially conscious business model.

Idea: Supplier Relationship Management

Analyze supplier relationships, negotiate contracts, and establish performance metrics to ensure effective collaboration and maximize value from suppliers.

Example Prompt 1:

As a business analyst, I need ChatGPT's advanced data processing functionality to analyze supplier relationships and provide insights on improving collaboration and maximizing value from suppliers. Please analyze the historical data of our supplier interactions, identify any patterns or trends, and suggest strategies to enhance our supplier relationship management process.

Example Prompt 2:

ChatGPT, using its advanced data processing capabilities, I need your support to negotiate contracts with our suppliers. Please review the terms and conditions of our existing contracts, identify any potential risks or areas for improvement, and provide recommendations on how to negotiate better terms to ensure effective collaboration and maximize value from our suppliers.

Example Prompt 3:

As a business analyst, I require ChatGPT's advanced data processing functionality to establish performance metrics for our suppliers. Please analyze the performance data of our suppliers, identify key performance indicators (KPIs) that align with our business goals, and suggest metrics that can be used to measure and evaluate the performance of our suppliers. Additionally, provide insights on how to effectively communicate these metrics to our suppliers to drive continuous improvement.

Example Prompt 4:

ChatGPT, I need your assistance as a business analyst to support our supplier relationship management efforts. Utilizing your advanced data processing capabilities, please analyze the feedback and satisfaction surveys from our internal stakeholders regarding our suppliers. Identify any areas of concern or improvement, and provide recommendations on how to address these issues to enhance collaboration and maximize value from our suppliers.

Idea: Cost Analysis

Conduct a comprehensive cost analysis of the supply chain, including procurement, transportation, warehousing, and inventory costs, to identify areas for cost reduction and process improvement.

Example Prompt 1:

Prompt: As a business analyst, I need ChatGPT to conduct a comprehensive cost analysis of our supply chain. Please provide a detailed breakdown of procurement, transportation, warehousing, and inventory costs, and identify areas where we can reduce costs and improve processes.

Example Prompt 2:

Prompt: ChatGPT, I require your assistance as a business analyst to perform a thorough cost analysis of our supply chain. Utilize advanced data processing capabilities to analyze the procurement, transportation, warehousing, and inventory costs. Identify specific areas where we can reduce costs and suggest process improvements to enhance efficiency.

Example Prompt 3:

Prompt: Business analyst support needed! ChatGPT, please

leverage your advanced data processing functionality to conduct a comprehensive cost analysis of our supply chain. Analyze the procurement, transportation, warehousing, and inventory costs in detail. Identify opportunities for cost reduction and process improvement, providing specific recommendations to optimize our operations.

Example Prompt 4:
Prompt: ChatGPT, as a business analyst, I require your expertise in performing a cost analysis of our supply chain. Utilize your advanced data processing capabilities to thoroughly examine procurement, transportation, warehousing, and inventory costs. Identify areas where we can reduce costs and suggest actionable process improvements to enhance our overall efficiency.

Idea: Order Fulfillment Analysis

Evaluate order fulfillment processes, including order processing time, picking and packing efficiency, and delivery accuracy, to enhance customer satisfaction and reduce order cycle times.

Example Prompt 1:
Prompt: As a business analyst, I need ChatGPT to analyze order fulfillment processes and provide insights on order processing time, picking and packing efficiency, and delivery accuracy. Please generate a report summarizing the current state of these metrics and suggest improvements to enhance customer satisfaction and reduce order cycle times.

Example Prompt 2:
Prompt: ChatGPT, I require your assistance as a business analyst to evaluate the order fulfillment processes of our company. Please analyze the historical data and identify any patterns or trends related to order processing time, picking and packing efficiency, and delivery accuracy. Additionally, provide recommendations on how we can optimize these processes to improve customer

satisfaction and reduce order cycle times.

Example Prompt 3:

Prompt: As a business analyst, I need ChatGPT to perform a comprehensive analysis of our order fulfillment processes. Please analyze the data to determine the average order processing time, picking and packing efficiency, and delivery accuracy. Based on these findings, suggest specific strategies or technologies that can be implemented to enhance customer satisfaction and reduce order cycle times.

Example Prompt 4:

Prompt: ChatGPT, I require your expertise as a business analyst to evaluate our order fulfillment processes. Please analyze the available data and provide a detailed breakdown of order processing time, picking and packing efficiency, and delivery accuracy. Additionally, suggest key performance indicators (KPIs) that can be tracked to monitor and improve these metrics, ultimately enhancing customer satisfaction and reducing order cycle times.

Idea: Supply Chain Visibility

Implement tools and technologies to enhance supply chain visibility, enabling real-time tracking of inventory, shipments, and demand, and facilitating proactive decision-making.

Example Prompt 1:

Prompt: As a business analyst, I need ChatGPT to provide insights on how implementing advanced data processing functionality can enhance supply chain visibility. Please explain the benefits of real-time tracking of inventory, shipments, and demand, and how it can facilitate proactive decision-making for businesses.

Example Prompt 2:

Prompt: ChatGPT, please outline the key tools and technologies that can be utilized to improve supply chain visibility. Describe how these tools enable real-time tracking of inventory, shipments, and demand, and how they contribute to proactive decision-making in supply chain management.

Example Prompt 3:
Prompt: As a business analyst, I want ChatGPT to provide examples of companies that have successfully implemented advanced data processing functionality to enhance supply chain visibility. Describe the specific tools and technologies they used, and how these implementations improved real-time tracking of inventory, shipments, and demand, leading to more informed and proactive decision-making.

Example Prompt 4:
Prompt: ChatGPT, please discuss the potential challenges and risks associated with implementing tools and technologies for supply chain visibility. Explain how advanced data processing functionality can help mitigate these challenges and risks, and provide examples of best practices for ensuring successful implementation and utilization of such tools in supply chain management.

Idea: Continuous Improvement Initiatives

Identify opportunities for process improvement within the supply chain, such as implementing lean principles, automation, or technology solutions, to drive efficiency and reduce waste.

Example Prompt 1:
As a business analyst, I need ChatGPT to analyze our supply chain processes and identify opportunities for improvement. Please provide a detailed report on how implementing lean principles can drive efficiency and reduce waste within our supply chain.

Example Prompt 2:
ChatGPT, help us identify potential areas within our supply chain where automation can be implemented to improve efficiency and reduce waste. Provide specific examples and recommendations for

automation solutions that align with our business goals.

Example Prompt 3:

We are looking to leverage technology solutions to optimize our supply chain processes. ChatGPT, analyze our current supply chain and suggest technology solutions that can enhance efficiency and reduce waste. Please provide a cost-benefit analysis for each recommended solution.

Example Prompt 4:

Our organization is committed to continuous improvement initiatives within our supply chain. ChatGPT, conduct a comprehensive analysis of our current processes and recommend specific actions we can take to drive efficiency and reduce waste. Consider both lean principles and technology solutions in your recommendations.

PRICING STRATEGY DEVELOPMENT

CRAFTING COMPETITIVE PRICING STRATEGIES

Developing effective pricing strategies is a complex task, requiring a deep understanding of market research, cost analysis, and competitive landscapes. Artificial Intelligence (AI), particularly tools like ChatGPT, plays a crucial role in enhancing this process, enabling business analysts to devise more informed and dynamic pricing strategies.

Take the example of Sophia, a business analyst at a consumer electronics company. Her challenge is to develop a pricing strategy for a new product. The traditional approach of solely relying on historical pricing data and basic competitor prices is no longer sufficient in today's fast-paced market. Sophia turns to AI for a more nuanced approach.

Utilizing ChatGPT, she inputs a wide array of data, including in-depth market research, production costs, competitor pricing, and consumer behavior trends. The AI tool processes this information, providing insights into optimal pricing points, potential market reactions, and competitive positioning. For instance, it suggests a tiered pricing strategy based on consumer segments, maximizing market reach and profitability.

Sophia's scenario illustrates the profound impact of AI in pricing strategy development. AI tools enable a more comprehensive analysis of various factors influencing pricing, leading to strategies that are not only competitive but also aligned with consumer expectations and market dynamics.

In conclusion, the integration of AI in pricing strategy development is a game-changer for business analysts. It empowers them to create more sophisticated and effective pricing models, essential for achieving business objectives in a competitive landscape. As AI technologies continue to evolve, their role in strategic pricing will only grow, offering unparalleled insights and capabilities.

Note: Please be aware that the strategies, tasks, and ideas discussed in this chapter can be further refined by taking advantage of ChatGPT's Advanced Data Analysis feature. If you require additional information about this tool, you can find comprehensive coverage in the previously authored chapter.

Task: Competitor analysis

ChatGPT can provide insights on competitor pricing strategies, market positioning, and pricing trends.

Example Prompt 1:
ChatGPT, analyze competitor pricing strategies for our industry and provide insights on any patterns or trends you identify.

Example Prompt 2:

Using ChatGPT's advanced data processing functionality, analyze our competitors' market positioning and provide recommendations on how we can differentiate ourselves.

Example Prompt 3:
ChatGPT, gather data on pricing trends in our industry and provide a comprehensive analysis of how our competitors' pricing strategies have evolved over the past year.

Example Prompt 4:
Utilizing ChatGPT's advanced data processing capabilities, analyze our competitors' pricing strategies and identify any potential gaps or opportunities for us to optimize our own pricing strategy.

Task: Customer segmentation

ChatGPT can assist in identifying customer segments based on various factors such as demographics, behavior, and preferences, which can inform pricing strategies.

Example Prompt 1:
Using ChatGPT's Advanced Data processing functionality, analyze customer data to identify distinct segments based on demographics, behavior, and preferences. How can these segments inform pricing strategies for our products/services?

Example Prompt 2:
Leverage ChatGPT's Advanced Data processing capabilities to segment our customer base by demographics, behavior, and preferences. How can these segments be utilized to optimize our pricing strategies and maximize profitability?

Example Prompt 3:
With the help of ChatGPT's Advanced Data processing functionality, analyze customer data to identify different segments based on demographics, behavior, and preferences. How can these segments guide us in developing targeted pricing

strategies to enhance customer satisfaction and drive sales?

Example Prompt 4:
Utilize ChatGPT's Advanced Data processing capabilities to segment our customers based on demographics, behavior, and preferences. How can these segments be leveraged to design personalized pricing strategies that cater to each segment's unique needs and preferences?

Task: Value proposition analysis

ChatGPT can help analyze the value proposition of your products or services and suggest pricing strategies that align with the perceived value.

Example Prompt 1:
ChatGPT can analyze customer feedback and market trends to identify the key value drivers of your products or services. Based on this analysis, it can suggest pricing strategies that align with the perceived value and maximize your profitability. How can ChatGPT assist you in understanding your value proposition and optimizing your pricing strategy?

Example Prompt 2:
With ChatGPT's advanced data processing functionality, it can analyze customer preferences, competitor offerings, and market dynamics to evaluate the perceived value of your products or services. By leveraging this analysis, ChatGPT can provide valuable insights and recommend pricing strategies that align with the perceived value. How can ChatGPT assist you in analyzing your value proposition and suggesting optimal pricing strategies?

Example Prompt 3:
ChatGPT's advanced data processing capabilities enable it to assess customer perceptions, market demand, and competitive landscape to evaluate the value proposition of your products or services. By leveraging this analysis, ChatGPT can offer data-driven recommendations for pricing strategies that align with the

perceived value. How can ChatGPT assist you in analyzing your value proposition and suggesting effective pricing strategies?

Example Prompt 4:
Leveraging ChatGPT's advanced data processing functionality, it can analyze customer behavior, market trends, and competitor pricing to evaluate the value proposition of your products or services. Based on this analysis, ChatGPT can provide insights and suggest pricing strategies that align with the perceived value, helping you optimize your pricing decisions. How can ChatGPT assist you in analyzing your value proposition and suggesting pricing strategies that maximize your profitability?

Task: Pricing research

ChatGPT can conduct market research to gather data on customer willingness to pay, price sensitivity, and demand elasticity, which can inform pricing decisions.

Example Prompt 1:
ChatGPT, conduct a survey to gather data on customer willingness to pay for our product range. Ask participants about their budget constraints, perceived value, and their maximum price threshold for each product category.

Example Prompt 2:
ChatGPT, analyze customer feedback and reviews from various online platforms to identify patterns related to price sensitivity. Provide insights on how customers perceive changes in pricing and their reactions to price adjustments.

Example Prompt 3:
ChatGPT, simulate conversations with potential customers to understand their preferences and expectations regarding pricing. Explore different pricing scenarios and gather data on customer reactions, including their likelihood to purchase at different price points.

Example Prompt 4:
ChatGPT, analyze historical sales data and customer purchase patterns to identify demand elasticity for our products. Provide insights on how changes in price have affected sales volume and revenue, and suggest optimal pricing strategies based on the analysis.

Task: Cost analysis

ChatGPT can assist in analyzing the cost structure of your business and provide insights on pricing strategies that ensure profitability.

Example Prompt 1:
ChatGPT, analyze the cost structure of our business and provide insights on the profitability of our current pricing strategies. Identify areas where we can reduce costs and suggest alternative pricing strategies to maximize profitability.

Example Prompt 2:
ChatGPT, utilize advanced data processing to analyze our cost structure and provide recommendations on pricing strategies that can improve our profitability. Consider factors such as fixed costs, variable costs, and market demand to suggest optimal pricing models.

Example Prompt 3:
ChatGPT, help us understand the cost breakdown of our business by analyzing various cost components such as production costs, overhead expenses, and marketing expenses. Based on this analysis, provide insights on pricing strategies that can ensure profitability while remaining competitive in the market.

Example Prompt 4:
ChatGPT, leverage its advanced data processing capabilities to conduct a comprehensive cost analysis of our business. Identify cost drivers, evaluate their impact on profitability, and suggest

pricing strategies that align with our cost structure. Additionally, provide insights on potential cost-saving measures that can be implemented to improve overall profitability.

Task: Pricing model development

ChatGPT can help in developing pricing models, such as cost-plus pricing, value-based pricing, or dynamic pricing, based on your business objectives and market dynamics.

Example Prompt 1:
Using ChatGPT's Advanced Data processing functionality, analyze market dynamics and customer preferences to develop a value-based pricing model for our new product line. Consider factors such as perceived value, competitive landscape, and customer segmentation to determine optimal pricing strategies.

Example Prompt 2:
Leverage ChatGPT's Advanced Data processing functionality to develop a dynamic pricing model that adjusts prices in real-time based on market demand and competitor pricing. Explore historical sales data, market trends, and customer behavior to identify pricing patterns and optimize revenue generation.

Example Prompt 3:
Utilize ChatGPT's Advanced Data processing functionality to develop a cost-plus pricing model for our manufacturing business. Analyze production costs, overhead expenses, and desired profit margins to determine the appropriate pricing structure that ensures profitability while remaining competitive in the market.

Example Prompt 4:
With the help of ChatGPT's Advanced Data processing functionality, develop a pricing model for our subscription-based service that maximizes customer acquisition and retention. Consider factors such as customer lifetime value, pricing elasticity, and market saturation to design a pricing strategy that balances revenue growth and customer satisfaction.

Task: Price optimization

ChatGPT can assist in optimizing prices by analyzing historical sales data, market conditions, and customer behavior to determine the most effective pricing strategies.

Example Prompt 1:
ChatGPT, analyze our historical sales data and market conditions to recommend pricing strategies that can maximize our revenue while considering customer behavior and market competition.

Example Prompt 2:
ChatGPT, based on our historical sales data and customer behavior, suggest dynamic pricing strategies that can help us optimize prices in real-time and increase our profitability.

Example Prompt 3:
ChatGPT, analyze our historical sales data and market conditions to identify pricing trends and patterns. Provide insights on how we can adjust our prices to stay competitive and maximize our market share.

Example Prompt 4:
ChatGPT, using advanced data processing, analyze our historical sales data, market conditions, and customer behavior to recommend personalized pricing strategies that can enhance customer satisfaction and drive repeat purchases.

Task: Promotional pricing

ChatGPT can provide suggestions for promotional pricing strategies, such as discounts, bundles, or loyalty programs, to attract customers and increase sales.

Example Prompt 1:
ChatGPT, analyze our customer data and suggest the most effective promotional pricing strategy to attract new customers and increase sales. Consider offering discounts on popular

products or creating bundle deals that encourage customers to purchase multiple items.

Example Prompt 2:
ChatGPT, based on our sales history and customer preferences, recommend a promotional pricing strategy that can help us retain existing customers and encourage repeat purchases. Explore options like loyalty programs or personalized discounts tailored to individual customer preferences.

Example Prompt 3:
ChatGPT, analyze market trends and competitor pricing to suggest a promotional pricing strategy that sets us apart from our competitors and attracts new customers. Consider offering limited-time discounts or exclusive bundle deals that provide added value to our customers.

Example Prompt 4:
ChatGPT, leverage our customer feedback and reviews to propose a promotional pricing strategy that addresses any pain points or concerns raised by our customers. Explore options like targeted discounts on specific products or services, or introducing a referral program to incentivize existing customers to refer new ones.

Task: Pricing communication

ChatGPT can help in developing effective pricing communication strategies, including pricing messages, pricing structures, and pricing presentation to customers.

Example Prompt 1:
How can ChatGPT's Advanced Data processing functionality be utilized to analyze customer feedback and preferences in order to develop effective pricing messages?

Example Prompt 2:
In what ways can ChatGPT's Advanced Data processing functionality assist in identifying optimal pricing structures based

on market trends and competitor analysis?

Example Prompt 3:
How can ChatGPT's Advanced Data processing functionality be leveraged to create personalized pricing presentations for different customer segments?

Example Prompt 4:
What are some examples of successful pricing communication strategies that have been developed using ChatGPT's Advanced Data processing functionality, and how can they be applied to our business?

Task: Pricing implementation plan

ChatGPT can assist in creating a detailed plan for implementing the pricing strategy, including timelines, responsibilities, and monitoring mechanisms.

Example Prompt 1:
ChatGPT, please generate a detailed timeline for implementing our pricing strategy, including key milestones and deadlines for each stage of the process.

Example Prompt 2:
ChatGPT, provide a breakdown of responsibilities and roles for each team member involved in the pricing implementation plan, including their specific tasks and deliverables.

Example Prompt 3:
ChatGPT, suggest monitoring mechanisms and metrics that can be used to track the effectiveness and success of our pricing strategy implementation. Include both qualitative and quantitative measures.

Example Prompt 4:
ChatGPT, analyze historical pricing data and customer feedback to identify potential risks and challenges that may arise during the implementation of our pricing strategy. Provide recommendations

on how to mitigate these risks and address customer concerns.

Idea: Competitive Pricing Analysis

ChatGPT can assist in analyzing competitors' pricing strategies, identifying pricing gaps, and recommending optimal pricing points.

Example Prompt 1:

Prompt: "As a business analyst, I need ChatGPT to assist me in conducting a competitive pricing analysis for our product line. Please analyze our competitors' pricing strategies, identify any pricing gaps, and recommend optimal pricing points for each product."

Example Prompt 2:

Prompt: "ChatGPT, as a business analyst, I require your support in analyzing our competitors' pricing strategies. Please provide a detailed analysis of their pricing structures, identify any gaps or discrepancies in comparison to our own pricing, and recommend optimal pricing points to maintain a competitive edge."

Example Prompt 3:

Prompt: "As a business analyst, I need ChatGPT to help me analyze our competitors' pricing strategies and identify any pricing gaps that exist. Please provide a comprehensive analysis of their pricing models, highlight any areas where our pricing is significantly higher or lower, and recommend optimal pricing points to maximize our competitiveness."

Example Prompt 4:

Prompt: "ChatGPT, I am a business analyst seeking your assistance in conducting a competitive pricing analysis. Please analyze our competitors' pricing strategies, identify any gaps or opportunities for improvement, and recommend optimal pricing points that will enable us to effectively position our products in the market."

Idea: Dynamic Pricing Implementation

ChatGPT can help in developing algorithms and models for dynamic pricing based on factors like demand, seasonality, and customer behavior.

Example Prompt 1:

As a business analyst, I need ChatGPT's advanced data processing functionality to develop an algorithm for dynamic pricing. Please provide a step-by-step guide on how to analyze historical sales data, customer behavior, and seasonal trends to create a pricing model that adjusts in real-time based on demand fluctuations.

Example Prompt 2:

ChatGPT, I require your assistance as a business analyst to implement dynamic pricing for our e-commerce platform. Can you help me understand how to leverage customer segmentation and purchase history data to personalize pricing for individual customers? Additionally, please guide me on how to integrate this pricing model into our existing system for seamless implementation.

Example Prompt 3:

As a business analyst, I'm looking for ChatGPT's support in developing a dynamic pricing strategy for our hotel chain. Could you provide insights on how to analyze market demand, competitor pricing, and customer reviews to determine optimal pricing levels for different seasons and customer segments? Please include recommendations on how to automate this process to ensure real-time adjustments.

Example Prompt 4:

ChatGPT, I need your expertise as a business analyst to implement dynamic pricing for our ride-sharing service. Can you guide me on how to utilize real-time data such as traffic conditions, driver availability, and customer demand to dynamically adjust pricing? Additionally, please advise on how to strike a balance between maximizing revenue and maintaining customer satisfaction through pricing optimization.

Idea: Value-Based Pricing Strategy

ChatGPT can aid in identifying customer segments, understanding their perceived value, and developing pricing strategies that align with the value delivered.

Example Prompt 1:

Prompt: As a business analyst, I need ChatGPT to assist in identifying customer segments for our value-based pricing strategy. Please provide insights on how different customer segments perceive the value of our product and suggest potential pricing strategies that align with their perceived value.

Example Prompt 2:

Prompt: ChatGPT, help me understand the perceived value of our product among different customer segments. Analyze customer feedback, reviews, and market trends to identify the key factors that influence their perception of value. Additionally, provide recommendations on pricing strategies that can effectively align with the value delivered to each segment.

Example Prompt 3:

Prompt: We are developing a value-based pricing strategy for our new product. ChatGPT, please analyze customer data and market research to identify distinct customer segments based on their perceived value. Furthermore, suggest pricing strategies that cater to each segment's unique value perception, ensuring maximum customer satisfaction and profitability.

Example Prompt 4:

Prompt: Our company aims to implement a value-based pricing strategy to optimize revenue and customer satisfaction. ChatGPT, assist us in understanding the perceived value of our product among different customer segments. Based on this analysis, recommend pricing strategies that effectively capture the value delivered to each segment, enabling us to achieve our business objectives.

Idea: Bundling and Packaging Strategies

ChatGPT can assist in analyzing customer preferences, market trends, and product portfolios to develop effective bundling and packaging strategies.

Example Prompt 1:
As a business analyst, I need ChatGPT's advanced data processing functionality to analyze customer preferences, market trends, and product portfolios in order to develop effective bundling and packaging strategies. Please provide insights on the most popular product combinations that customers tend to purchase together, and suggest potential bundling options that could increase sales and customer satisfaction.

Example Prompt 2:
ChatGPT, using its advanced data processing capabilities, I need your assistance in analyzing customer preferences, market trends, and product portfolios to identify any emerging patterns or trends in bundling and packaging strategies. Please provide recommendations on how we can optimize our product offerings by bundling complementary items together, taking into consideration customer preferences and market demand.

Example Prompt 3:
As a business analyst, I rely on ChatGPT's advanced data processing functionality to analyze customer preferences, market trends, and product portfolios. Please provide insights on the most effective packaging strategies that can enhance the perceived value of our products and drive customer engagement. Additionally, suggest any potential cross-selling opportunities that can be leveraged through strategic bundling and packaging.

Example Prompt 4:
ChatGPT, I need your support as a business analyst to analyze

customer preferences, market trends, and product portfolios for developing effective bundling and packaging strategies. Please provide recommendations on how we can create attractive product bundles that align with customer preferences and capitalize on market trends. Additionally, suggest any innovative packaging ideas that can differentiate our products and increase their appeal to customers.

Idea: Price Optimization for Revenue Maximization

ChatGPT can help in developing pricing optimization models to maximize revenue by considering factors like price elasticity, cost structures, and market conditions.

Example Prompt 1:
As a business analyst, I need ChatGPT's advanced data processing functionality to develop a pricing optimization model for our product line. Please provide guidance on how to incorporate price elasticity, cost structures, and market conditions to maximize revenue.

Example Prompt 2:
ChatGPT, using its advanced data processing capabilities, can you assist in analyzing our historical sales data and market trends to identify the optimal price points for our products? Consider factors such as price elasticity, cost structures, and market conditions to help us maximize revenue.

Example Prompt 3:
We are looking to optimize our pricing strategy to maximize revenue. With ChatGPT's advanced data processing functionality, please provide insights on how we can leverage price elasticity, cost structures, and market conditions to determine the most profitable pricing for our products.

Example Prompt 4:

ChatGPT, as a business analyst, I need your support in developing a pricing optimization model that takes into account price elasticity, cost structures, and market conditions. Utilizing your advanced data processing capabilities, please provide recommendations on how we can adjust our prices to maximize revenue while considering these factors.

Idea: Promotional Pricing Campaigns

ChatGPT can support in designing and evaluating promotional pricing campaigns, including discounts, coupons, and limited-time offers.

Example Prompt 1:
As a business analyst, I need ChatGPT's advanced data processing functionality to design a promotional pricing campaign for a new product launch. Please provide me with a step-by-step plan on how to create an effective campaign that includes discounts, coupons, and limited-time offers. Additionally, evaluate the potential impact of this campaign on sales and customer engagement.

Example Prompt 2:
ChatGPT, using its advanced data processing capabilities, help me analyze customer data to identify the most effective promotional pricing strategy for our upcoming seasonal sale. Consider incorporating discounts, coupons, and limited-time offers to maximize customer acquisition and revenue generation. Provide insights on the optimal discount percentage, coupon distribution, and duration of the campaign.

Example Prompt 3:
I require ChatGPT's support in evaluating the success of our ongoing promotional pricing campaign. Utilizing its advanced data processing functionality, analyze the sales data, customer feedback, and engagement metrics to determine the effectiveness of the discounts, coupons, and limited-time offers. Suggest any necessary adjustments or improvements to optimize the

campaign's performance.

Example Prompt 4:

As a business analyst, I need ChatGPT to assist me in designing a promotional pricing campaign for our loyal customer base. Utilize advanced data processing techniques to segment our customers based on their purchase history and preferences. Recommend personalized discounts, coupons, and limited-time offers tailored to each customer segment to enhance customer loyalty and drive repeat purchases. Evaluate the potential impact of this campaign on customer retention and lifetime value.

Idea: Price Discrimination Strategies

ChatGPT can aid in developing strategies to implement price discrimination based on factors like customer segments, geographical regions, or purchase history.

Example Prompt 1:

Prompt: As a business analyst, I need ChatGPT's advanced data processing functionality to develop price discrimination strategies based on customer segments. Please provide insights on how ChatGPT can help identify customer segments and recommend pricing strategies accordingly.

Example Prompt 2:

Prompt: ChatGPT's advanced data processing functionality can assist in implementing price discrimination strategies based on geographical regions. Please analyze the data and suggest ways in which ChatGPT can help identify regional pricing variations and optimize pricing strategies accordingly.

Example Prompt 3:

Prompt: As a business analyst, I require ChatGPT's advanced data processing capabilities to develop price discrimination strategies based on purchase history. Please provide insights on how ChatGPT can analyze customer purchase patterns and recommend personalized pricing strategies to maximize revenue.

Example Prompt 4:
Prompt: ChatGPT's advanced data processing functionality can aid in implementing price discrimination strategies. Please analyze customer data and suggest ways in which ChatGPT can help identify key factors influencing price sensitivity, enabling the development of targeted pricing strategies for different customer segments, geographical regions, or purchase history.

Idea: Psychological Pricing Techniques

ChatGPT can assist in exploring and implementing psychological pricing techniques such as charm pricing, decoy pricing, or anchoring to influence customer perception.

Example Prompt 1:
As a business analyst, I need ChatGPT to provide insights on implementing charm pricing techniques. Please explain how charm pricing works and suggest specific strategies that can be used to influence customer perception and increase sales.

Example Prompt 2:
ChatGPT, I require your assistance in exploring decoy pricing techniques. Please provide examples of how decoy pricing can be used effectively to influence customer decision-making and encourage higher-value purchases. Additionally, suggest ways to implement decoy pricing in our pricing strategy.

Example Prompt 3:
In order to influence customer perception and increase sales, I would like ChatGPT to help me understand anchoring techniques. Please explain how anchoring works and provide real-world examples of how businesses have successfully used anchoring to their advantage. Furthermore, suggest ways we can incorporate anchoring into our pricing strategy.

Example Prompt 4:
As a business analyst, I need ChatGPT to assist me in

implementing psychological pricing techniques. Please provide a comprehensive overview of charm pricing, decoy pricing, and anchoring, including their benefits and potential drawbacks. Additionally, suggest a step-by-step approach to implementing these techniques in our pricing strategy, considering our specific industry and target market.

Idea: Pricing for New Product Launches

ChatGPT can help in determining optimal pricing strategies for new product launches, considering factors like market positioning, competitive landscape, and target customer segments.

Example Prompt 1:

Prompt: "You are a business analyst working for a consumer electronics company. Use ChatGPT's advanced data processing functionality to analyze the market positioning, competitive landscape, and target customer segments for our new smartphone launch. Based on this information, provide recommendations for an optimal pricing strategy."

Example Prompt 2:

Prompt: "As a business analyst for a fashion retail company, leverage ChatGPT's advanced data processing capabilities to evaluate the market positioning, competitive landscape, and target customer segments for our upcoming clothing line launch. Considering these factors, suggest a pricing strategy that maximizes profitability while maintaining a competitive edge."

Example Prompt 3:

Prompt: "Imagine you are a business analyst assisting a food and beverage company in launching a new energy drink. Utilize ChatGPT's advanced data processing functionality to assess the market positioning, competitive landscape, and target customer segments. Based on this analysis, propose a pricing strategy that ensures a successful product launch and captures the intended market share."

Example Prompt 4:
Prompt: "You are a business analyst working for a software development company. Utilize ChatGPT's advanced data processing capabilities to analyze the market positioning, competitive landscape, and target customer segments for our new productivity software launch. Considering these factors, provide insights on an optimal pricing strategy that balances profitability and market penetration."

Idea: Pricing for International Markets

ChatGPT can support in analyzing market dynamics, currency fluctuations, and cultural differences to develop pricing strategies for international markets.

Example Prompt 1:
As a business analyst, I need ChatGPT to analyze market dynamics, currency fluctuations, and cultural differences to develop pricing strategies for international markets. Please provide insights on how different factors impact pricing decisions in international markets and suggest strategies to optimize pricing for maximum profitability.

Example Prompt 2:
ChatGPT, using its advanced data processing functionality, I need your support in analyzing market dynamics, currency fluctuations, and cultural differences to develop pricing strategies for international markets. Please provide a comprehensive analysis of the target market's economic conditions, competitive landscape, and consumer behavior to help determine the optimal pricing strategy for our products or services.

Example Prompt 3:
In my role as a business analyst, I require ChatGPT's assistance in understanding market dynamics, currency fluctuations, and cultural differences to develop pricing strategies for international

markets. Please analyze the impact of local economic conditions, purchasing power parity, and cultural preferences on pricing decisions. Additionally, suggest pricing strategies that can help us gain a competitive edge in each target market.

Example Prompt 4:

As a business analyst, I rely on ChatGPT's advanced data processing functionality to support me in analyzing market dynamics, currency fluctuations, and cultural differences for developing pricing strategies in international markets. Please provide a detailed analysis of the target market's inflation rates, exchange rates, and cultural nuances that influence consumer behavior. Based on this analysis, recommend pricing strategies that align with local market conditions and maximize profitability.

Idea: Pricing Analytics and Reporting

ChatGPT can aid in developing pricing dashboards, generating reports, and performing data analysis to monitor pricing performance and identify areas for improvement.

Example Prompt 1:

Prompt: "As a business analyst, I need ChatGPT to assist in developing a pricing dashboard for our company's products. Please provide step-by-step instructions on how to create a pricing dashboard that includes key metrics such as average price, price variance, and price elasticity. Additionally, suggest any visualizations or charts that would be helpful in monitoring pricing performance."

Example Prompt 2:

Prompt: "ChatGPT, please generate a report on our pricing performance for the past quarter. Include an analysis of pricing trends, customer segmentation based on price sensitivity, and any recommendations for optimizing our pricing strategy. The report should also highlight any outliers or anomalies in pricing data that *may require further investigation."*

Example Prompt 3:

Prompt: "We are looking to improve our pricing strategy for a specific product category. Can you assist in performing data analysis to identify pricing opportunities and potential areas for improvement? Please analyze historical sales data, competitor pricing, and customer feedback to provide insights on pricing optimization strategies, such as dynamic pricing or bundling options."

Example Prompt 4:

Prompt: "ChatGPT, we need your support in conducting a pricing sensitivity analysis for our new product launch. Please analyze customer survey data, historical sales data, and competitor pricing to determine the price elasticity of demand for the new product. Additionally, provide recommendations on pricing tiers or promotional strategies that would maximize revenue and market penetration."

SOCIAL MEDIA ANALYTICS

LEVERAGING SOCIAL MEDIA INSIGHTS

In the digital age, social media analytics is critical for understanding brand perception and customer sentiment. Artificial Intelligence (AI), especially tools like ChatGPT, is transforming this analysis, providing deeper insights into consumer behavior and trends.

Meet Laura, a business analyst at a lifestyle brand. Her challenge is to analyze social media data to understand how customers perceive their latest product line. Traditional methods of manual analysis are time-consuming and often miss subtle nuances in sentiment. Laura employs AI-driven analytics for a more efficient and comprehensive approach.

Using ChatGPT, Laura inputs vast amounts of social media data, including comments, likes, and shares related to their products. The AI tool adeptly processes this data, distinguishing between positive, negative, and neutral sentiments. It even identifies specific trends in customer feedback, such as high praise for product design but concerns over durability.

This nuanced analysis is invaluable for Laura. It enables her to provide actionable insights to the marketing and product development teams, leading to strategies that align closely with customer preferences and enhance brand reputation.

Laura's experience underscores the significance of AI in social media analytics. AI tools not only streamline data analysis but also offer a deeper understanding of customer sentiment, critical for strategic decision-making. In a world where social media plays a pivotal role in shaping brand perception, AI-driven analytics is an indispensable tool for business analysts.

In conclusion, AI's role in social media analytics represents a significant advancement in understanding and responding to customer sentiment. It equips analysts with the tools to extract meaningful insights from vast social media data, ensuring that strategies are data-driven and customer-focused. As AI technology continues to evolve, its impact on social media analytics and strategic decision-making will only deepen.

Note: Please be aware that the strategies, tasks, and ideas discussed in this chapter can be further refined by taking advantage of ChatGPT's Advanced Data Analysis feature. If you require additional information about this tool, you can find comprehensive coverage in

the previously authored chapter.

Task: Sentiment analysis

Analyzing the sentiment of social media posts or comments to determine whether they are positive, negative, or neutral.

Example Prompt 1:
Develop a ChatGPT model that can accurately analyze the sentiment of social media posts or comments. The model should be able to classify the sentiment as positive, negative, or neutral with a high degree of accuracy. Use ChatGPT's advanced data processing functionality to preprocess the social media data and extract relevant features for sentiment analysis.

Example Prompt 2:
Create a ChatGPT-based sentiment analysis system that can handle large volumes of social media data in real-time. Utilize ChatGPT's advanced data processing capabilities to efficiently process and analyze the sentiment of social media posts or comments, providing real-time insights into the overall sentiment trends.

Example Prompt 3:
Design a ChatGPT-powered sentiment analysis tool that can accurately identify and classify the sentiment of social media posts or comments in multiple languages. Leverage ChatGPT's advanced data processing functionality to handle multilingual data and ensure accurate sentiment analysis across different languages.

Example Prompt 4:
Build a ChatGPT-based sentiment analysis solution that can detect and analyze the sentiment of social media posts or comments in specific domains or industries. Utilize ChatGPT's advanced data processing capabilities to train the model on domain-specific data and improve the accuracy of sentiment analysis for industry-specific social media content.

Task: Trend analysis

Identifying and analyzing popular topics or trends on social media platforms to gain insights into customer preferences and market trends.

Example Prompt 1:

Develop a ChatGPT model that can analyze social media data to identify and categorize popular topics or trends based on customer preferences and market trends. The model should be able to provide insights into the frequency, sentiment, and engagement levels of these trends.

Example Prompt 2:

Create a ChatGPT system that can process and analyze large volumes of social media data in real-time to identify emerging trends and popular topics. The system should be able to generate reports highlighting the key trends, their growth patterns, and potential impact on customer preferences and market trends.

Example Prompt 3:

Design a ChatGPT-based solution that can perform sentiment analysis on social media conversations related to specific topics or trends. The solution should be able to identify the sentiment distribution, key influencers, and potential opportunities or risks associated with these trends.

Example Prompt 4:

Build a ChatGPT model that can predict the future popularity of specific topics or trends on social media platforms. The model should leverage advanced data processing techniques to analyze historical data, identify patterns, and provide insights into the potential growth or decline of these trends.

Task: Influencer identification

Identifying influential individuals or accounts on social media platforms who can potentially impact brand perception or drive engagement.

Example Prompt 1:
Develop a model using ChatGPT's Advanced Data processing functionality to analyze social media data and identify influential individuals or accounts based on their engagement metrics, such as number of followers, likes, comments, and shares.

Example Prompt 2:
Design a prompt that leverages ChatGPT's Advanced Data processing functionality to analyze user-generated content on social media platforms and identify influential individuals or accounts based on the sentiment and tone of their posts, as well as the level of engagement they generate.

Example Prompt 3:
Create a prompt utilizing ChatGPT's Advanced Data processing functionality to analyze social media data and identify influential individuals or accounts by considering their domain expertise, credibility, and the extent of their reach within specific target audiences.

Example Prompt 4:
Utilize ChatGPT's Advanced Data processing functionality to develop a prompt that can analyze social media data and identify influential individuals or accounts based on their ability to drive brand perception and engagement, considering factors such as the frequency and quality of their interactions with followers, as well as their ability to create viral content.

Task: Competitor analysis

Monitoring and analyzing the social media activities of competitors to identify their strategies, strengths, and weaknesses.

Example Prompt 1:

Develop a ChatGPT model that can analyze and summarize competitor social media activities, highlighting their key strategies, strengths, and weaknesses.

Example Prompt 2:
Create a ChatGPT system that can track and compare competitor social media engagement metrics, such as likes, shares, and comments, to identify trends and patterns.

Example Prompt 3:
Design a ChatGPT solution that can extract and analyze competitor social media content, including posts, hashtags, and user interactions, to uncover their content strategy and messaging.

Example Prompt 4:
Build a ChatGPT tool that can generate competitor social media performance reports, providing insights on their audience demographics, engagement rates, and overall social media presence.

Task: Content performance analysis

Evaluating the performance of social media content, such as posts or campaigns, by analyzing metrics like engagement, reach, and conversions.

Example Prompt 1:
Develop a ChatGPT model that can analyze social media content performance by extracting key metrics such as engagement, reach, and conversions. The model should be able to process large datasets and provide insights on the effectiveness of different posts or campaigns.

Example Prompt 2:
Design a ChatGPT system that can automatically generate reports on social media content performance. The system should be capable of processing raw data, calculating engagement rates, reach, and conversions, and presenting the results in a clear and

concise manner.

Example Prompt 3:
Create a ChatGPT solution that can identify patterns and trends in social media content performance. The system should be able to analyze historical data, detect correlations between different metrics, and provide actionable recommendations for improving future campaigns.

Example Prompt 4:
Build a ChatGPT model with advanced data processing capabilities to evaluate the impact of social media content on conversions. The model should be able to analyze conversion rates, identify factors that contribute to successful conversions, and suggest optimization strategies for maximizing conversion rates.

Task: Customer segmentation

Segmenting social media users based on their demographics, interests, or behavior to better understand target audiences and tailor marketing strategies.

Example Prompt 1:
Develop a data processing pipeline using ChatGPT's Advanced Data processing functionality to segment social media users based on their demographics, interests, and behavior. Provide a step-by-step guide on how to collect and preprocess social media data, extract relevant features, and apply clustering algorithms to identify distinct customer segments.

Example Prompt 2:
Design a ChatGPT-powered chatbot that interacts with social media users to collect data on their demographics, interests, and behavior. Utilize the Advanced Data processing functionality to analyze the collected data and generate customer segments. Provide recommendations on how to integrate the chatbot into social media platforms and leverage the segmented data for targeted marketing campaigns.

Example Prompt 3:
Explore the capabilities of ChatGPT's Advanced Data processing functionality to analyze social media data and identify key demographic, interest, and behavioral attributes that can be used for customer segmentation. Develop a comprehensive framework that combines natural language processing techniques, machine learning algorithms, and data visualization to effectively segment social media users and inform marketing strategies.

Example Prompt 4:
Leverage ChatGPT's Advanced Data processing functionality to build a predictive model that segments social media users based on their demographics, interests, and behavior. Provide a detailed analysis of the model's accuracy, precision, and recall metrics, along with recommendations on how to interpret and utilize the segmented data for targeted marketing campaigns. Additionally, discuss potential challenges and limitations of using AI-powered data processing for customer segmentation in the social media domain.

Task: Brand reputation monitoring

Tracking and analyzing mentions of a brand or product on social media to assess brand sentiment and identify potential reputation risks.

Example Prompt 1:
Develop a ChatGPT model that can analyze social media mentions of a brand or product to determine sentiment and identify potential reputation risks. The model should be able to process large volumes of data and provide real-time insights.

Example Prompt 2:
Create a ChatGPT system that can track and monitor social media conversations related to a specific brand or product. The system should be able to identify key themes, sentiment trends, and potential reputation risks, and provide regular reports or alerts to

the business analyst.

Example Prompt 3:
Design a ChatGPT-based solution that can automatically categorize social media mentions of a brand or product based on sentiment (positive, negative, neutral) and identify specific keywords or phrases that may indicate reputation risks. The solution should be scalable and able to handle a high volume of data.

Example Prompt 4:
Implement a ChatGPT-powered chatbot that can engage with social media users discussing a brand or product, gather feedback, and analyze sentiment in real-time. The chatbot should be able to identify potential reputation risks and escalate urgent issues to the appropriate stakeholders for immediate action.

Task: Social listening

Monitoring social media platforms for mentions of specific keywords, topics, or hashtags to gather insights about customer opinions, needs, or preferences.

Example Prompt 1:
Develop a ChatGPT model that can efficiently process and analyze social media data to identify customer sentiments, preferences, and needs related to specific keywords, topics, or hashtags. Provide a detailed report on the most frequently mentioned keywords and sentiments associated with them.

Example Prompt 2:
Create a ChatGPT system that can monitor social media platforms in real-time and generate alerts whenever there is a significant increase in mentions of specific keywords, topics, or hashtags. The system should also provide a summary of the overall sentiment and key themes associated with the mentions.

Example Prompt 3:

Design a ChatGPT-based solution that can categorize social media mentions based on customer opinions, needs, or preferences related to specific keywords, topics, or hashtags. The system should provide an interactive dashboard with visualizations to help stakeholders understand the distribution of sentiments and identify emerging trends.

Example Prompt 4:
Build a ChatGPT model that can analyze historical social media data to identify patterns and trends in customer opinions, needs, or preferences related to specific keywords, topics, or hashtags. The model should provide insights on how these preferences have evolved over time and recommend strategies to address emerging customer needs.

Task: Campaign tracking

Tracking the performance of social media campaigns by analyzing metrics like click-through rates, conversions, or return on investment (ROI).

Example Prompt 1:
ChatGPT, analyze the click-through rates of our recent social media campaign and identify any significant trends or patterns that could help us optimize our future campaigns.

Example Prompt 2:
ChatGPT, calculate the conversion rates for each social media platform we used in our campaign and provide insights on which platforms performed the best in terms of driving conversions.

Example Prompt 3:
ChatGPT, analyze the return on investment (ROI) for our social media campaign by comparing the cost of the campaign to the revenue generated. Additionally, provide recommendations on how we can improve the ROI for future campaigns.

Example Prompt 4:

ChatGPT, compare the performance metrics of our current social media campaign with our previous campaigns and identify any areas where we have seen improvements or declines. Additionally, suggest strategies to enhance the overall performance of our social media campaigns.

Task: Customer feedback analysis

Analyzing customer feedback or reviews on social media platforms to identify common issues, improve products or services, and enhance customer satisfaction.

Example Prompt 1:
Develop a ChatGPT model that can process and analyze customer feedback from social media platforms to identify common issues, improve products or services, and enhance customer satisfaction. The model should be able to extract sentiment, categorize feedback into different topics, and provide actionable insights for the business.

Example Prompt 2:
Create a ChatGPT system that can automatically collect and analyze customer reviews from various social media platforms. The system should be able to identify key themes and sentiments expressed by customers, highlight recurring issues, and suggest potential improvements to enhance customer satisfaction.

Example Prompt 3:
Design a ChatGPT-based solution that can process and analyze customer feedback in real-time from social media platforms. The solution should be able to identify emerging trends, detect sentiment changes, and provide timely recommendations to address customer concerns and improve overall customer satisfaction.

Example Prompt 4:
Build a ChatGPT model with advanced data processing capabilities to analyze customer feedback and reviews on social media

platforms. The model should be able to identify sentiment, extract key phrases, and categorize feedback into different topics. Additionally, it should provide actionable insights and recommendations to help businesses improve their products or services and enhance customer satisfaction.

Idea: Sentiment Analysis

Use ChatGPT to analyze social media posts and comments to determine the sentiment (positive, negative, neutral) towards your business or brand. This can help you gauge customer satisfaction and identify areas for improvement.

Example Prompt 1:
As a business analyst, I need ChatGPT to analyze social media posts and comments related to our brand and determine the sentiment (positive, negative, neutral) towards our business. Please provide a step-by-step guide on how to use ChatGPT's advanced data processing functionality to perform sentiment analysis on a dataset of social media posts and comments.

Example Prompt 2:
Our company wants to gauge customer satisfaction and identify areas for improvement by analyzing social media posts and comments about our brand. Can ChatGPT's advanced data processing functionality be used to perform sentiment analysis on a large dataset of social media data? If so, please explain the process and provide any necessary code or resources.

Example Prompt 3:
We are interested in using ChatGPT's advanced data processing functionality to analyze social media posts and comments to determine the sentiment towards our business. Could you provide a tutorial or example on how to preprocess the data, train a sentiment analysis model using ChatGPT, and evaluate its performance on our dataset?

Example Prompt 4:

As a business analyst, I want to leverage ChatGPT's advanced data processing functionality to analyze social media posts and comments about our brand and identify the sentiment (positive, negative, neutral) expressed by customers. Can you guide me on how to preprocess the data, fine-tune ChatGPT for sentiment analysis, and generate insights from the results?

Idea: Competitor Analysis

Utilize ChatGPT to gather insights on your competitors' social media presence. It can help you identify their strategies, engagement levels, and customer sentiment, allowing you to refine your own social media approach.

Example Prompt 1:

Prompt: "As a business analyst, I need ChatGPT to analyze my competitors' social media presence and provide insights on their strategies, engagement levels, and customer sentiment. Please gather information on the top three competitors in my industry and summarize their social media approach, including the platforms they are active on, the frequency of their posts, the types of content they share, and any notable engagement metrics."

Example Prompt 2:

Prompt: "ChatGPT, I require your assistance as a business analyst to evaluate my competitors' social media presence. Please analyze the sentiment of customer comments and reviews on their social media platforms and provide an overview of the overall customer sentiment towards each competitor. Additionally, identify any recurring themes or topics that customers frequently discuss in relation to my competitors' brands."

Example Prompt 3:

Prompt: "As a business analyst, I need ChatGPT to help me understand my competitors' social media strategies. Please analyze the engagement levels of my top three competitors by examining the number of likes, shares, comments, and followers they have on their social media platforms. Based on this analysis, provide recommendations on how I can refine my own social media approach to increase engagement and attract a larger audience."

Example Prompt 4:

Prompt: "ChatGPT, I require your expertise as a business analyst to conduct a comprehensive competitor analysis of their social media presence. Please analyze the content strategy of my top three competitors by identifying the most frequently used hashtags, keywords, and topics in their social media posts. Additionally, provide insights on the types of influencers or partnerships they engage with to enhance their social media reach and brand visibility."

Idea: Influencer Identification

ChatGPT can assist in identifying relevant influencers in your industry by analyzing their social media presence, engagement rates, and audience demographics. This can help you form partnerships and reach a wider audience.

Example Prompt 1:

As a business analyst, I need ChatGPT to assist me in identifying relevant influencers in the fashion industry. Please analyze their social media presence, engagement rates, and audience demographics to help me form partnerships and reach a wider audience.

Example Prompt 2:

ChatGPT, I require your advanced data processing functionality to help me identify influencers in the fitness and wellness industry. Analyze their social media presence, engagement rates, and audience demographics to assist me in forming partnerships and expanding my reach.

Example Prompt 3:

In my role as a business analyst, I need ChatGPT's support to identify relevant influencers in the technology sector. Please analyze their social media presence, engagement rates, and audience demographics to help me form strategic partnerships and reach a wider audience.

Example Prompt 4:
As a business analyst, I'm looking for ChatGPT's assistance in identifying influencers in the food and beverage industry. Utilize your advanced data processing functionality to analyze their social media presence, engagement rates, and audience demographics, enabling me to form valuable partnerships and expand my brand's reach.

Idea: Content Optimization

Use ChatGPT to analyze social media content and identify the most engaging posts. It can provide recommendations on optimizing content, such as using specific keywords, hashtags, or multimedia elements to increase reach and engagement.

Example Prompt 1:
As a business analyst, I need ChatGPT's advanced data processing functionality to analyze social media content and identify the most engaging posts. Please provide recommendations on optimizing content to increase reach and engagement. Specifically, suggest specific keywords or phrases that are currently popular and likely to resonate with the target audience.

Example Prompt 2:
ChatGPT, as a business analyst, I require your assistance in content optimization for social media. Analyze the existing posts and identify the most engaging ones. Provide recommendations on incorporating relevant hashtags that are currently trending and likely to boost reach and engagement. Additionally, suggest multimedia elements, such as images or videos, that can be used to enhance the content's appeal.

Example Prompt 3:
As a business analyst, I need ChatGPT's advanced data

processing capabilities to optimize social media content. Analyze the existing posts and identify the most engaging ones. Provide recommendations on incorporating specific keywords or phrases that are popular among the target audience. Additionally, suggest multimedia elements, such as infographics or GIFs, that can be used to make the content more visually appealing and increase its reach.

Example Prompt 4:
ChatGPT, I require your support as a business analyst to optimize social media content. Analyze the current posts and identify the most engaging ones. Provide recommendations on incorporating relevant hashtags that are currently trending and likely to increase reach and engagement. Additionally, suggest multimedia elements, such as interactive polls or quizzes, that can be used to make the content more interactive and encourage audience participation.

Idea: Customer Segmentation

ChatGPT can help in segmenting your social media audience based on their interests, demographics, and behavior. This information can be used to tailor marketing messages and create personalized campaigns.

Example Prompt 1:
Prompt: "As a business analyst, use ChatGPT's advanced data processing functionality to segment our social media audience based on their interests, demographics, and behavior. Provide insights on how we can tailor marketing messages and create personalized campaigns."

Example Prompt 2:
Prompt: "ChatGPT, analyze our social media audience and segment them based on their interests, demographics, and behavior. Provide recommendations on how we can effectively tailor marketing messages and create personalized campaigns to

engage each segment."

Example Prompt 3:

Prompt: "With the help of ChatGPT's advanced data processing capabilities, analyze our social media audience and segment them based on their interests, demographics, and behavior. Suggest strategies to tailor marketing messages and create personalized campaigns that resonate with each segment."

Example Prompt 4:

Prompt: "As a business analyst, leverage ChatGPT's advanced data processing functionality to segment our social media audience by their interests, demographics, and behavior. Provide actionable insights on how we can optimize marketing messages and create personalized campaigns to drive better engagement and conversions."

Idea: Social Listening

Utilize ChatGPT to monitor social media conversations related to your business or industry. It can help you identify customer pain points, emerging trends, and potential opportunities for product or service enhancements.

Example Prompt 1:

As a business analyst, use ChatGPT's advanced data processing functionality to monitor social media conversations related to our industry and identify customer pain points. Provide a summary of the top three pain points mentioned and suggest potential solutions or enhancements to address them.

Example Prompt 2:

Utilize ChatGPT's advanced data processing capabilities to monitor social media conversations about our business and industry. Identify emerging trends mentioned by customers and provide a report highlighting the top three trends, along with recommendations on how we can leverage these trends to enhance our products or services.

Example Prompt 3:

As a business analyst, leverage ChatGPT's advanced data processing functionality to monitor social media conversations related to our business or industry. Identify potential opportunities for product or service enhancements mentioned by customers and provide a detailed analysis of the top three opportunities, including suggestions on how we can capitalize on them.

Example Prompt 4:

Use ChatGPT's advanced data processing capabilities to monitor social media conversations about our business or industry. Identify customer pain points, emerging trends, and potential opportunities for product or service enhancements. Provide a comprehensive report summarizing the findings, along with actionable recommendations on how we can improve our offerings based on the insights gathered.

Idea: Crisis Management

ChatGPT can support in monitoring social media during a crisis or negative event. It can help identify and analyze customer complaints, sentiment, and public perception, allowing you to respond effectively and mitigate reputational damage.

Example Prompt 1:

Prompt: As a Crisis Management Analyst, use ChatGPT's Advanced Data processing functionality to monitor social media during a crisis or negative event. Identify and analyze customer complaints, sentiment, and public perception to help respond effectively and mitigate reputational damage.

Example Prompt 2:

Prompt: You are a Crisis Management professional seeking assistance from ChatGPT's Advanced Data processing functionality. Task ChatGPT to monitor social media platforms during a crisis or negative event. Analyze customer complaints, sentiment, and public perception to provide insights for an effective response and reputation management.

Example Prompt 3:
Prompt: As a Business Analyst specializing in Crisis Management, leverage ChatGPT's Advanced Data processing functionality to monitor social media during a crisis or negative event. Instruct ChatGPT to identify and analyze customer complaints, sentiment, and public perception. Utilize the insights to develop strategies for effective response and reputation mitigation.

Example Prompt 4:
Prompt: You are a Crisis Management expert relying on ChatGPT's Advanced Data processing functionality. Direct ChatGPT to monitor social media platforms during a crisis or negative event. Task ChatGPT to identify and analyze customer complaints, sentiment, and public perception. Leverage the insights to formulate an effective response plan and minimize reputational damage.

Idea: Influencer Campaign Evaluation
Use ChatGPT to evaluate the effectiveness of influencer marketing campaigns by analyzing engagement rates, sentiment, and conversions generated through social media. This can help optimize future campaigns and measure ROI.

Example Prompt 1:
Prompt: As a business analyst, I need your help to evaluate the effectiveness of our recent influencer marketing campaign. Please analyze the engagement rates, sentiment, and conversions generated through social media to provide insights that can help optimize future campaigns and measure ROI.

Example Prompt 2:
Prompt: Our company is investing in influencer marketing campaigns, and we need your expertise as a business analyst

to evaluate their effectiveness. Can you analyze the engagement rates, sentiment, and conversions generated through social media for these campaigns? Your insights will be crucial in optimizing future campaigns and measuring ROI accurately.

Example Prompt 3:

Prompt: We are looking to assess the impact of our influencer marketing campaigns, and we need your assistance as a business analyst. By analyzing the engagement rates, sentiment, and conversions generated through social media, you can provide valuable insights that will help us optimize future campaigns and measure ROI effectively. Please support us in this evaluation process.

Example Prompt 4:

Prompt: As a business analyst, we rely on your expertise to evaluate the effectiveness of our influencer marketing campaigns. By analyzing the engagement rates, sentiment, and conversions generated through social media, you can provide insights that will help us optimize future campaigns and measure ROI accurately. Your support in this evaluation process is highly appreciated.

Idea: Social Media ROI Analysis

ChatGPT can assist in analyzing the return on investment (ROI) of your social media efforts. It can help track key metrics such as conversions, website traffic, and customer acquisition costs, enabling you to measure the impact of your social media activities.

Example Prompt 1:

Prompt: "As a business analyst, I need ChatGPT to assist in analyzing the return on investment (ROI) of our social media efforts. Please provide a step-by-step guide on how to track key metrics such as conversions, website traffic, and customer acquisition costs using advanced data processing functionality."

Example Prompt 2:

Prompt: "ChatGPT, we are looking to measure the impact of our social media activities. Can you help us analyze the return on investment (ROI) by providing insights on how to effectively track conversions, website traffic, and customer acquisition costs? Please explain the advanced data processing techniques we can utilize for this analysis."

Example Prompt 3:

Prompt: "Our company wants to evaluate the success of our social media campaigns by measuring the return on investment (ROI). How can ChatGPT assist us in tracking key metrics such as conversions, website traffic, and customer acquisition costs? Please provide a detailed explanation of the advanced data processing functionality we can leverage for this analysis."

Example Prompt 4:

Prompt: "As a business analyst, I need ChatGPT's support in analyzing the ROI of our social media efforts. Can you guide me on how to utilize advanced data processing techniques to track and measure key metrics like conversions, website traffic, and customer acquisition costs? Please provide step-by-step instructions on how to perform this analysis using ChatGPT's capabilities."

INVESTMENT
ANALYSIS

MASTERING INVESTMENT ANALYSIS

In the intricate field of investment analysis, Artificial Intelligence (AI), particularly tools like ChatGPT, is redefining how business analysts evaluate potential investments, estimate ROI, and assess risks.

Imagine David, a business analyst in a venture capital firm. His task is to evaluate potential start-up investments. Traditionally, this involves manual analysis of financial statements, market trends, and competitor activities, a process often limited by human biases and the sheer volume of data. David, however, leverages AI to enhance his analysis.

Utilizing ChatGPT, he inputs extensive data sets, including financial models, market analysis, and historical performance metrics of similar startups. The AI tool processes this data efficiently, providing insights into potential ROI and highlighting risk factors. For example, it identifies a high-risk factor in a start-up's scalability model, which might have been overlooked in a manual review.

David's experience highlights the impact of AI in investment analysis. It's not just about crunching numbers; it's about gaining a holistic view of the investment landscape. AI tools like ChatGPT provide a more objective and comprehensive analysis, leading to better-informed investment decisions.

In conclusion, AI's integration into investment analysis is transforming the role of business analysts. It enables a more accurate and efficient evaluation of potential investments, crucial for making strategic decisions in the fast-paced investment world. As AI continues to advance, its role in investment analysis and decision-making will only grow, providing analysts with an ever-more sophisticated toolkit.

Note: It's important to remember that the strategies, tasks, and ideas presented in this chapter can be enhanced with the use of ChatGPT's Advanced Data Analysis feature. For a comprehensive understanding of this tool, kindly review the chapter that expounds on its functionalities.

Task: Financial statement analysis

Analyzing the financial statements of companies to assess their financial health and performance.

Example Prompt 1:
Using ChatGPT's Advanced Data processing functionality, analyze the financial statements of Company X for the past five years and identify any significant trends or patterns in their revenue growth, profitability, and liquidity ratios. Provide insights into the company's financial health and performance based on these

findings.

Example Prompt 2:
Leveraging ChatGPT's Advanced Data processing functionality, compare the financial statements of Company A and Company B for the latest fiscal year. Evaluate their key financial ratios, such as return on assets, debt-to-equity ratio, and current ratio, to determine which company is in a better financial position and why.

Example Prompt 3:
With the help of ChatGPT's Advanced Data processing functionality, conduct a comprehensive financial statement analysis of Company Y. Assess their income statement, balance sheet, and cash flow statement to identify any potential red flags or areas of concern. Provide recommendations on how the company can improve its financial health and performance.

Example Prompt 4:
Utilizing ChatGPT's Advanced Data processing functionality, perform a vertical and horizontal analysis of the financial statements of Company Z. Analyze their income statement and balance sheet over the past three years to identify any significant changes in revenue, expenses, assets, and liabilities. Interpret the findings to evaluate the company's financial stability and growth potential.

Task: Industry analysis

Evaluating the industry trends, competitive landscape, and market dynamics to identify investment opportunities.

Example Prompt 1:
Using ChatGPT's Advanced Data processing functionality, analyze the current industry trends in the technology sector and identify potential investment opportunities. Consider factors such as emerging technologies, market demand, and competitive landscape to provide insights for decision-making.

Example Prompt 2:
Leveraging ChatGPT's Advanced Data processing functionality, evaluate the competitive landscape and market dynamics of the healthcare industry. Identify key players, market share, and growth potential to assist in identifying investment opportunities in this sector.

Example Prompt 3:
Utilizing ChatGPT's Advanced Data processing functionality, conduct an industry analysis of the renewable energy sector. Assess market trends, government policies, and competitive forces to identify potential investment opportunities in this rapidly growing industry.

Example Prompt 4:
With the help of ChatGPT's Advanced Data processing functionality, analyze the current market dynamics and competitive landscape of the e-commerce industry. Evaluate consumer behavior, emerging trends, and competitive advantages of major players to identify potential investment opportunities in this highly competitive sector.

Task: Company valuation

Assessing the value of a company by analyzing its financials, market position, and growth prospects.

Example Prompt 1:
Using ChatGPT's Advanced Data processing functionality, analyze the financial statements of Company XYZ for the past five years and provide a comprehensive assessment of its financial health, including key financial ratios, profitability, liquidity, and solvency indicators. Additionally, evaluate the company's market position and growth prospects based on industry trends and competitive analysis.

Example Prompt 2:

Leveraging ChatGPT's Advanced Data processing functionality, conduct a comparative analysis of Company ABC and its competitors in terms of financial performance, market share, and growth potential. Provide insights on how Company ABC's financials, market position, and growth prospects compare to its industry peers, and identify any areas of strength or weakness that may impact its valuation.

Example Prompt 3:
Utilizing ChatGPT's Advanced Data processing functionality, evaluate the impact of macroeconomic factors on Company XYZ's valuation. Analyze the company's financials in relation to economic indicators such as GDP growth, interest rates, inflation, and consumer sentiment. Assess how these factors influence the company's market position and growth prospects, and provide recommendations on potential valuation adjustments.

Example Prompt 4:
With the help of ChatGPT's Advanced Data processing functionality, perform a comprehensive SWOT analysis of Company ABC to assess its strengths, weaknesses, opportunities, and threats. Analyze the company's financials, market position, and growth prospects to identify internal and external factors that may impact its valuation. Provide actionable insights on how the company can leverage its strengths and opportunities while mitigating weaknesses and threats to enhance its overall value.

Task: Risk assessment

Identifying and evaluating potential risks associated with an investment, such as market risks, regulatory risks, or operational risks.

Example Prompt 1:
Using ChatGPT's Advanced Data processing functionality, analyze and identify potential market risks associated with the investment opportunity. Provide insights on market trends,

competitor analysis, and economic indicators that may impact the investment's performance.

Example Prompt 2:
Leveraging ChatGPT's Advanced Data processing functionality, evaluate regulatory risks associated with the investment. Assess the current regulatory landscape, identify potential legal or compliance issues, and provide recommendations to mitigate these risks.

Example Prompt 3:
Utilizing ChatGPT's Advanced Data processing functionality, conduct a comprehensive assessment of operational risks related to the investment. Analyze factors such as supply chain vulnerabilities, operational inefficiencies, and potential disruptions to identify and evaluate potential risks.

Example Prompt 4:
With the help of ChatGPT's Advanced Data processing functionality, perform a holistic risk assessment for the investment opportunity. Consider market risks, regulatory risks, and operational risks, and provide a detailed analysis of the potential impact of these risks on the investment's success. Offer recommendations to mitigate and manage these risks effectively.

Task: Investment portfolio analysis
Analyzing the performance and composition of an investment portfolio to optimize asset allocation and diversification.

Example Prompt 1:
ChatGPT, analyze the historical performance of my investment portfolio and provide insights on the returns, volatility, and risk-adjusted metrics of each asset within the portfolio.

Example Prompt 2:
ChatGPT, evaluate the composition of my investment portfolio and suggest potential adjustments to optimize asset allocation

and diversification based on historical data and market trends.

Example Prompt 3:
ChatGPT, compare the performance of my investment portfolio against relevant benchmarks and provide recommendations on potential changes to enhance its risk-adjusted returns.

Example Prompt 4:
ChatGPT, analyze the correlation and covariance between different assets in my investment portfolio to identify potential diversification opportunities and suggest adjustments to minimize risk.

Task: Return on investment (ROI) analysis

Calculating and assessing the potential return on investment for a particular investment opportunity.

Example Prompt 1:
Using ChatGPT's Advanced Data processing functionality, analyze the financial data and investment details provided to calculate the potential return on investment (ROI) for the investment opportunity. Consider factors such as initial investment amount, projected cash flows, and estimated time horizon. Provide a comprehensive report outlining the ROI analysis and highlight any potential risks or uncertainties associated with the investment.

Example Prompt 2:
Leveraging ChatGPT's Advanced Data processing functionality, evaluate the historical financial performance of similar investment opportunities to estimate the potential ROI. Analyze relevant financial metrics, such as net present value (NPV), internal rate of return (IRR), and payback period. Present your findings in a clear and concise manner, including any assumptions made during the analysis.

Example Prompt 3:
Utilize ChatGPT's Advanced Data processing functionality to

conduct a comparative ROI analysis for multiple investment opportunities. Gather and analyze financial data for each opportunity, considering factors such as expected returns, risk levels, and investment timeframes. Present a detailed comparison of the potential ROI for each opportunity, along with recommendations on the most favorable investment option.

Example Prompt 4:
With the help of ChatGPT's Advanced Data processing functionality, perform a sensitivity analysis on the potential ROI for the investment opportunity. Explore different scenarios by adjusting key variables such as revenue growth rates, cost structures, and discount rates. Present a comprehensive analysis of how changes in these variables impact the ROI, enabling a better understanding of the investment's potential risks and rewards.

Task: Cash flow analysis

Evaluating the cash flow patterns of an investment to determine its profitability and sustainability.

Example Prompt 1:
Develop a ChatGPT model that can analyze the cash flow patterns of an investment over a specified time period. The model should be able to identify and categorize different types of cash flows such as operating activities, investing activities, and financing activities. Additionally, it should provide insights into the profitability and sustainability of the investment based on the cash flow analysis.

Example Prompt 2:
Create a ChatGPT system that can extract relevant financial data from a given investment portfolio and perform a comprehensive cash flow analysis. The system should be capable of calculating key financial metrics such as net cash flow, cash flow from operations, and free cash flow. It should also provide an assessment of the investment's profitability and sustainability based on the cash flow patterns observed.

Example Prompt 3:

Design a ChatGPT solution that can analyze the cash flow statements of multiple investments simultaneously. The solution should be able to compare and contrast the cash flow patterns of different investments, highlighting any significant differences or similarities. Additionally, it should provide recommendations on which investments are more profitable and sustainable based on their respective cash flow analyses.

Example Prompt 4:

Build a ChatGPT model that can predict future cash flow patterns of an investment based on historical data. The model should be trained on a dataset of past cash flows and be able to forecast future cash flows for a given investment. It should also provide insights into the potential profitability and sustainability of the investment based on the predicted cash flow patterns.

Task: Investment strategy development

Assisting in the development of investment strategies based on market research, risk assessment, and financial analysis.

Example Prompt 1:

ChatGPT, analyze the historical performance of various investment portfolios and identify the key factors that contributed to their success or failure. Based on this analysis, provide recommendations for developing investment strategies that maximize returns while minimizing risks.

Example Prompt 2:

ChatGPT, gather real-time market data and news articles related to specific industries or sectors. Process and summarize this information to identify emerging trends, potential risks, and investment opportunities. Based on your analysis, suggest investment strategies that align with the current market conditions.

Example Prompt 3:
ChatGPT, assess the risk profiles of different investment options, such as stocks, bonds, and mutual funds. Utilize advanced data processing techniques to analyze historical volatility, correlation, and other risk indicators. Provide insights and recommendations on constructing diversified investment portfolios that balance risk and return.

Example Prompt 4:
ChatGPT, conduct a comprehensive financial analysis of companies within a specific industry. Utilize advanced data processing capabilities to evaluate key financial metrics, such as revenue growth, profitability, and debt levels. Based on this analysis, assist in developing investment strategies that focus on companies with strong financial fundamentals and growth potential.

Task: Investment performance tracking

Monitoring and analyzing the performance of investments over time to assess their success and make informed decisions.

Example Prompt 1:
Develop a chat-based investment performance tracking system using ChatGPT's Advanced Data processing functionality. The system should allow users to input their investment details, such as asset type, purchase date, and purchase price. It should then provide real-time updates on the investment's performance, including current value, return on investment, and any relevant market news or trends. Additionally, the system should offer personalized insights and recommendations based on historical data and market analysis to assist users in making informed investment decisions.

Example Prompt 2:
Design a conversational interface powered by ChatGPT's Advanced Data processing functionality to track and monitor investment

performance. The interface should enable users to input their investment portfolio details, including asset allocation, investment amounts, and timeframes. It should then generate comprehensive reports and visualizations, highlighting key performance metrics such as annualized returns, volatility, and risk-adjusted returns. The system should also provide comparative analysis against relevant benchmarks and suggest potential adjustments to optimize portfolio performance.

Example Prompt 3:
Create an interactive chatbot leveraging ChatGPT's Advanced Data processing functionality to assist users in monitoring and analyzing their investment performance. The chatbot should allow users to input their investment transactions, including buy/sell orders, dividends, and fees. It should then generate personalized performance reports, including metrics like total return, annualized return, and portfolio diversification. The chatbot should also provide insights on investment trends, market news, and potential investment opportunities based on historical data and market analysis.

Example Prompt 4:
Build a dynamic investment performance monitoring tool using ChatGPT's Advanced Data processing functionality. The tool should enable users to import their investment data from various sources, such as brokerage accounts or spreadsheets. It should then process and analyze the data to generate comprehensive performance dashboards, including visualizations of portfolio growth, asset allocation breakdowns, and historical returns. The tool should also offer advanced features like scenario analysis, stress testing, and risk assessment to help users make informed investment decisions and optimize their portfolio performance.

Task: Investment recommendation

Providing recommendations on potential investment opportunities based on thorough analysis and evaluation.

Example Prompt 1:

ChatGPT, analyze the historical performance and financial indicators of Company X and provide an investment recommendation based on your evaluation.

Example Prompt 2:

Using ChatGPT's advanced data processing functionality, assess the market trends and growth potential of Industry Y. Provide an investment recommendation for potential opportunities within this industry.

Example Prompt 3:

ChatGPT, analyze the risk factors and financial stability of Company Z. Based on your evaluation, recommend whether it is a suitable investment option for long-term growth.

Example Prompt 4:

Leveraging ChatGPT's advanced data processing capabilities, evaluate the macroeconomic factors and industry dynamics affecting the renewable energy sector. Provide investment recommendations for sustainable energy companies with high growth potential.

Idea: Portfolio Optimization

ChatGPT can assist in analyzing investment portfolios by providing insights on asset allocation, risk assessment, and diversification strategies.

Example Prompt 1:

Prompt: As a business analyst, I need ChatGPT to assist in analyzing investment portfolios by providing insights on asset allocation, risk assessment, and diversification strategies. Please generate a report summarizing the asset allocation of a given portfolio and suggest any necessary adjustments to optimize the portfolio's performance.

Example Prompt 2:

Prompt: ChatGPT, as a business analyst, I require your assistance in evaluating the risk associated with a given investment portfolio. Please analyze the historical performance of the assets within the portfolio and provide insights on the risk levels, including volatility, standard deviation, and correlation coefficients. Additionally, suggest any diversification strategies that could help mitigate risk.

Example Prompt 3:
Prompt: As a business analyst, I need ChatGPT to help me optimize an investment portfolio by suggesting asset allocation strategies. Please provide recommendations on the ideal allocation percentages for different asset classes, such as stocks, bonds, and commodities, based on historical data and risk-return trade-offs. Additionally, consider any specific investment goals or constraints provided.

Example Prompt 4:
Prompt: ChatGPT, I require your expertise as a business analyst to assist in rebalancing an investment portfolio. Please analyze the current asset allocation and suggest adjustments to bring the portfolio back to its target allocation. Consider factors such as the portfolio's risk tolerance, investment objectives, and any specific constraints. Additionally, provide insights on the potential impact of the proposed changes on the portfolio's risk and return characteristics.

Idea: Risk Management
ChatGPT can help in evaluating and quantifying investment risks, such as market volatility, credit risk, and liquidity risk, to support decision-making.

Example Prompt 1:
Prompt: As a business analyst, I need ChatGPT to evaluate market volatility and its impact on investment risks. Please provide a detailed analysis of the current market conditions, highlighting

any potential risks and their potential consequences for decision-making.

Example Prompt 2:
Prompt: ChatGPT, as a risk management tool, I need your assistance in quantifying credit risk associated with potential investments. Please analyze the creditworthiness of a specific company or industry, considering factors such as financial statements, credit ratings, and market trends. Provide an assessment of the credit risk level and suggest appropriate risk mitigation strategies.

Example Prompt 3:
Prompt: ChatGPT, I require your support in evaluating liquidity risk for a portfolio of investments. Please analyze the liquidity of various assets within the portfolio, considering factors such as trading volume, bid-ask spreads, and market depth. Provide insights on potential liquidity risks and recommend strategies to manage and mitigate these risks effectively.

Example Prompt 4:
Prompt: As a business analyst, I need ChatGPT to assist in decision-making by evaluating and quantifying investment risks associated with specific financial instruments. Please analyze the risk-return profile of a particular investment, considering factors such as historical performance, volatility, and correlation with other assets. Provide an assessment of the investment's risk level and suggest suitable risk management techniques to optimize decision-making.

Idea: Performance Measurement

ChatGPT can provide analysis on investment performance metrics, such as return on investment (ROI), Sharpe ratio, and alpha, to assess the effectiveness of investment strategies.

Example Prompt 1:
Calculate the return on investment (ROI) for a given investment

strategy and provide an analysis of its effectiveness. Please include the formula used to calculate ROI and any assumptions made in the analysis.

Example Prompt 2:
Evaluate the Sharpe ratio for a portfolio of investments and provide insights into the risk-adjusted performance. Please explain the formula used to calculate the Sharpe ratio and interpret the results in terms of the investment strategy's effectiveness.

Example Prompt 3:
Assess the alpha of a specific investment strategy and provide an analysis of its ability to outperform the market. Please describe the methodology used to calculate alpha and provide insights into the strategy's performance relative to the benchmark.

Example Prompt 4:
Analyze the performance metrics, including ROI, Sharpe ratio, and alpha, for a diversified investment portfolio. Please provide a comprehensive assessment of the portfolio's effectiveness in generating returns and managing risk, highlighting any notable strengths or weaknesses.

Idea: Valuation Analysis

ChatGPT can assist in conducting valuation analysis for various investment assets, including stocks, bonds, real estate, and derivatives, by considering factors like cash flows, market trends, and comparable transactions.

Example Prompt 1:
Prompt: "Perform a valuation analysis for a specific stock by considering its cash flows, market trends, and comparable transactions. Provide a comprehensive report outlining the estimated value and potential investment opportunities."

Example Prompt 2:
Prompt: "Conduct a valuation analysis for a real estate

property by analyzing its cash flows, market trends, and comparable transactions. Generate a detailed report highlighting the property's estimated value, potential rental income, and investment prospects."

Example Prompt 3:

Prompt: "Assist in evaluating the valuation of a bond by analyzing its cash flows, market trends, and comparable transactions. Provide insights on the bond's estimated value, yield, and potential risks associated with the investment."

Example Prompt 4:

Prompt: "Perform a valuation analysis for a derivative instrument by considering its cash flows, market trends, and comparable transactions. Generate a comprehensive report outlining the estimated value, potential risks, and investment opportunities associated with the derivative."

Idea: Industry and Market Research

ChatGPT can support business analysts in conducting research on specific industries or markets to identify investment opportunities, analyze competitive landscapes, and assess market trends.

Example Prompt 1:

Prompt: As a business analyst, I need ChatGPT's advanced data processing functionality to conduct industry research on the renewable energy sector. Please provide an analysis of investment opportunities, competitive landscapes, and market trends in this industry.

Example Prompt 2:

Prompt: ChatGPT, as a business analyst, I require your support in researching the e-commerce market. Utilize your advanced data processing capabilities to identify potential investment opportunities, analyze the competitive landscape, and assess the latest market trends in this industry.

Example Prompt 3:
Prompt: As a business analyst, I need ChatGPT to assist me in conducting market research on the healthcare sector. Please leverage your advanced data processing functionality to identify promising investment opportunities, analyze the competitive landscape, and provide insights into the latest market trends in this industry.

Example Prompt 4:
Prompt: ChatGPT, as a business analyst, I require your expertise in researching the technology industry. Utilize your advanced data processing capabilities to identify lucrative investment opportunities, analyze the competitive landscape, and assess the current market trends in this sector.

Idea: Financial Modeling

ChatGPT can aid in building financial models to forecast investment returns, assess the impact of different scenarios, and perform sensitivity analysis to guide investment decisions.

Example Prompt 1:
Prompt: "As a business analyst, I need assistance from ChatGPT to build a financial model for forecasting investment returns. Please provide step-by-step guidance on how to structure the model, identify relevant variables, and apply appropriate forecasting techniques to make accurate predictions."

Example Prompt 2:
Prompt: "ChatGPT, I require your support in assessing the impact of different scenarios on investment returns. Please help me analyze various market conditions, economic factors, and industry trends to determine how they influence investment outcomes. Additionally, suggest suitable sensitivity analysis techniques to evaluate the robustness of the model."

Example Prompt 3:

Prompt: "I am a business analyst seeking ChatGPT's expertise in building a financial model that can guide investment decisions. Please assist me in identifying key performance indicators (KPIs) and developing a comprehensive framework to evaluate investment opportunities. Furthermore, provide insights on how to incorporate risk assessment and probability analysis into the model."

Example Prompt 4:

Prompt: "ChatGPT, I need your assistance in leveraging advanced data processing capabilities to build a financial model that accurately forecasts investment returns. Please guide me on how to gather and preprocess relevant financial data, select appropriate statistical techniques for modeling, and validate the model's accuracy using historical data. Additionally, suggest methods to incorporate external factors such as market sentiment and regulatory changes into the model."

Idea: Due Diligence

ChatGPT can assist in conducting due diligence on potential investment opportunities, including analyzing financial statements, assessing management capabilities, and evaluating legal and regulatory compliance.

Example Prompt 1:

As a business analyst, I need ChatGPT to assist me in conducting due diligence on a potential investment opportunity. Please analyze the financial statements of Company XYZ, assess their management capabilities, and evaluate their legal and regulatory compliance. Provide me with a comprehensive report summarizing your findings.

Example Prompt 2:

ChatGPT, I require your advanced data processing functionality to support me in performing due diligence on a potential investment opportunity. *Please analyze the financial statements of Company ABC, assess the competence of their management team, and evaluate their adherence to legal and regulatory requirements. Present your analysis in a structured format, highlighting any potential risks or concerns.*

Example Prompt 3:
In my role as a business analyst, I need ChatGPT's assistance in conducting due diligence on a potential investment opportunity. Please analyze the financial statements of Company DEF, assess the effectiveness of their management team, and evaluate their compliance with legal and regulatory frameworks. Provide me with a detailed assessment, including any red flags or areas of concern.

Example Prompt 4:
ChatGPT, I require your support as a business analyst to conduct due diligence on a potential investment opportunity. Please analyze the financial statements of Company GHI, assess the capabilities of their management team, and evaluate their adherence to legal and regulatory obligations. Generate a comprehensive due diligence report, highlighting any key findings or potential risks that may impact the investment decision.

Idea: Investment Strategy Development

ChatGPT can provide insights and recommendations on developing investment strategies tailored to specific goals, risk tolerance, and time horizons.

Example Prompt 1:
As a business analyst, I need assistance from ChatGPT to develop an investment strategy for a client who has a moderate risk tolerance and a long-term time horizon. Please provide insights and recommendations on how to tailor the investment strategy to meet these specific requirements.

Example Prompt 2:

ChatGPT, I require your expertise as a business analyst to help me develop an investment strategy for a client who has a short-term time horizon and a low risk tolerance. Please provide insights and recommendations on how to create an investment strategy that aligns with these specific goals.

Example Prompt 3:

I'm working on developing an investment strategy for a client with a high risk tolerance and a medium-term time horizon. As a business analyst, I would appreciate your insights and recommendations on how to tailor the investment strategy to suit these specific requirements.

Example Prompt 4:

ChatGPT, I need your assistance as a business analyst to develop an investment strategy for a client who has a conservative risk tolerance and a long-term time horizon. Please provide insights and recommendations on how to create an investment strategy that aligns with these specific goals.

Idea: Investment Decision Support

ChatGPT can provide decision support by analyzing investment opportunities, conducting cost-benefit analysis, and assessing the alignment of investments with business objectives.

Example Prompt 1:

Prompt: As a business analyst, I need ChatGPT to analyze an investment opportunity and provide decision support. Please assess the potential return on investment (ROI) for investing in a new technology platform and evaluate its alignment with our business objectives.

Example Prompt 2:

Prompt: ChatGPT, I require your assistance as a business analyst to conduct a cost-benefit analysis for a potential investment opportunity. Please evaluate the financial costs and benefits of expanding our manufacturing facilities and determine if it aligns with our business objectives.

Example Prompt 3:
Prompt: As a business analyst, I need ChatGPT to provide decision support by analyzing an investment opportunity. Please assess the market potential and profitability of investing in a renewable energy project, considering its alignment with our business objectives.

Example Prompt 4:
Prompt: ChatGPT, I require your expertise as a business analyst to evaluate an investment opportunity and provide decision support. Please analyze the risks and rewards associated with investing in a new product line and assess its alignment with our business objectives.

Idea: Regulatory Compliance Analysis

ChatGPT can assist in analyzing investment activities to ensure compliance with relevant regulations, such as securities laws, anti-money laundering (AML) regulations, and investor protection guidelines.

Example Prompt 1:
Prompt: As a business analyst, I need ChatGPT to assist in analyzing investment activities to ensure compliance with relevant regulations. Please provide a summary of the key provisions of the securities laws that apply to investment activities.

Example Prompt 2:
Prompt: ChatGPT, please analyze a given investment portfolio and identify any potential violations of anti-money laundering (AML) regulations. Provide recommendations on how to address these violations and ensure compliance.

Example Prompt 3:
Prompt: As a business analyst, I require ChatGPT's assistance

in analyzing investment activities to ensure compliance with investor protection guidelines. Please provide an evaluation of a specific investment product's compliance with these guidelines, highlighting any areas of concern or non-compliance.

Example Prompt 4:

Prompt: ChatGPT, please analyze a series of investment transactions and identify any potential regulatory compliance issues, such as violations of securities laws or investor protection guidelines. Provide a detailed report outlining the identified issues and suggest corrective actions to ensure compliance.

REGULATORY COMPLIANCE CHECK

NAVIGATING REGULATORY COMPLIANCE

In the complex realm of regulatory compliance, Artificial Intelligence (AI), particularly tools like ChatGPT, is revolutionizing the way business analysts ensure adherence to relevant laws and regulations. It provides a more comprehensive and efficient approach to compliance checks.

Consider Sarah, a business analyst at a financial institution. Her role involves ensuring that the company's financial practices comply with evolving financial regulations. Traditional compliance checks involve laborious manual reviews, which may lead to oversight. Sarah turns to AI for a more rigorous and systematic approach.

Using ChatGPT, she inputs the latest regulatory documents, financial reports, and transaction data. The AI tool analyzes this information swiftly and accurately, flagging any potential compliance issues. For instance, it identifies a discrepancy in transaction reporting that could have led to regulatory fines.

Sarah's experience underscores the transformative power of AI in regulatory compliance checks. It doesn't just automate the process; it enhances accuracy and ensures compliance in an ever-changing regulatory landscape. AI tools empower business analysts to identify and address compliance issues proactively, reducing the risk of costly violations.

In conclusion, the integration of AI in regulatory compliance checks is indispensable for business analysts. It offers a more robust and efficient means of ensuring adherence to laws and regulations, safeguarding a company's reputation and financial stability. As AI technology continues to advance, its role in regulatory compliance will become increasingly critical, providing analysts with a vital ally in navigating the intricacies of regulatory compliance.

Task: Researching regulatory requirements

ChatGPT can provide information on specific regulations and their implications for your business.

Example Prompt 1:
Can you provide an overview of the regulatory requirements for businesses operating in the healthcare industry? Please include any specific regulations that impact patient data privacy and security.

Example Prompt 2:
What are the key regulatory requirements that businesses need to comply with when operating in the financial services sector? Please highlight any regulations related to anti-money laundering and consumer protection.

Example Prompt 3:
Could you provide information on the regulatory requirements for businesses involved in the production and distribution of food products? Specifically, I'm interested in understanding the regulations related to food safety and labeling.

Example Prompt 4:
What are the current regulatory requirements for businesses operating in the technology sector? Please focus on any regulations related to data protection and privacy, as well as cybersecurity.

Task: Identifying applicable regulations

ChatGPT can help you determine which regulations are relevant to your industry and operations.

Example Prompt 1:
ChatGPT, please provide a list of regulations that are applicable to the [insert industry] industry and our specific operations.

Example Prompt 2:
Can you help me identify the key regulations that we need to comply with in our industry? Please consider our operations and any specific requirements.

Example Prompt 3:
I need assistance in determining the regulations that are relevant to our industry and operations. Could you provide a summary of the most important ones?

Example Prompt 4:
ChatGPT, please analyze our industry and operations to identify the regulations that we should be aware of and comply with. Additionally, provide any specific requirements or guidelines associated with these regulations.

Task: Analyzing regulatory changes

ChatGPT can assist in monitoring and understanding updates to regulations that may impact your business.

Example Prompt 1:
Can you provide me with the latest updates on regulatory changes in the [specific industry] sector that may affect our business

operations?

Example Prompt 2:
How can ChatGPT help us stay informed about regulatory changes and their potential impact on our business?

Example Prompt 3:
What are the key regulations that have been recently introduced or modified, and how might they impact our compliance requirements?

Example Prompt 4:
In what ways can ChatGPT assist us in analyzing and interpreting complex regulatory language to ensure our business remains compliant with the latest changes?

Task: Assessing compliance gaps

ChatGPT can help identify areas where your business may not be fully compliant with regulatory requirements.

Example Prompt 1:
ChatGPT, please analyze our current data privacy practices and identify any potential compliance gaps with relevant data protection regulations such as GDPR or CCPA.

Example Prompt 2:
Can you help me assess our company's adherence to financial regulations? Please identify any areas where we may not be fully compliant with laws such as Sarbanes-Oxley or Anti-Money Laundering (AML) regulations.

Example Prompt 3:
ChatGPT, please review our advertising and marketing strategies and highlight any potential non-compliance with consumer protection laws, such as false advertising or unfair competition practices.

Example Prompt 4:

Assist me in evaluating our cybersecurity measures and identify any potential compliance gaps with industry-specific regulations like HIPAA (Health Insurance Portability and Accountability Act) or PCI DSS (Payment Card Industry Data Security Standard).

Task: Developing compliance strategies

ChatGPT can provide insights and suggestions for developing effective strategies to ensure regulatory compliance.

Example Prompt 1:
ChatGPT, what are some key considerations for developing compliance strategies in the financial industry? Provide insights and suggestions on how businesses can ensure regulatory compliance while maintaining operational efficiency.

Example Prompt 2:
ChatGPT, can you provide examples of compliance challenges faced by businesses in the healthcare sector? Offer insights and suggestions on how organizations can develop effective strategies to meet regulatory requirements and protect patient data privacy.

Example Prompt 3:
ChatGPT, what are the current regulatory trends in the technology industry? Provide insights and suggestions on how businesses can develop compliance strategies to address emerging regulations such as data protection, cybersecurity, and privacy.

Example Prompt 4:
ChatGPT, how can businesses ensure compliance with environmental regulations and sustainability standards? Offer insights and suggestions on developing effective strategies to minimize environmental impact, promote sustainable practices, and meet regulatory requirements in industries such as manufacturing or energy.

Task: Creating compliance documentation

ChatGPT can assist in generating compliance reports, policies, and procedures to meet regulatory standards.

Example Prompt 1:
Please generate a compliance report for our organization's financial operations, ensuring that it aligns with the latest regulatory standards in the industry.

Example Prompt 2:
ChatGPT, help me draft a comprehensive policy document that outlines our company's data protection and privacy measures, in accordance with relevant data protection laws and regulations.

Example Prompt 3:
Assist me in creating a set of procedures that ensure our organization's adherence to anti-money laundering (AML) regulations. The procedures should cover customer due diligence, transaction monitoring, and reporting suspicious activities.

Example Prompt 4:
Please generate a compliance checklist for our organization's HR department, outlining the necessary steps and documentation required to ensure compliance with employment laws, including hiring practices, employee contracts, and workplace safety regulations.

Task: Conducting compliance audits

ChatGPT can help in designing audit checklists and providing guidance on conducting compliance audits.

Example Prompt 1:
Can you provide a checklist for conducting compliance audits in the financial industry? Include key areas to assess, such as risk management, internal controls, and regulatory compliance.

Example Prompt 2:
Please guide me on how to conduct a compliance audit for data privacy regulations, specifically focusing on areas like data

collection, storage, and sharing practices.

Example Prompt 3:
Design an audit checklist for assessing compliance with environmental regulations in manufacturing industries. Include criteria related to waste management, emissions control, and adherence to sustainability standards.

Example Prompt 4:
Assist me in creating a comprehensive compliance audit checklist for healthcare organizations, covering areas like patient data protection, HIPAA compliance, and adherence to medical billing and coding regulations.

Task: Evaluating risk and impact

ChatGPT can assist in assessing the potential risks and impacts of non-compliance with specific regulations.

Example Prompt 1:
ChatGPT, please evaluate the potential risks and impacts of non-compliance with the General Data Protection Regulation (GDPR) for our organization. Consider both financial and reputational consequences.

Example Prompt 2:
ChatGPT, assess the potential risks and impacts of non-compliance with the Health Insurance Portability and Accountability Act (HIPAA) in our healthcare organization. Focus on the legal penalties and potential loss of patient trust.

Example Prompt 3:
ChatGPT, analyze the potential risks and impacts of non-compliance with the Payment Card Industry Data Security Standard (PCI DSS) for our e-commerce platform. Consider the financial losses due to data breaches and the potential damage to our brand reputation.

Example Prompt 4:

ChatGPT, help us evaluate the potential risks and impacts of non-compliance with the Sarbanes-Oxley Act (SOX) for our publicly traded company. Focus on the legal consequences, financial penalties, and potential loss of investor confidence.

Task: Providing compliance training

ChatGPT can offer guidance and resources for training employees on regulatory compliance.

Example Prompt 1:
Can you provide an overview of the key regulations and compliance requirements that our employees need to be aware of in their day-to-day work?

Example Prompt 2:
How can ChatGPT assist in delivering interactive compliance training sessions to our employees, ensuring they understand the importance of regulatory compliance?

Example Prompt 3:
What are some effective strategies or resources that ChatGPT can recommend for creating engaging compliance training materials?

Example Prompt 4:
In what ways can ChatGPT help in assessing the effectiveness of our compliance training programs and identifying areas for improvement?

Task: Monitoring compliance activities

ChatGPT can help in setting up systems to monitor ongoing compliance efforts and provide alerts for potential issues.

Example Prompt 1:
How can ChatGPT assist in monitoring compliance activities and providing real-time alerts for potential issues?

Example Prompt 2:

What are the key features or functionalities that ChatGPT can offer to support ongoing compliance monitoring?

Example Prompt 3:
Can ChatGPT help in automating the identification and reporting of compliance violations or deviations?

Example Prompt 4:
In what ways can ChatGPT be integrated with existing compliance systems to enhance monitoring and alerting capabilities?

Idea: Compliance Checklist Generator

Develop a tool that generates customized compliance checklists based on specific regulatory requirements, helping businesses ensure they are meeting all necessary compliance standards.

Example Prompt 1:
As a business analyst, I need ChatGPT to assist in developing a Compliance Checklist Generator tool. Please provide step-by-step instructions on how to create a customized compliance checklist based on specific regulatory requirements. Include details on how the tool will help businesses ensure they meet all necessary compliance standards.

Example Prompt 2:
ChatGPT, please explain the importance of compliance checklists for businesses in meeting regulatory requirements. Describe how a Compliance Checklist Generator tool can streamline the process of creating customized checklists based on specific regulations. Highlight the benefits this tool can offer to businesses in terms of time-saving and accuracy.

Example Prompt 3:
As a business analyst, I require ChatGPT's support in designing a user-friendly interface for the Compliance Checklist Generator tool. Please provide recommendations on the key features and

functionalities that should be included in the tool to make it intuitive and efficient for businesses to generate customized compliance checklists. Consider factors such as ease of use, accessibility, and the ability to track compliance progress.

Example Prompt 4:
ChatGPT, please outline the potential challenges that businesses may face when trying to meet compliance standards. Explain how the Compliance Checklist Generator tool can address these challenges and assist businesses in ensuring they are meeting all necessary regulatory requirements. Provide examples of how the tool's features can help overcome common compliance obstacles and improve overall compliance management.

Idea: Compliance Document Repository

Create a centralized repository where businesses can store and manage all their compliance-related documents, making it easier to access and track regulatory information.

Example Prompt 1:
As a business analyst, I need ChatGPT to provide a step-by-step guide on how to design and develop a compliance document repository. Please outline the key features and functionalities that should be included in this centralized repository.

Example Prompt 2:
ChatGPT, can you assist in identifying the potential challenges and risks associated with implementing a compliance document repository? Please provide insights on how businesses can mitigate these risks and ensure the security and integrity of their regulatory information.

Example Prompt 3:
Businesses often struggle with organizing and categorizing their compliance-related documents. How can ChatGPT help in developing an efficient tagging system for the repository, ensuring easy retrieval and tracking of regulatory information?

Example Prompt 4:
ChatGPT, please provide recommendations on the best practices for integrating the compliance document repository with existing business systems and processes. How can businesses ensure seamless integration and maximize the benefits of this centralized repository?

Idea: Compliance Training Assistant

Build a virtual assistant that provides on-demand training and guidance on regulatory compliance topics, helping businesses educate their employees and stay up-to-date with changing regulations.

Example Prompt 1:

Prompt: "As a Compliance Training Assistant, provide an overview of the latest regulatory compliance updates in the financial industry and explain how these changes impact businesses. Additionally, suggest best practices for businesses to ensure compliance with these regulations."

Example Prompt 2:

Prompt: "As a Compliance Training Assistant, create a step-by-step training guide on data privacy regulations, such as GDPR or CCPA. Include key concepts, compliance requirements, and practical examples to help businesses understand and implement necessary measures to protect customer data."

Example Prompt 3:

Prompt: "As a Compliance Training Assistant, simulate a conversation between an employee and a supervisor regarding a potential compliance violation. Guide the employee through the appropriate steps to report the incident, ensuring confidentiality and protection against retaliation, and explain the importance of whistleblowing in maintaining a compliant work environment."

Example Prompt 4:

Prompt: "As a Compliance Training Assistant, develop a series of interactive quizzes to test employees' knowledge and understanding of regulatory compliance topics. Include questions on various compliance areas, such as anti-money laundering, workplace safety, or environmental regulations, and provide immediate feedback to reinforce learning and identify areas for improvement."

Idea: Compliance Risk Assessment Tool

Design a tool that assesses the level of compliance risk for different business processes and identifies areas that require immediate attention, enabling businesses to proactively address compliance gaps.

Example Prompt 1:
Design a compliance risk assessment tool that analyzes various business processes and provides a comprehensive report highlighting potential compliance gaps. The tool should offer recommendations on how businesses can proactively address these gaps to mitigate compliance risks. Please describe the key features and functionalities of this tool.

Example Prompt 2:
Develop a chat-based compliance risk assessment tool that allows businesses to input their specific business processes and receive real-time feedback on the level of compliance risk associated with each process. The tool should also identify areas that require immediate attention and suggest actionable steps to address compliance gaps. Please outline the user interface and interaction flow for this chat-based tool.

Example Prompt 3:
Create an interactive compliance risk assessment tool that integrates with existing business systems and databases to gather relevant data for analysis. The tool should evaluate the compliance risk level for different business processes based on

predefined criteria and generate a visual dashboard highlighting areas that require immediate attention. Please explain how this tool can effectively integrate with various business systems and databases.

Example Prompt 4:
Imagine a compliance risk assessment tool that utilizes machine learning algorithms to continuously monitor and assess the level of compliance risk for different business processes. The tool should learn from historical data and adapt its risk assessment capabilities over time. Additionally, it should provide real-time alerts and notifications to businesses, enabling them to proactively address compliance gaps. Please elaborate on the machine learning techniques and data sources that can be utilized to build such a dynamic compliance risk assessment tool.

Idea: Compliance Reporting Dashboard

Develop a dashboard that consolidates compliance data from various sources and presents it in a visually appealing format, allowing businesses to monitor their compliance status in real-time.

Example Prompt 1:
Design a Compliance Reporting Dashboard that integrates data from multiple sources, such as financial systems, HR databases, and regulatory platforms. The dashboard should provide real-time updates on businesses' compliance status, highlighting any potential risks or violations. Please describe the key features and visual elements you would include in this dashboard.

Example Prompt 2:
Develop a ChatGPT-powered Compliance Reporting Dashboard that enables businesses to interactively explore and analyze their compliance data. The dashboard should allow users to ask questions about specific compliance metrics, generate compliance reports on-demand, and receive proactive alerts for any

compliance issues. Please outline the conversational capabilities and user interface components you would incorporate into this dashboard.

Example Prompt 3:
Create a visually appealing Compliance Reporting Dashboard that consolidates compliance data from various sources, such as audit logs, incident reports, and policy documentation. The dashboard should provide an intuitive overview of businesses' compliance status, including trend analysis, compliance scores, and key performance indicators. Please outline the data visualization techniques and interactive elements you would utilize to enhance the user experience.

Example Prompt 4:
Build an AI-powered Compliance Reporting Dashboard that leverages natural language processing to extract and analyze compliance data from unstructured sources, such as emails, contracts, and legal documents. The dashboard should offer businesses the ability to search and filter compliance information, identify potential compliance gaps, and generate comprehensive compliance reports. Please describe the AI capabilities and data processing techniques you would employ to ensure accurate and efficient compliance monitoring.

Idea: Compliance Audit Tracker

Create a system that tracks and manages compliance audits, including scheduling, documentation, and follow-up actions, streamlining the audit process for businesses.

Example Prompt 1:
Prompt: "As a compliance audit tracker, help businesses streamline their audit process by providing a comprehensive system that manages scheduling, documentation, and follow-up actions. Design a user-friendly interface that allows businesses to easily schedule audits, upload and store relevant documentation, and

track the progress of each audit. Additionally, ensure the system generates automated reminders for upcoming audits and follow-up actions, reducing the risk of non-compliance."

Example Prompt 2:

Prompt: "Develop an efficient compliance audit tracker that assists businesses in managing their audit process. Enable the system to generate customizable audit schedules based on regulatory requirements and business preferences. Implement a centralized document management feature that allows businesses to securely store and organize audit-related documents. Furthermore, provide an intuitive dashboard that displays real-time audit progress, highlights pending follow-up actions, and generates comprehensive reports for management review."

Example Prompt 3:

Prompt: "Create a user-friendly compliance audit tracking system that simplifies the audit process for businesses. Incorporate an intelligent scheduling module that considers various factors such as audit frequency, regulatory deadlines, and resource availability to generate optimized audit schedules. Implement a document repository that supports version control, document sharing, and collaboration among audit stakeholders. Additionally, enable the system to automatically assign and track follow-up actions, ensuring timely resolution and compliance."

Example Prompt 4:

Prompt: "Design a comprehensive compliance audit tracker that streamlines the audit process for businesses. Develop an intuitive interface that allows businesses to easily schedule audits, assign auditors, and allocate resources. Implement a centralized repository for storing audit-related documents, ensuring easy access and retrieval. Furthermore, enable the system to generate automated notifications and reminders for upcoming audits, pending follow-up actions, and approaching regulatory deadlines, enhancing compliance and reducing administrative burden."

Idea: Compliance Policy Review Assistant

Build an AI-powered assistant that analyzes and reviews compliance policies, highlighting any inconsistencies or gaps, and suggesting improvements to ensure alignment with regulatory requirements.

Example Prompt 1:

As a compliance policy review assistant, help me analyze and review a compliance policy document to identify any inconsistencies or gaps in alignment with regulatory requirements. Provide suggestions for improvements to ensure compliance with the relevant regulations.

Example Prompt 2:

Develop an AI-powered assistant that can review and analyze compliance policies, highlighting any inconsistencies or gaps that may exist in relation to regulatory requirements. Additionally, provide recommendations on how to improve the policy to ensure full compliance.

Example Prompt 3:

Create a chatbot assistant capable of analyzing compliance policies and identifying any inconsistencies or gaps that may exist in relation to regulatory requirements. The assistant should then suggest improvements to ensure the policy aligns with the necessary regulations.

Example Prompt 4:

Build an AI-powered assistant that specializes in reviewing compliance policies. The assistant should be able to analyze a policy document, identify any inconsistencies or gaps, and provide actionable recommendations to ensure the policy aligns with regulatory requirements.

Idea: Compliance Change Management Tool

Design a tool that helps businesses manage regulatory changes by tracking updates, assessing their impact on existing processes, and facilitating the implementation of necessary changes.

Example Prompt 1:

Prompt: "As a compliance change management tool, help businesses track regulatory updates and assess their impact on existing processes. Provide step-by-step guidance on implementing necessary changes."

Example Prompt 2:

Prompt: "Design a tool that assists businesses in managing regulatory changes by tracking updates, assessing their impact on existing processes, and facilitating the implementation of necessary changes. Provide a user-friendly interface that allows users to easily navigate through the tool's features and access relevant information."

Example Prompt 3:

Prompt: "As a compliance change management tool, support businesses in staying up-to-date with regulatory changes by providing real-time notifications and alerts. Additionally, help users assess the impact of these changes on their existing processes and guide them through the implementation of required modifications."

Example Prompt 4:

Prompt: "Design a comprehensive compliance change management tool that enables businesses to effectively manage regulatory updates. Develop a system that allows users to track changes, evaluate their impact on existing processes, and collaborate with relevant stakeholders to implement necessary modifications. Ensure the tool provides detailed reporting and analytics to support decision-making processes."

Idea: Compliance Incident Reporting System

Develop a system that enables businesses to report compliance incidents, track their resolution, and generate comprehensive incident reports, ensuring transparency and accountability.

Example Prompt 1:

Prompt: *"Design a user-friendly interface for a Compliance Incident Reporting System that allows businesses to easily report compliance incidents. The system should include features such as incident categorization, severity levels, and the ability to attach relevant documents or evidence. Provide step-by-step instructions on how to navigate and utilize the system effectively."*

Example Prompt 2:

Prompt: *"Develop an automated tracking mechanism within the Compliance Incident Reporting System that enables businesses to monitor the progress and resolution of reported incidents. The system should allow users to assign responsible parties, set deadlines, and receive real-time notifications on updates or escalations. Describe how this tracking mechanism ensures transparency and accountability throughout the incident resolution process."*

Example Prompt 3:

Prompt: *"Create a comprehensive incident reporting template within the Compliance Incident Reporting System that generates detailed incident reports. The template should capture essential information such as incident description, date and time, individuals involved, and any corrective actions taken. Explain how this template promotes consistency in reporting and facilitates the generation of accurate and standardized incident reports."*

Example Prompt 4:

Prompt: *"Integrate data analytics capabilities into the Compliance Incident Reporting System to provide businesses with valuable insights. Develop a dashboard that visualizes incident trends, identifies recurring compliance issues, and highlights areas for improvement. Discuss how these analytics empower businesses to proactively address compliance risks and enhance overall transparency and accountability."*

Idea: Compliance Knowledge Base

Create a knowledge base that contains comprehensive information on regulatory compliance requirements, serving as a valuable resource for businesses seeking guidance and clarification.

Example Prompt 1:

As a compliance-focused business analyst, I need ChatGPT to help me create a comprehensive knowledge base on regulatory compliance requirements. Please provide a detailed overview of the key regulatory frameworks and standards that businesses should be aware of, along with their specific compliance requirements and implications.

Example Prompt 2:

ChatGPT, I need your assistance in building a valuable resource for businesses seeking guidance on regulatory compliance. Can you compile a list of common compliance challenges faced by organizations across different industries? Include practical tips and best practices to address these challenges effectively, ensuring businesses can navigate the complex landscape of regulatory requirements.

Example Prompt 3:

In order to support businesses in their compliance efforts, I want ChatGPT to help me develop a knowledge base that covers various compliance documentation and reporting obligations. Please provide a comprehensive list of the essential documents and reports that businesses should maintain to demonstrate compliance with regulatory requirements. Include any specific deadlines or frequency of reporting, if applicable.

Example Prompt 4:

As a business analyst working on the compliance knowledge base project, I need ChatGPT to assist me in creating a section that focuses on emerging compliance trends and regulatory updates. Please gather information on recent regulatory changes, upcoming compliance requirements, and any industry-specific updates that businesses should be aware of. Additionally, provide insights on how these changes may impact businesses and suggest proactive measures to ensure ongoing compliance.

Idea: Compliance Workflow Automation

Implement an automated workflow system that streamlines compliance-related processes, such as document approvals, policy reviews, and compliance training, reducing manual effort and ensuring consistency.

Example Prompt 1:
Prompt: "As a compliance officer, I need an automated workflow system to streamline compliance-related processes. Please describe how ChatGPT can assist in implementing an efficient compliance workflow automation solution that reduces manual effort and ensures consistency. Provide step-by-step guidance on how to set up the system, including document approvals, policy reviews, and compliance training."

Example Prompt 2:
Prompt: "Imagine you are a business owner who wants to implement an automated workflow system to streamline compliance processes. Explain how ChatGPT can help in designing and implementing a compliance workflow automation solution. Discuss the benefits of such a system, including reducing manual effort, ensuring consistency, and improving overall compliance efficiency."

Example Prompt 3:
Prompt: "You are a compliance manager responsible for implementing an automated workflow system to streamline

compliance-related processes. Describe how ChatGPT can assist in developing a comprehensive compliance workflow automation solution. Highlight the key features and functionalities that should be included in the system to effectively manage document approvals, policy reviews, and compliance training."

Example Prompt 4:
Prompt: "As a business analyst, you have been assigned the task of recommending an automated workflow system for compliance-related processes. Explain how ChatGPT can support in identifying the best practices and tools required to implement a compliance workflow automation solution. Discuss the potential challenges and considerations that should be taken into account while designing and implementing the system, ensuring it reduces manual effort and maintains consistency."

Idea: Compliance Data Analytics

Utilize data analytics techniques to analyze compliance-related data and identify patterns, trends, and potential risks, empowering businesses to make data-driven decisions and enhance their compliance strategies.

Example Prompt 1:
Prompt: "As a compliance data analytics expert, I need ChatGPT to assist me in analyzing compliance-related data. Please provide step-by-step guidance on how to utilize data analytics techniques to identify patterns, trends, and potential risks within the data. Additionally, suggest ways in which businesses can leverage these insights to make data-driven decisions and enhance their compliance strategies."

Example Prompt 2:
Prompt: "ChatGPT, I require your support in understanding the various data analytics techniques that can be applied to compliance-related data. Please explain how businesses can use these techniques to identify patterns, trends, and potential risks.

Furthermore, provide examples of how data-driven decisions based on these insights can enhance compliance strategies and ensure regulatory compliance."

Example Prompt 3:

Prompt: "As a business analyst specializing in compliance data analytics, I need ChatGPT's assistance in exploring the benefits of utilizing data analytics techniques for compliance purposes. Please elaborate on the specific patterns, trends, and potential risks that can be identified through data analysis. Additionally, suggest ways in which businesses can effectively implement these insights to enhance their compliance strategies and mitigate compliance-related risks."

Example Prompt 4:

Prompt: "ChatGPT, I require your expertise in compliance data analytics to guide me on the best practices for analyzing compliance-related data. Please outline the key steps involved in utilizing data analytics techniques to identify patterns, trends, and potential risks. Furthermore, provide insights on how businesses can leverage these findings to make informed, data-driven decisions and strengthen their compliance strategies."

STAKEHOLDER ENGAGEMENT ANALYSIS

ENGAGING WITH STAKEHOLDERS EFFECTIVELY

In the domain of stakeholder engagement analysis, Artificial Intelligence (AI), particularly tools like ChatGPT, is reshaping how business analysts identify and understand the needs and expectations of key stakeholders. It offers a more comprehensive and data-driven approach to stakeholder engagement.

Meet Alex, a business analyst tasked with assessing stakeholder expectations for a software development project. Traditional methods of stakeholder interviews and surveys can be time-consuming and may not capture all nuances. Alex leverages AI to gain deeper insights.

Using ChatGPT, he inputs data from stakeholder interactions, project documents, and past communication records. The AI tool processes this information, identifying recurring themes and sentiments among stakeholders. It even suggests potential areas of concern that might have been overlooked.

Alex's experience highlights AI's transformative role in stakeholder engagement analysis. It provides a data-driven foundation for understanding stakeholder needs and expectations, ensuring that projects are aligned with stakeholder interests.

In conclusion, AI's integration into stakeholder engagement analysis equips business analysts with tools to derive more insightful and data-driven insights from stakeholder interactions. This is essential for building strong relationships and ensuring project success. As AI technologies continue to advance, their impact on stakeholder engagement will only deepen, offering more sophisticated means of understanding and meeting stakeholder needs.

Task: Stakeholder identification

ChatGPT can help in brainstorming and identifying potential stakeholders for a project or initiative.

Example Prompt 1:

ChatGPT, let's brainstorm and identify potential stakeholders for a new software development project aimed at improving our customer support system. Who are the key individuals or groups that might have an interest or be affected by this initiative?

Example Prompt 2:

ChatGPT, help me identify stakeholders for a marketing campaign targeting a new product launch. Who are the individuals or teams within our organization, as well as external parties, that we should consider involving or consulting with?

Example Prompt 3:

ChatGPT, let's explore potential stakeholders for a sustainability initiative within our company. Who are the employees, departments, or external organizations that might have a vested interest in this project and could contribute to its success?

Example Prompt 4:

ChatGPT, assist me in identifying stakeholders for a process improvement project in our manufacturing department. Which individuals or teams within our organization, including suppliers or customers, should be considered as stakeholders for this initiative?

Task: Stakeholder mapping

ChatGPT can assist in creating a visual representation of stakeholders and their relationships, helping to identify key influencers and decision-makers.

Example Prompt 1:
Can you provide a detailed description of the stakeholders involved in your project or organization? Please include their roles, responsibilities, and any known relationships or dependencies between them.

Example Prompt 2:
Please describe the decision-making process within your project or organization. How do stakeholders contribute to the decision-making process, and are there any specific influencers or key decision-makers?

Example Prompt 3:
Could you provide a list of stakeholders who have a direct impact on your project or organization? Additionally, please indicate any stakeholders who have a strong influence or control over the outcomes.

Example Prompt 4:
In order to create a visual representation of stakeholders and their relationships, it would be helpful to understand the communication channels and interactions between stakeholders. Can you describe how stakeholders communicate and collaborate with each other?

Task: Stakeholder analysis

ChatGPT can provide insights and perspectives on stakeholders' interests, needs, and concerns, helping to prioritize engagement strategies.

Example Prompt 1:

ChatGPT, analyze the interests and needs of our stakeholders in the context of our current project. Provide insights on how we can prioritize our engagement strategies accordingly.

Example Prompt 2:

ChatGPT, identify the key concerns and potential challenges that our stakeholders might have regarding our upcoming initiative. Suggest effective ways to address these concerns and prioritize our engagement efforts.

Example Prompt 3:

ChatGPT, analyze the different stakeholder groups involved in our project and provide insights on their respective interests, needs, and concerns. Help us develop a comprehensive engagement strategy that prioritizes the most critical stakeholders.

Example Prompt 4:

ChatGPT, assess the level of influence and power that each stakeholder holds in our project. Provide insights on how we can prioritize our engagement strategies based on stakeholder importance and potential impact on project outcomes.

Task: Stakeholder communication planning

ChatGPT can assist in developing communication plans tailored to different stakeholder groups, considering their preferences and communication channels.

Example Prompt 1:

ChatGPT, help me develop a communication plan for our executive stakeholders. Consider their preferences and communication channels, and provide recommendations on the most effective ways to engage with them.

Example Prompt 2:
ChatGPT, assist me in creating a communication plan for our project team members. Take into account their preferences and communication channels, and suggest strategies to ensure effective and timely information sharing within the team.

Example Prompt 3:
ChatGPT, I need your support in developing a communication plan for our external stakeholders, such as customers and partners. Consider their preferences and communication channels, and provide guidance on how to effectively engage with them to build strong relationships and address their needs.

Example Prompt 4:
ChatGPT, help me create a communication plan for our internal stakeholders, including employees and managers. Take into consideration their preferences and communication channels, and suggest strategies to foster transparent and efficient communication within the organization.

Task: Stakeholder engagement strategy development

ChatGPT can help in formulating strategies to engage stakeholders effectively, considering their level of influence and potential impact on the project.

Example Prompt 1:
ChatGPT, based on the project objectives and stakeholder analysis, suggest strategies to engage stakeholders with high influence and high potential impact on the project. Consider both direct and indirect methods of engagement.

Example Prompt 2:
Develop a stakeholder engagement strategy that prioritizes

stakeholders with low influence but high potential impact on the project. Provide recommendations on how to effectively communicate and involve these stakeholders in decision-making processes.

Example Prompt 3:

ChatGPT, propose strategies to engage stakeholders with high influence but low potential impact on the project. Consider approaches such as regular updates, seeking their input on non-critical aspects, and leveraging their networks to influence other stakeholders.

Example Prompt 4:

Formulate a stakeholder engagement strategy that focuses on stakeholders with both high influence and high potential impact on the project. Provide specific tactics to build strong relationships, gain their support, and ensure their active involvement throughout the project lifecycle.

Task: Stakeholder feedback collection

ChatGPT can aid in designing surveys or questionnaires to gather feedback from stakeholders, ensuring their opinions and suggestions are considered.

Example Prompt 1:

As a business analyst, you are tasked with gathering stakeholder feedback to improve our products/services. Design a survey using ChatGPT that includes open-ended questions to capture stakeholders' opinions and suggestions on how we can enhance our offerings.

Example Prompt 2:

ChatGPT can assist you in creating a questionnaire to collect stakeholder feedback on our recent product launch. Develop a set of multiple-choice questions that cover various aspects such as usability, features, and overall satisfaction, allowing stakeholders to provide their input easily.

Example Prompt 3:
In order to understand stakeholders' preferences and expectations, create a survey using ChatGPT that includes Likert scale questions. Design a series of statements related to our business processes or customer experience and ask stakeholders to rate their level of agreement or satisfaction.

Example Prompt 4:
As a business analyst, you need to gather feedback from stakeholders on a new marketing campaign. Utilize ChatGPT to design a questionnaire that includes both qualitative and quantitative questions. Incorporate a mix of open-ended questions to capture detailed feedback and rating-based questions to measure stakeholders' perception of the campaign's effectiveness.

Task: Stakeholder relationship management

ChatGPT can provide guidance on building and maintaining positive relationships with stakeholders, fostering trust and collaboration.

Example Prompt 1:
How can I effectively communicate with stakeholders to build trust and collaboration?

Example Prompt 2:
What strategies can I employ to identify and understand the needs and expectations of different stakeholders?

Example Prompt 3:
Can you provide examples of successful stakeholder engagement practices that have led to positive relationships?

Example Prompt 4:
How can I proactively address conflicts or disagreements with stakeholders to maintain positive relationships?

Task: Stakeholder conflict resolution

ChatGPT can offer suggestions and approaches to address conflicts or disagreements among stakeholders, aiming for mutually beneficial resolutions.

Example Prompt 1:

Prompt: "Two stakeholders in a project have conflicting opinions on the project timeline. One stakeholder believes the timeline is too aggressive, while the other stakeholder insists it is too lenient. Discuss the concerns of both stakeholders and propose a compromise that ensures project success while addressing their individual needs."

Example Prompt 2:

Prompt: "A stakeholder is concerned about the allocation of resources in a project, feeling that their department is not receiving adequate support. Another stakeholder believes the resource allocation is fair and necessary for the project's overall success. Engage in a conversation with both stakeholders, understand their perspectives, and suggest a solution that balances resource allocation while meeting project objectives."

Example Prompt 3:

Prompt: "Two stakeholders have differing opinions on the prioritization of project features. One stakeholder believes certain features are critical for success, while the other stakeholder argues for different features to be prioritized. Engage in a dialogue with both stakeholders, explore the rationale behind their preferences, and propose a prioritization strategy that incorporates their concerns and maximizes project value."

Example Prompt 4:

Prompt: "A stakeholder is dissatisfied with the communication channels established for project updates, feeling that they are not receiving timely and relevant information. Another stakeholder believes the current communication channels are sufficient and efficient. Engage in a conversation with both stakeholders, understand their communication needs, and suggest an improved communication plan that addresses their concerns and ensures effective information flow."

Task: Stakeholder engagement evaluation

ChatGPT can assist in developing metrics and methods to evaluate the effectiveness of stakeholder engagement activities, helping to identify areas for improvement.

Example Prompt 1:
How can ChatGPT be utilized to measure the level of stakeholder engagement in a given project or initiative?

Example Prompt 2:
What metrics or indicators can ChatGPT generate to evaluate the effectiveness of stakeholder engagement activities?

Example Prompt 3:
In what ways can ChatGPT assist in identifying areas for improvement in stakeholder engagement strategies?

Example Prompt 4:
Can ChatGPT provide insights or recommendations on how to enhance stakeholder engagement based on the evaluation of past activities?

Task: Stakeholder engagement reporting

ChatGPT can help in preparing reports or presentations summarizing stakeholder engagement efforts, outcomes, and recommendations for future actions.

Example Prompt 1:
Please provide a summary of the stakeholder engagement activities conducted during the past quarter, including the key stakeholders involved, the methods used for engagement, and the main topics discussed.

Example Prompt 2:
Can you generate a report outlining the outcomes and feedback received from stakeholders regarding a specific project or initiative? Please include any concerns, suggestions, or recommendations provided by the stakeholders.

Example Prompt 3:
Prepare a presentation summarizing the key findings and insights gathered from stakeholder engagement efforts. Include any notable trends, patterns, or recurring themes identified during the engagement process.

Example Prompt 4:
Create a report that highlights the effectiveness of stakeholder engagement strategies employed by the organization. Include metrics such as stakeholder satisfaction levels, participation rates, and the impact of stakeholder feedback on decision-making processes.

Idea: Stakeholder Mapping

Use ChatGPT to assist in identifying and categorizing stakeholders based on their interests, influence, and level of engagement with the business.

Example Prompt 1:
Prompt: "As a business analyst, I need assistance in stakeholder mapping. Please help me identify and categorize stakeholders based on their interests, influence, and level of engagement with the business. Provide a comprehensive list of stakeholders and their corresponding attributes."

Example Prompt 2:
Prompt: "ChatGPT, I require your support in stakeholder mapping for our business. Please analyze the various stakeholders involved and categorize them based on their interests, influence, and level of engagement. Additionally, provide insights on how these

stakeholders may impact our business strategy and decision-making process."

Example Prompt 3:
Prompt: "As a business analyst, I'm seeking assistance in stakeholder mapping. Help me identify and categorize stakeholders based on their interests, influence, and level of engagement with our organization. Furthermore, provide recommendations on how to effectively engage and manage these stakeholders to ensure successful business outcomes."

Example Prompt 4:
Prompt: "ChatGPT, I need your expertise in stakeholder mapping for our business analysis. Please assist me in identifying and categorizing stakeholders based on their interests, influence, and level of engagement. Additionally, provide insights on potential conflicts of interest among stakeholders and suggest strategies to mitigate them for better business alignment."

Idea: Stakeholder Needs Assessment

ChatGPT can help in conducting surveys or interviews with stakeholders to gather their feedback, opinions, and requirements, enabling a comprehensive analysis of their needs.

Example Prompt 1:
As a business analyst, I need ChatGPT to assist in conducting stakeholder surveys to gather their feedback and requirements. Please design a conversation where ChatGPT acts as an interviewer and asks stakeholders relevant questions to assess their needs and expectations.

Example Prompt 2:
ChatGPT can play a crucial role in conducting stakeholder interviews to gather their opinions and feedback. Create a prompt where ChatGPT acts as a facilitator, guiding stakeholders through a conversation to understand their requirements and preferences

in detail.

Example Prompt 3:

Stakeholder needs assessment is a critical step in any project. Utilize ChatGPT to simulate a survey scenario where it interacts with stakeholders, collects their feedback, and compiles a comprehensive analysis of their needs. The prompt should encourage stakeholders to provide detailed responses to ensure accurate requirements gathering.

Example Prompt 4:

ChatGPT's conversational abilities can be leveraged to conduct stakeholder interviews and gather their feedback effectively. Develop a prompt where ChatGPT acts as a virtual interviewer, engaging stakeholders in a conversation to understand their needs, expectations, and any specific requirements they may have.

Idea: Stakeholder Engagement Metrics

ChatGPT can assist in defining key performance indicators (KPIs) and metrics to measure the effectiveness of stakeholder engagement activities, such as response rates, satisfaction levels, or participation rates.

Example Prompt 1:

As a business analyst, I need ChatGPT to assist in defining key performance indicators (KPIs) and metrics to measure the effectiveness of stakeholder engagement activities. Please provide a list of potential KPIs and metrics that can be used to evaluate response rates during stakeholder engagement initiatives.

Example Prompt 2:

ChatGPT plays a crucial role in stakeholder engagement activities. Can you help me identify KPIs and metrics that can be used to measure satisfaction levels of stakeholders when interacting with ChatGPT? Please provide a comprehensive list of potential metrics that can be used for this purpose.

Example Prompt 3:
Stakeholder participation rates are essential for evaluating the success of engagement activities. How can ChatGPT contribute to defining KPIs and metrics that accurately measure the level of stakeholder participation during interactions? Please suggest a range of metrics that can be used to assess participation rates effectively.

Example Prompt 4:
As a business analyst, I need ChatGPT's support in establishing KPIs and metrics to measure the effectiveness of stakeholder engagement activities. Can you provide a set of metrics that can be used to evaluate the overall impact and success of stakeholder engagement initiatives, considering factors such as response rates, satisfaction levels, and participation rates?

Idea: Stakeholder Influence Analysis

Use ChatGPT to analyze the level of influence each stakeholder holds within the organization or industry, helping prioritize engagement efforts accordingly.

Example Prompt 1:
Prompt: "As a business analyst, I need ChatGPT to perform a stakeholder influence analysis within an organization. Please analyze the level of influence each stakeholder holds and provide insights to help prioritize engagement efforts accordingly. Consider factors such as their role, decision-making power, relationships, and past actions."

Example Prompt 2:
Prompt: "ChatGPT, I require your assistance as a business analyst to conduct a stakeholder influence analysis in the industry we operate in. Analyze the level of influence each stakeholder holds and provide recommendations on how to prioritize engagement efforts. Consider their position in the industry, reputation, connections, and any significant actions they have taken."

Example Prompt 3:

Prompt: "In my role as a business analyst, I need ChatGPT to help me analyze the level of influence each stakeholder holds within our organization. Please assess their influence based on factors such as their hierarchical position, access to resources, decision-making authority, and relationships with other stakeholders. Provide insights to guide our prioritization of engagement efforts."

Example Prompt 4:

Prompt: "As a business analyst, I require ChatGPT's support to conduct a stakeholder influence analysis in our organization or industry. Please evaluate the level of influence each stakeholder holds by considering their expertise, network, financial resources, and involvement in key projects. Provide recommendations on how to prioritize engagement efforts based on these insights."

Idea: Stakeholder Engagement Training

ChatGPT can support the development of training materials or interactive modules to educate employees on effective stakeholder engagement techniques and best practices.

Example Prompt 1:

Prompt: "As a business analyst, I need ChatGPT to support the development of training materials for stakeholder engagement. Please provide a step-by-step guide on how to effectively engage with stakeholders during project planning and execution. Include key techniques, best practices, and real-life examples to make the training interactive and engaging."

Example Prompt 2:

Prompt: "ChatGPT, we need your assistance in creating an interactive module for stakeholder engagement training. Design a module that covers the importance of stakeholder identification, analysis, and prioritization. Include practical exercises and case studies to help employees understand how to effectively engage with different types of stakeholders. Provide tips on building trust, managing conflicts, and maintaining positive relationships throughout the engagement process."

Example Prompt 3:

Prompt: "As a business analyst, I require ChatGPT's support in developing training materials for stakeholder engagement. Create a comprehensive training package that focuses on effective communication strategies for engaging stakeholders. Include guidance on active listening, clear and concise messaging, and adapting communication styles to different stakeholders. Provide examples of successful communication techniques and pitfalls to avoid."

Example Prompt 4:

Prompt: "ChatGPT, we need your expertise in creating training materials for stakeholder engagement. Develop an interactive workshop that educates employees on the importance of continuous stakeholder engagement throughout the project lifecycle. Include modules on stakeholder mapping, feedback collection, and incorporating stakeholder input into decision-making processes. Provide practical tips on maintaining ongoing communication channels and adapting engagement strategies based on stakeholder needs and expectations."

Idea: Stakeholder Feedback Analysis

Utilize ChatGPT to analyze and interpret stakeholder feedback, identifying patterns, trends, and areas of improvement for the business.

Example Prompt 1:

Prompt: "As a business analyst, I need ChatGPT's assistance to analyze and interpret stakeholder feedback for our business. Please provide a detailed analysis of the feedback received from our customers, highlighting any patterns, trends, and areas of improvement that can help us enhance our products and services."

Example Prompt 2:

Prompt: "ChatGPT, we require your support in analyzing stakeholder feedback to gain insights into our business's strengths and weaknesses. Please analyze the feedback received from our stakeholders, identify any recurring themes or patterns, and suggest actionable recommendations to improve our overall performance."

Example Prompt 3:

Prompt: "As a business analyst, I rely on ChatGPT to help me analyze stakeholder feedback effectively. Please review the feedback provided by our stakeholders and identify any emerging trends, sentiments, or areas of concern. Additionally, provide recommendations on how we can address these concerns and enhance our business operations."

Example Prompt 4:

Prompt: "ChatGPT, we need your expertise in analyzing stakeholder feedback to drive continuous improvement in our business. Please analyze the feedback received from our stakeholders, identify any significant trends or patterns, and provide actionable insights to help us make informed decisions and enhance our overall stakeholder satisfaction."

Idea: Stakeholder Engagement Technology Evaluation

Use ChatGPT to evaluate and recommend suitable technology platforms or tools for enhancing stakeholder engagement, such as CRM systems or collaboration platforms.

Example Prompt 1:

As a business analyst, evaluate and recommend suitable technology platforms or tools for enhancing stakeholder engagement, such as CRM systems or collaboration platforms. Provide an overview of the key features and benefits of each recommended platform, and explain how they can effectively improve stakeholder engagement.

Example Prompt 2:
ChatGPT, analyze and compare different CRM systems or collaboration platforms available in the market for enhancing stakeholder engagement. Consider factors such as ease of use, scalability, integration capabilities, and customization options. Provide a detailed evaluation of each platform, highlighting their strengths and weaknesses.

Example Prompt 3:
Evaluate and recommend technology platforms or tools that can effectively enhance stakeholder engagement in a remote work environment. Consider features like virtual meeting capabilities, document sharing, task management, and communication channels. Explain how these platforms can facilitate effective collaboration and engagement among stakeholders.

Example Prompt 4:
As a business analyst, assess and recommend technology platforms or tools that can improve stakeholder engagement across multiple channels, such as email, social media, and customer support. Analyze the integration capabilities of these platforms with existing systems and evaluate their ability to provide a seamless and personalized experience for stakeholders.

Idea: Stakeholder Engagement Benchmarking

ChatGPT can support the comparison of stakeholder engagement practices with industry benchmarks, identifying areas where the business can improve or excel.

Example Prompt 1:
As a business analyst, I need ChatGPT to analyze our stakeholder engagement practices and compare them with industry benchmarks. Please provide insights on how our current practices align with the benchmarks and identify areas where we can improve or excel.

Example Prompt 2:
ChatGPT, help us benchmark our stakeholder engagement efforts against industry standards. Analyze our current practices and provide a detailed comparison with the benchmarks, highlighting areas where we can enhance our engagement strategies.

Example Prompt 3:
ChatGPT, we want to assess our stakeholder engagement practices by comparing them to industry benchmarks. Please analyze our current strategies and provide a comprehensive report on how we fare against the benchmarks, suggesting areas for improvement or opportunities for excellence.

Example Prompt 4:
As a business analyst, I require ChatGPT's assistance in benchmarking our stakeholder engagement practices. Evaluate our current strategies and compare them with industry benchmarks, offering actionable insights on how we can enhance our engagement efforts and potentially outperform the competition.

Idea: Stakeholder Engagement Policy Development

Utilize ChatGPT to develop comprehensive policies and guidelines for stakeholder engagement, ensuring consistency and alignment with organizational objectives.

Example Prompt 1:
As a business analyst, I need your assistance in developing a stakeholder engagement policy that aligns with our organizational objectives. Please provide a step-by-step guide on how to create comprehensive policies and guidelines for stakeholder engagement, ensuring consistency throughout the organization.

Example Prompt 2:
ChatGPT, help me draft a stakeholder engagement policy that promotes effective communication and collaboration with

our stakeholders. Ensure that the policy includes guidelines on identifying and prioritizing stakeholders, establishing communication channels, and measuring the success of engagement efforts.

Example Prompt 3:
I require your expertise as a business analyst to develop a stakeholder engagement framework that aligns with our organizational objectives. Please outline the key components of the framework, including strategies for stakeholder identification, engagement methods, and mechanisms for feedback and continuous improvement.

Example Prompt 4:
ChatGPT, assist me in creating a comprehensive set of guidelines for stakeholder engagement that can be easily understood and implemented by our organization. Include best practices for stakeholder communication, conflict resolution, and maintaining transparency. Additionally, provide recommendations on how to integrate stakeholder feedback into decision-making processes.

Idea: Stakeholder Engagement Reporting

ChatGPT can assist in generating regular reports on stakeholder engagement activities, summarizing key findings, progress, and recommendations for management and stakeholders.

Example Prompt 1:
As a business analyst, I need ChatGPT to generate a monthly stakeholder engagement report. Please provide a detailed summary of the key findings from recent stakeholder interactions, including any emerging trends or concerns. Additionally, include progress updates on ongoing engagement initiatives and provide recommendations for management and stakeholders based on the findings.

Example Prompt 2:

ChatGPT, please assist in creating a quarterly stakeholder engagement report. Summarize the outcomes of stakeholder meetings, surveys, and feedback received during the quarter. Highlight any significant changes in stakeholder sentiment or priorities, and provide an analysis of the progress made in addressing their concerns. Finally, offer recommendations for management and stakeholders to enhance future engagement efforts.

Example Prompt 3:
As a business analyst, I require ChatGPT's support in generating an annual stakeholder engagement report. Compile a comprehensive overview of all stakeholder interactions throughout the year, including details of meetings, workshops, and feedback received. Summarize the key themes, challenges, and opportunities identified during these engagements. Provide an analysis of the progress made in addressing stakeholder expectations and offer strategic recommendations for management and stakeholders to improve engagement in the upcoming year.

Example Prompt 4:
ChatGPT, please assist in creating a customized stakeholder engagement report for a specific project or initiative. Incorporate stakeholder feedback, survey results, and any other relevant data to provide a comprehensive analysis of stakeholder engagement activities. Summarize the project's impact on stakeholders, identify areas of improvement, and offer recommendations to enhance future engagement efforts. Additionally, include progress updates on the project's objectives and milestones, ensuring alignment with stakeholder expectations.

HOW YOU CAN AUTOMATE PARTS OF YOUR BUSINESS ANALYSTS JOB

INTRODUCTION

The Significance of Automation

Envision stepping into a workspace of the future—your future —where the burden of mundane tasks no longer weighs you down. A place where you can truly excel at what you do best. Welcome to the realm of Business Analysts, where technology is not just a convenience, but a game-changing force for transformation. In this chapter, we will explore the profound impact of automation and AI, two revolutionary forces that are reshaping industries. If you're a Business Analyst, it's time to sit up and take notice.

The Goals of this Chapter

Let's be clear: we're not merely scratching the surface here. We will dive deep into the core principles of AI and automation, specifically tailored for Business Analysts. By the end of this chapter, you will discover a vast horizon of opportunities that can enhance your productivity and, most importantly, fortify your job security.

The Advantages of Automation for Business Analysts

Imagine this: fewer hours spent on mind-numbing data entry and more time dedicated to strategic thinking. Does it sound too good to be true? Well, it's not. Automation is not just a buzzword for tech enthusiasts; it's a practical tool that is readily available to enrich your work life, boost your efficiency, and safeguard your career.

THE DIFFERENCES BETWEEN AI AND AUTOMATION

Introducing your new digital co-workers: automation and AI. Automation is here to handle the mundane, repetitive tasks that hold you back, allowing you to focus on more nuanced and creative endeavors. AI, on the other hand, takes things to the next level by offering intelligent suggestions and even predicting future trends. Together, they form a powerful duo.

But what exactly is the difference between AI and automation, and why does it matter for business analysts like yourself? Well, automation is all about tackling those dreaded, rule-based tasks that seem to never end. It's here to free up your time and energy. On the other hand, AI is designed to handle complex decisions and analytics, taking care of the more intricate aspects of your work.

As a business analyst, understanding the dynamics between automation and AI is crucial. It's the first step towards becoming an automation champion within your organization. So, let's dive in and explore the world of automation and AI, and discover how they can revolutionize your role as a business analyst.

IMPLEMENTING AI AUTOMATIONS

Now that you have a solid understanding of the background of AI Automation, it's time to delve into the practical aspects. In this chapter, we will explore various pathways for applying what you've learned, taking into consideration your comfort level, time availability, and resource allocation.

Let's start by introducing you to two game-changing tools: Zapier.com and Make.com. If you enjoy the satisfaction of doing things yourself, you're in luck. These platforms act as your own digital task forces, available 24/7 to carry out your commands. Zapier excels at connecting multiple apps you already use, streamlining repetitive tasks. On the other hand, Make.com offers the flexibility to develop more complex, custom workflows. The best part? Both platforms are designed for individuals without a coding background, and they provide a range of tutorials to help you get started.

If the DIY approach isn't your style or you're short on time, don't worry. There are other excellent options available to you. My website, jeroenerne.com/aiautomation, serves as a one-stop hub for outsourcing your automation needs to specialized companies. These experts can tailor solutions that perfectly align with your business requirements. Additionally, if you're eager to enhance your automation skill set, the site offers personal training options to help you elevate your game.

FUTURE-PROOFING YOUR BUSINESS ANALYSTS ROLE

Strategies for Continuous Learning and Adaptation
Welcome to the era of evolving technology, where the question of whether it will replace you is irrelevant. Instead, view this as an opportunity to thrive, not a threat to your existence. By continuously learning and adapting, you not only secure your place in the business world but also elevate your role to new heights.

Embracing automation and AI doesn't jeopardize your position; it empowers it. In the upcoming chapters, we will delve into a treasure trove of automation ideas that have the potential to skyrocket your company's growth. It is your responsibility to lead the way and seize these opportunities. While other companies in your industry may eventually catch up, rest assured that your foresight and decisive action will make you indispensable.

Remember, the key to success lies in embracing change, staying ahead of the curve, and continuously honing your skills. By doing so, you will not only secure your place in the business world but also become a driving force behind your company's success. So, let's embark on this journey together and unlock the full potential of your role as a business analyst.

AUTOMATION IDEAS AND CASE STUDIES

Equipped with a solid understanding of the fundamentals and a visionary outlook, you are now poised to embark on the truly game-changing phase of this expedition. Within this chapter, you will discover a collection of pragmatic automation strategies specifically designed for individuals in the realm of Business Analysts. Rest assured, this is not merely about simplifying your own workload; it is about propelling your organization towards enhanced competitiveness and fortified security.

DATA GATHERING AND ANALYSIS

Data gathering and analysis is a crucial aspect of business decision-making. With the advent of artificial intelligence (AI), this process can now be automated, enabling companies to collect and analyze vast amounts of data effortlessly. By leveraging AI, business analysts can shift their focus from tedious data collection to interpreting the results and providing strategic recommendations. This automation not only saves time but also enhances the accuracy and efficiency of data analysis, leading to more informed decision-making.

For instance, let's consider a fictive company called "TechSolutions." TechSolutions specializes in developing software solutions for various industries. To stay ahead of the competition, they need to constantly monitor market trends, customer preferences, and competitor strategies. By implementing AI-powered automation, TechSolutions can effortlessly gather data from multiple sources, such as social media, customer feedback, and industry reports. The AI algorithms then analyze this data, identifying patterns, trends, and potential opportunities. With the automated data gathering and analysis process, TechSolutions' business analysts can now focus on interpreting the insights and recommending strategic actions to improve their products and services. This automation empowers TechSolutions to make data-driven decisions swiftly and effectively, giving them a competitive edge in the market.

REPORT GENERATION

Report generation is made effortless with the help of AI. By extracting pertinent information from multiple sources, AI can format and generate visually captivating and enlightening reports. This automation streamlines the process, saving time and effort for businesses.

For instance, let's consider a fictitious company called "TechSolutions." TechSolutions specializes in providing IT solutions to various clients. With the implementation of AI-powered report generation, the company can effortlessly compile data from customer feedback surveys, sales figures, and market trends. The AI system then processes this information, formats it into a comprehensive report, and presents it in an engaging visual format. This automation not only saves TechSolutions valuable time but also ensures that their reports are consistently accurate, insightful, and visually appealing.

TREND ANALYSIS

Trend analysis is a powerful tool that utilizes AI algorithms to automatically detect patterns and trends within data. By employing this technology, business analysts can swiftly identify market trends, customer preferences, and potential opportunities. This automation enables companies to stay ahead of the competition and make informed decisions based on accurate insights.

For instance, let's consider a fictive company called "TechSolutions." As a leading provider of technology solutions, TechSolutions implements trend analysis automation to gain a competitive edge. By analyzing vast amounts of customer data, their AI algorithms identify a rising trend in the demand for smart home devices. Recognizing this opportunity, TechSolutions quickly develops and launches a new line of innovative smart home products, capturing a significant market share and boosting their revenue. Thanks to trend analysis automation, TechSolutions successfully anticipates customer preferences and capitalizes on emerging trends, solidifying their position as an industry leader.

FORECASTING AND PREDICTIVE MODELING

Forecasting and predictive modeling are crucial tools for businesses to anticipate future outcomes and make informed decisions. With the advent of AI, this process can now be automated, enabling business analysts to build accurate predictive models based on historical data. By leveraging AI algorithms, companies can forecast market trends, customer behavior, and other relevant factors, empowering them to make data-driven decisions with confidence.

For instance, let's consider a fictive retail company called "SmartMart." SmartMart wants to optimize its inventory management by accurately predicting customer demand for various products. By implementing AI-powered forecasting and predictive modeling, SmartMart can analyze historical sales data, market trends, and external factors like weather conditions. The AI system can then generate accurate predictions on future demand, allowing SmartMart to adjust its inventory levels accordingly. This automation not only saves time and resources but also ensures that SmartMart always has the right products in stock, leading to improved customer satisfaction and increased profitability.

DATA CLEANSING AND VALIDATION

Data cleansing and validation is a crucial process in ensuring the accuracy and reliability of data for analysis purposes. With the advent of artificial intelligence (AI), this task can now be automated, saving time and effort for businesses. AI algorithms can identify and rectify errors, inconsistencies, and duplicates in datasets, resulting in cleaner and more reliable data.

For instance, let's consider a fictive company called "TechSolutions." TechSolutions is a software development firm that collects customer data for market analysis. By implementing AI-powered data cleansing and validation, TechSolutions can automatically detect and correct any inaccuracies or inconsistencies in their customer database. This automation not only saves time but also ensures that the company's analysis is based on accurate and reliable data, leading to better decision-making and improved customer insights.

REQUIREMENT GATHERING AND DOCUMENTATION

Requirement gathering and documentation is a crucial process for businesses to understand the needs and expectations of their stakeholders. With the advent of AI-powered chatbots, this task has become more efficient and accurate. These chatbots can assist business analysts by engaging with stakeholders, collecting their requirements, and documenting them in a structured manner. Moreover, these intelligent chatbots can even suggest potential solutions based on predefined rules and patterns, saving time and effort for analysts.

For instance, let's consider a fictive company called "TechSolutions." They specialize in developing software solutions for various industries. To streamline their requirement gathering process, TechSolutions implements an AI-powered chatbot named "ReqBot." When stakeholders interact with ReqBot, it engages in natural language conversations, asking relevant questions to gather their requirements. It then documents these requirements in a centralized system, ensuring accuracy and easy access for the business analysts. Additionally, based on predefined rules and patterns, ReqBot suggests potential solutions, enabling analysts to explore different options quickly. This automation not only enhances the efficiency of TechSolutions' requirement gathering process but also improves the overall quality of their software solutions.

PROCESS OPTIMIZATION

Process optimization is a powerful tool that leverages AI technology to enhance business operations. By analyzing various business processes, AI can identify bottlenecks and propose improvements to streamline operations. This enables business analysts to concentrate on implementing and monitoring these changes, rather than spending time on identifying inefficiencies.

For instance, let's consider a fictive company called "TechSolutions." They specialize in providing IT support services to various clients. TechSolutions implemented process optimization using AI to enhance their ticket resolution process. The AI system analyzed the entire workflow, identified areas where tickets were getting stuck, and suggested improvements to expedite the resolution process. As a result, TechSolutions experienced a significant reduction in ticket resolution time, leading to improved customer satisfaction and increased productivity for their support team.

RISK ASSESSMENT

Risk assessment is a crucial aspect of any business, and now, with the help of AI algorithms, this process can be automated for greater efficiency. By analyzing historical data, these algorithms can identify potential risks and offer recommendations for effective risk mitigation strategies. For instance, imagine a fictive company, XYZ Corp, which specializes in manufacturing electronic devices. By implementing AI-powered risk assessment, XYZ Corp can analyze past incidents, such as product recalls or supply chain disruptions, to proactively identify potential risks. The algorithms can then suggest measures like diversifying suppliers or implementing stricter quality control to mitigate these risks, ensuring smoother operations and enhanced business resilience.

CUSTOMER SEGMENTATION

Customer segmentation is a powerful tool that enables businesses to understand their customers better and deliver personalized experiences. With the help of AI, companies can automatically segment their customers based on factors like demographics, behavior, and preferences. This automation empowers business analysts to tailor marketing strategies and improve customer targeting, resulting in higher customer satisfaction and increased sales.

For instance, let's consider a fictive company called "GloboTech," an online fashion retailer. By implementing AI-driven customer segmentation, GloboTech can analyze customer data to identify different segments such as young professionals, fashion enthusiasts, and bargain hunters. With this information, GloboTech's marketing team can create targeted campaigns for each segment, showcasing relevant products and offering personalized discounts. As a result, young professionals receive tailored recommendations for office wear, fashion enthusiasts get updates on the latest trends, and bargain hunters receive exclusive deals on discounted items. This automation not only enhances customer engagement but also boosts sales by delivering a more personalized shopping experience.

COMPETITIVE ANALYSIS

Competitive analysis is a crucial aspect of business strategy, and AI has revolutionized this process by automating the collection and analysis of competitor data. By leveraging AI technology, business analysts can gain valuable insights into market trends, pricing strategies, and competitive advantages. This automation enables companies to make informed decisions and stay ahead in the market.

For instance, let's consider a fictive company called "TechPro," a leading technology firm. TechPro implements AI automation for competitive analysis, allowing their business analysts to effortlessly gather and analyze data on their competitors. The AI system continuously monitors competitor websites, social media platforms, and industry news, extracting relevant information and providing real-time insights. With this automation, TechPro gains a comprehensive understanding of their competitors' product offerings, pricing strategies, and customer feedback. Armed with these valuable insights, TechPro can swiftly adapt their business strategies, launch innovative products, and maintain a competitive edge in the dynamic technology market.

PERFORMANCE MONITORING

Performance monitoring is a crucial aspect of any business, and with the help of AI, it has become even more efficient. AI technology can constantly track and analyze key performance indicators (KPIs) and promptly notify business analysts of any noteworthy deviations or anomalies. This enables them to swiftly respond and take proactive actions to address potential issues or capitalize on emerging opportunities.

For instance, let's consider a fictitious retail company called "SmartMart." SmartMart utilizes AI-powered performance monitoring to keep a close eye on its sales figures, inventory levels, and customer satisfaction ratings. One day, the AI system detects a sudden drop in sales for a particular product category. It immediately alerts the business analysts, who quickly investigate the issue. They discover that a competitor has launched a similar product at a lower price, attracting SmartMart's customers. Armed with this information, SmartMart promptly adjusts its pricing strategy and launches a targeted marketing campaign to regain its market share. Thanks to AI-driven performance monitoring, SmartMart was able to identify and address the problem swiftly, minimizing potential losses and maintaining its competitive edge.

NATURAL LANGUAGE PROCESSING (NLP)

Natural language processing (NLP) refers to the use of AI-powered algorithms that can automatically analyze unstructured data, including customer feedback, social media posts, and online reviews. By implementing NLP automation, business analysts can extract valuable insights from textual data, enabling them to make informed decisions and improve their products or services.

For instance, let's consider a fictive company called "GlobeTech," a global e-commerce platform. GlobeTech decides to implement NLP automation to analyze customer feedback and online reviews. By utilizing AI-powered NLP algorithms, they can automatically process thousands of customer reviews in various languages, extracting sentiments, identifying common issues, and categorizing feedback. This automation allows GlobeTech's business analysts to quickly identify areas for improvement, address customer concerns, and enhance their overall customer experience. As a result, GlobeTech sees an increase in customer satisfaction, loyalty, and ultimately, their bottom line.

EPILOGUE

Dear Reader,

Congratulations on completing "The Artificial Intelligence Handbook for Business Analysts." I hope this book has provided you with valuable insights into the world of AI and its potential for revolutionizing the field of business analysis.

Throughout this book, we have explored the capabilities of ChatGPT, a powerful AI tool that can automate various aspects of your job as a business analyst. From analyzing market trends to predicting financial performance, ChatGPT has the potential to enhance your efficiency and effectiveness in delivering valuable insights to your organization.

By leveraging ChatGPT, you can automate tasks such as examining competitors' strategies, identifying opportunities for process improvement, and assessing potential risks to the business. This AI tool can also aid in decision-making processes by estimating future sales volumes, analyzing product performance, and optimizing the supply chain.

Furthermore, ChatGPT can assist in developing pricing strategies, evaluating brand perception through social media analysis, and assessing potential investments. It ensures that your business practices adhere to relevant laws and regulations while understanding the needs and expectations of key stakeholders.

As you embark on your AI journey, I encourage you to sign

up for my newsletter at www.jeroenerne.com/ainewsletter. By doing so, you will receive regular updates on the latest advancements in AI and how they can benefit your role as a business analyst.

If you have any questions or would like to discuss specific AI applications further, please feel free to contact me via www.jeroenerne.com/contact/. I am always eager to engage with fellow professionals and share knowledge and experiences.

Remember, AI is not meant to replace human expertise but to augment it. By embracing the power of AI, you can elevate your role as a business analyst and become a catalyst for positive change within your organization.

Thank you for joining me on this AI journey, and I wish you all the best in your future endeavors.

Sincerely,

Jeroen Erné

ABOUT THE AUTHOR & COMPLETE AI TRAINING

Jeroen's journey in the field of technology and digital innovation is a profound testament to what passion, dedication, and a forward-thinking mindset can achieve. Not just an individual working in the AI sector, Jeroen stands out as a pioneer, whose initiatives have significantly impacted thousands of individuals across a multitude of professions. At the helm of Nexibeo AI and Complete AI Training, he has been instrumental in demonstrating the transformative potential of integrating AI into our daily workflows, proving that it is not merely a futuristic concept but a tangible, game-changing reality.

Jeroen's commitment to digital innovation has catalyzed the ascent of over a thousand companies to unprecedented levels of success through his leadership at his agencies: JoyGroup Web Design, Nova Interactive, and Nexibeo Development. His ventures as (Co-)Founder of startups like SimplySocial, MobileRevolution, and Coincheckup.com further illustrate his keen insight into the tech landscape and his ability to innovate and drive positive change within it.

Central to Jeroen founded CompleteAiTraining.com in 2023, where his ambition extends beyond mere instruction to the empowerment of professionals. Here, he equips thousands with the knowledge and tools necessary for weaving AI into their daily activities. The platform provides an exhaustive suite of resources tailored to various professions, including custom ChatGPTs, thousands of specific prompts, in-depth courses, video tutorials, audiobooks, eBooks, reference guides, and unlimited inquiries to an AI strategy GPT. These resources are made available through the purchase of his book on platforms like Amazon, which also offers a month of complimentary access to Complete AI Training for further exploration at https://completeaitraining.com/free-resources-amazon.

Jeroen's influence extends well beyond his training platform. Having authored 240 AI-focused books for a broad spectrum of professions, he has armed a myriad of individuals with the capabilities to seamlessly integrate AI into their work environments. These publications are accessible on Amazon (https://www.amazon.com/stores/author/B0CKRXVNB2) and via subscriptions on CompleteAITraining.com.

With Jeroen guiding Nexibeo AI, the company plays a crucial role in helping businesses incorporate AI into their daily operations effectively, ensuring they remain leaders in innovation.

Jeroen is more than an author or an entrepreneur; he is a visionary who is pushing the boundaries in the technology, AI, and innovation sectors. His journey and insights can be followed on LinkedIn at https://www.linkedin.com/in/jeroenerne/.

His narrative is not just about the accomplishments of an individual but highlights the capacity of AI to revolutionize our world—making it more intelligent, efficient, and interconnected. Jeroen's work is about simplifying complexity, making innovation practical, and bringing the future within our reach, one step at a time.

Could you help me grow with a Review?

Hello, amazing reader, may I ask you for a favour? I hope you've found valuable insights and enjoyed your journey through the pages of this AI handbook, dedicated to you. If you feel inspired, I'd be truly thrilled if you could spare a moment to share your experience on Amazon or wherever you purchased your copy. Your feedback not only brightens our day—it also helps others discover the book's value. So, could you kindly light up the stars with your review? Thank you for being so awesome and for all your support!

"HELLO, AMAZING READER, MAY I ASK YOU FOR A FAVOUR TO HELP ME GROW?"

COULD YOU SHARE YOUR REVIEW ON AMAZON?